THE NOVEL IN TRANSITION

THE NOVEL IN TRANSITION

Gender and Literature in
Early Colonial Korea

JOOYEON RHEE

East Asia Program
Cornell University
Ithaca, New York 14853

The Cornell East Asia Series is published by the Cornell University East Asia Program (distinct from Cornell University Press). We publish books on a variety of scholarly topics relating to East Asia as a service to the academic community and the general public. Address submission inquiries to CEAS Editorial Board, East Asia Program, Cornell University, 140 Uris Hall, Ithaca, New York 14853-7601.

Cover:
Front image provided by Pak Chinyŏng. Seoul: Hoedong sŏgwan (1913)
Back image provided by Ham T'aeyŏng. Seoul: Sech'ang sŏgwan (1952)
Previously published materials used with permission from:
The Journal of Korean Studies
Sungkyun Journal of East Asian Studies

Number 196 in the Cornell East Asia Series
Copyright ©2019 Cornell East Asia Program. All rights reserved.
ISSN: 1050-2955
ISBN: 978-1-939161-06-2 hardcover
ISBN: 978-1-939161-96-3 paperback
ISBN: 978-1-942242-96-3 e-book
Library of Congress Control Number: 2018966298
Printed in the United States of America

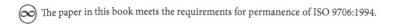 The paper in this book meets the requirements for permanence of ISO 9706:1994.

CONTENTS

Acknowledgments

THE WRITING OF THIS BOOK was carried out on three different continents, and just as each journey was not always prepared for or anticipated, so too were my feelings about the progress of the writing. At each stage, however, I encountered numerous souls who provided me with their intellectual insights, useful advice, and emotional support, which ultimately helped me to complete this book. I thank them for their generosity, time, and encouragement, all of which convinced me that this book was worth publishing.

I am indebted to my exemplary committee members Theresa Hyun, Ted Goossen, Sharon Hayashi, Hong Kal, and Andre Schmid. Theresa Hyun introduced me to the world of translation studies and guided me on my dissertation with her kind heart and helpful advice; Ted Goossen encouraged me to make meaningful connections between Korean and Japanese culture through literature; Sharon Hayashi and Hong Kal showed me how I could enrich my reading of literary texts by incorporating visual images taken from newspapers and books. Andre Schmid gave me extensive advice on how to develop the dissertation into a book. Joan Judge encouraged me to examine the topic from a cross-cultural perspective and helped me expand the horizon of my knowledge of women's history in early twentieth-century East Asia. John Lie kindly offered to take a look at my monograph, and his comments and suggestions enabled me to articulate key points during the revision process. Theodore Jun Yoo painstakingly read my monograph chapter by chapter, helping me clear up theoretical issues and improve the overall structure of the monograph. I also thank the anonymous reviewers whose detailed comments and thoughtful questions helped me make clearer connections between literature and gender in the colonial context.

I have attended a number of seminars and conferences in Japan and Korea, where I learned so much from scholars in the field of colonial culture and literature. Youngjae Lee introduced me to one of the most active and productive academic groups on Korean history and culture in Japan, *Jinbun hyōronkai*. It was at such venues that I met inspiring individuals such as Taeyeong Ham, Hoduk Hwang, Hyoungduck Kwak, Youngmin Kim, Aimee Nayoung Kwon, Kyunghoon Lee, Jiyoung Shin, and Chunghee Ryu. Watanabe Naoki, who has been leading the *hyōronkai*, has always been my great *sensei*, friend, and supporter who generously shared his knowledge with me and connected me to many interesting researchers. Many scholars in Korea shared their expertise and experience with me and I thank them for their generosity and kindness: Jaehee Bak, Moonim Baek, Kim Chul, Hyejong Kang, Sungyeon Kim, Hyunjoo Kim, Chinyoung Park, and Hyunseon Park.

I feel truly lucky to have a community of colleagues at The Hebrew University of Jerusalem whose passion for research and teaching has envigorated me. Many thanks to Nissim Otmazgin for having been my mentor ever since I arrived in the university. Nissim has shared his experience and knowledge with me selflessly. With Nissim's constant support and Junko Nakajima Otmazgin's kind help on various matters, I feel at home in the community. I also thank my wonderful colleagues at the university who provided academic advice, useful information, and advice on everyday life. Because of them, my life in Jerusalem has been fulfilling in many ways: Naomi Alshech, Reuven Amitai, Michal Biran, Shalmit Bejarano, Menachem Blondheim, Yigal Bronner, Rotem Geva, Helena Grinshpun, Jewan Rosman Kim, Minjeong Ko, Alon Levkowitz, Ira Lyan, Orna Naftali, Danny Orbach, Yuri Pines, Lihi Yariv-Laor, Kineret Levy, Noa Oppenheim, Ronit Ricci, Hanoch Roniger, Gideon Shelach, Evyatar Shulman, Marina Shusterman, Merav Yaacobi, and Kumiko Yayama.

I feel very fortunate to have friends and colleagues in many parts of the world whose work and life stories have been a source of inspiration for me as I move forward with my research: Shelley Chan, Sookja Cho, Howard Choy, Terumi Imai, Sunny Jeong, Sueen Noh Kelly, Yuri Keum, Minjeong Kim, Uliana Kobyakova, Jongim Lim, Anna Lim, Janet Lee, Jinkyung Lee, Myungsook Lee, Seung Hyok Lee, Doug Lehman, Jongim Lim, Natsue Haji Oh, Sunji Park, Guy Podoler, Baryon Tensor Posadas, Liora Sarfati, Hijoo Son, Ayumi Togashi, Barbara Wall, Carmiele Wilkerson, Youngshil

Yoon, and Dafna Zur. During my years of graduate study in Toronto I had tremendously supportive, fun, brilliant, and interesting friends. Many of them are now dispersed to different parts of the world, but I think of them often and my heart is always with them wherever they are: John Carlaw, Alicia Filipowich, Naoko Ikeda, Ike Itani, Inhye Kang, Sungjo Kim, Sunho Ko, Minna Lee, Eric Li, Brandon Moores, Chikako Nagayama, Nori Onuki, Tomoe Otsuki, Nedra Rodrigo, Doris Sung, Akiko Takesue, and Katsunari Tsuchiya.

A generous and patient soul who has helped with numerous writings—including this book for over a decade—is my editor, Nina Hoeschele, deserves high praise for her professionalism and expertise. My years of research in Korea and Japan were made possible by the generous support of several funding agencies: the Social Science and Humanities Research Council, Daesan Foundation, the Northeast Asia Council, the Israeli Science Foundation, and the Research Centre for Korean Studies at Kyushu University.

The discussion of *Maeil sinbo*'s utilization of the novel in the early 1910s in Chapter 3 originally appeared in *The Journal of Korean Studies* 22, no. 1 (2017); and the comparative analysis of a Korean translation of the Japanese domestic novel, *The Gold Demon*, in Chapter 4 originally appeared in *Sungkyun Journal of East Asian Studies* 15, no. 1 (2015). I thank these two journals for permitting me to publish materials that I used in the articles. Unless otherwise stated, all translations are my own.

My family in Korea has been patiently waiting to see this book, and I want to tell them that their love has been a great source of strength. I dedicate this book to my courageous, hardworking, and loving mother whose intelligence and wisdom inspire me always.

INTRODUCTION

The Ambiguity of Modern Korean Literature

Reading and talking about indecent matters are common folks' best pastime while they pay little to no attention to the study of words of sages. These people love going to wild parties while avoiding places where they are expected to observe decorum. The novel (*sosŏl*) and play (*yŏnhi*), therefore, are two most popular forms of pastime among women and ignorant men.[1]

The novel (*sosŏl*) is the compass for national subjects (*kungmin*). Even ignorant laborers can enjoy reading the novel if worldly affairs are skillfully written in it. Thus novelists must be aware of their duty to lead *kungmin* to a right place through their works since their works can shape the character of *kungmin*.[2]

These statements are from *Taehan maeil sinbo* (*The Korea Daily News*), one of the most popular newspapers in the early 1900s, which was run by reformist intellectuals during the Taehan cheguk (Great Korean Empire, 1897–1910) period. While the author of the first statement is unknown, the second was written by Sin Ch'aeho, a nationalist historian who was actively writing fiction during this period. Despite their seemingly contradictory views on the readership of fictional narratives—narratives generally referred to as *sosŏl*—these two writers represent the era during which the concept and the value of the novel were changing dramatically. It was the time when "women and ignorant men" would become "national subjects" whose reading practices would determine the nation's fate. Fictional narratives, in other words, would affect the real lives of the national subjects tremendously—a daunting task that had never been expected of the

---

1. "Sosŏl kwa yŏnhi ga p'ungsok e yugwan" (The relationship between social custom and the novel and play), *Taehan maeil sinbo*, 20 July 1910.
2. Sin Ch'aeho, "Sosŏlga ŭi ch'use" (A trend among fiction writers), *Taehan maeil sinbo*, 2 December 1909.

genre in the previous era. This is not to say that the literary space of fantasy disappeared, but that fantasy would take a different form and content, continuously producing imaginations about the society called *nation*.

Although both authors used the same term for the novel (*sosŏl*), the former author perceives "the novel" as it has been while Sin perceives it as it should be. Their contrasting views also apply to narrative forms; they refer to fictional narratives generally, including oral literature, for the former and written texts only for the latter. It would take time for the term *sosŏl* to mean what we understand as the "novel" now, a transformation that began around this time through experiments with the genre undertaken by writers and translators. *Sosŏl* was considered a pastime for women and the lower classes, existing on the periphery of literary culture proper in Chosŏn, but by the end of the nineteenth century this perception was changing quickly, as nationalist intellectuals found fictional narratives valuable for transforming the masses into national subjects.

The Japanese colonial state also enthusiastically promoted *sosŏl* to establish and maintain colonial order immediately after the annexation of Korea. Caught in the clash between nationalism and colonialism and amid fervent discourses on the nature of civilization, the concept and function of the novel would undergo tremendous changes; it is in this historical context that writers articulated their immediate reality through fiction writing and translation. How could the novel reflect reality differently than the fiction works of Chosŏn? Why did the genre matter to the elites as far as nation building was concerned? What were the social, political, and cultural implications of writing and reading novels at the turn of the twentieth century? These are the essential questions this book raises, answers to which provide important clues about literature's crucial role in affirming, challenging, and negotiating the historical forces at a critical juncture in Korean history.

This book focuses on "the novel"—an English translation of *sosŏl*—apart from other literary genres because it is through investigating the formation of the novel, I argue, that we understand the ambiguous morphology of modern Korean literature at the turn of the twentieth century. "Modern Korean literature" needs to be deconstructed in order for us to better understand the meaning of the modern. What students and researchers refer to as modern Korean literature in fact retains many remnants of the premodern. This period witnessed the expression of a strong desire to overthrow cultural traditions of the past but it also saw the impossibility of doing so. Elements of the past—residues, as Williams called them—were still effective, and were incorporated into a literary culture that would become dominant in the first two decades of the twentieth century.[3] The process whereby cultural residues become effective needs to be examined in order to understand the "newness" associated with modern Korean literature. Second, modern Korean literature is ambiguous because scholarly discussions on the subject have brushed aside writing and reading practices that are crucial in historicizing the modern. Without exploring these practices, which were hugely influenced by modern print-media and transnational literary forces at the time, it is futile to discuss the "modern-ness" of Korean literature.

The third and most important reason to call modern Korean literature ambiguous is its gendered imagination of modernity that reified the gender boundary. By gendered imagination I do not mean only the representation of gender relations and roles in literature, but also the tropes of modernity manifested in ideological descriptions of national culture and history that resulted in the legitimization of gender boundaries both within and outside of the literary scene. In the selected works I investigate, male writers describe women as symbols of arbitrarily constructed traditions and futures. For example, young women's strong desire for education is suggested as a model for Koreans to follow for national growth, while their possession of Confucian female virtues is represented as a continuity of traditions. In reality, however, although women were brought to the public discourse of civilization, the space for them to participate in the nation building became narrower, limiting their role exclusively to the domestic sphere as mothers. This reification of gender boundaries became even more rigid during the 1920s when a coterie of female writers was ignored, marginalized, and suppressed by their male counterparts. It is often pointed out that women in colonized societies were doubly colonized by the colonial force and patriarchy.[4] In this case, the group of female writers was marginalized by the male-dominated publishing industry in the colony,

---

3. Raymond Williams, *Marxism and Literature* (London: Oxford University Press, 1977), 122.

4. Ch'oe Myŏngp'yo, "Somun ŭro Kusŏng toen Kim Myŏngsun ŭi sam kwa munhak" (The life and works of Kim Myŏngsun, which has been constructed by rumors), *Hyŏndae munhakiron yŏn'gu* 30 (April 2007): 224–228.

and their works and private lives became objects of criticism and control by male writers. Their economic and cultural lives, in other words, were tremendously limited in the doubly colonized social structure.

Most of these fiction writers, especially right before Japan's full annexation of Chosŏn, were not professional novelists in today's understanding of the term; they were thinkers, journalists, educators, and reformers who did not necessarily view fiction writing as a literary endeavor but rather as a political act. Viewed as enlightenment texts rather than literature, the novels that I investigate in this book are thus not usually read as the "novel" proper in Korea. For some time, the label of "the first modern novel" has been indisputably applied to a later work, Yi Kwangsu's *The Heartless* (*Mujŏng*, 1917). However, writers' utilization of the novel form from 1900 through the 1910s must be examined outside the realm of intellectual history and beyond the previously dominant view on this body of works as enlightenment texts. A close examination of this body of works will help us to comprehend the process by which modern Korean literature was formed between the premodern and the modern and between the local and global. As Moretti rightly observes, "theories of the novel have been theories of modernity," but modernity did not emerge from a vacuum; it was influenced by the premodern and modern imagination.[5] Practice precedes theories, and the in-between literary space this book investigates is a dialogic space, showings how new utterances apprehend old utterances while anticipating future utterances.[6]

Gender played a crucial role in turn-of-the-twentieth-century Korea in shaping the dominant idea of nation and modernity in the field of literature. The concept is not used as a sexual difference in this book but as a "useful category of historical analysis"[7] of modernity that enables us to see how the hegemony of gender was constructed at the intersection of nationalism and colonialism—a place in which imaginations of modernity were produced mostly in the hands of men. Fiction represents the way people imagine their social reality as "shared by large group of people, [a]

---

5. Franco Moretti, "History of the Novel, Theory of the Novel," *Novel: A Forum on Fiction* 43, no. 1 (2010): 8.

6. Mikhail Bakhtin, *The Dialogic Imagination: Four Essays* (Austin: University of Texas Press, 1992).

7. Joan W. Scott, "Introduction to Revisiting 'Gender: A Useful Category of Historical Analysis,'" *The American Historical Review* 113 no. 5 (2008): 1344–1345.

common understanding that makes possible common practices and a widely shared sense of intimacy."[8] Despite the native writers' and translators' attempts to construct a shared sense of intimacy among people through novels, the intimacy was not gender neutral. In addition, gender had the capacity to challenge, destabilize, or interrupt the colonial regime.[9] Korean translators' and writers' constructions of mobile, vengeful, and murderous masculinity, for example, embodied critical views of colonialism. The nation-focused historiography, so deeply inscribed in the scholarship of colonial culture in South Korea, thus needs to be deconstructed in order to explicate the instability of modernity, as scholars have pointed out.[10] At the same time, any investigation should consider gender when examining how the instability and ambiguity of modernity is embedded in modern Korean literature.

In the literary history scholarship on colonial Korea there is a tendency to dismiss the gender dimension in literary development of the 1900s and 1910s. When gender is discussed most scholarship focuses on the ideological descriptions of women's roles as good wives and wise mothers in a national context. However, writers' and translators' representations of gender in their works had a function far beyond defining the roles of men and women. Their handling of gender encompassed multiple issues concerning national community and culture, and a close examination of their texts reveals numerous instances where they engaged with historical forces, namely colonialism, capitalism, and nationalism. My special interest is in tracing the ways in which they negotiated with these forces since this speaks to their visions for the nation and national community, which were articulated in their works.

This book investigates the novel genre with three methodological approaches that articulate the relationship between gender and literature. First, this study avoids the binary of nationalism and colonialism so inherent in the scholarship of colonial literature in Korea. This binary fails

---

8. Charles Taylor, *Modern Social Imaginaries* (Durham, NC: Duke University Press, 2004), 23.

9. Antoinette Burton, "The Unfinished Business of Colonial Modernities," in *Gender, Sexuality, and Colonial Modernities*, ed. Antoinette Burton (New York: Routledge, 1999), 1.

10. Prasenjit Duara, *Rescuing History from the Nation* (Chicago: University of Chicago Press, 1997); Gi-Wook Shin and Michael Robinson (eds.), *Colonial Modernity in Korea* (Cambridge, MA: Harvard University Press, 1999).

to delineate the role literature played in expressing Korean writers' ambiguous attitude toward the Japan-led modernization while simultaneously undermining writers' agency as an important factor in literary history.[11] Nationalist intellectuals certainly had more freedom of expression prior to Japan's annexation of Korea in 1910; however, the embodiment of the historical consciousness about nation and modernity did not evaporate at the onset of Japan's colonization of Korea. Instead, it continuously underpinned native writers' literary production in which ambiguous experiences of modernity were manifest through their handling of gender representations.

Second, this book views gender as an apparatus for native writers and translators in negotiating with the colonial force. These writers' and translators' representations of women as patriotic mothers, educated daughters, and chaste wives did not mean that they attempted to ensure gender equality; rather, "woman" was a convenient category to present their political visions for nation and modernity. To follow Teresa de Lauretis, gender "is the product and process of a number of various social technologies."[12] The novel was a technology where gender hierarchy, roles, relations, and sexuality were constructed and hegemonized; and where native writers and translators as well as the colonial state attempted to authenticate their voices on the issues of nation and modernity.

Third, the selected novels in this book will be examined in terms of their association with transnational literary forces and modern print media. Transnational literature helped native Korean writers and translators in negotiating with the Japanese imperial force.[13] Newspapers played a decisive role in altering consciousness and disseminating "specific modes

---

11. Even under the most oppressive colonial domination during the Pacific War, Korean writers, by writing in the language of the empire, could express their ambiguous attitude toward nation and modernity in their works, thus directing us to see the complexity of modernity experienced by colonized writers. Aimee Nayoung Kwon, *Intimate Empire: Collaboration and Colonial Modernity in Korea and Japan* (Durham, NC: Duke University Press, 2015).

12. Teresa de Lauretis, *Technologies of Gender: Essays on Film, Theory and Fiction* (Bloomington: Indiana University Press, 1987), 2.

13. Karen L. Thornber, *Empire of Texts in Motion: Chinese, Korean, and Taiwanese Transculturations of Japanese Literature* (Cambridge, MA: The Harvard-Yenching Institute, 2009).

of knowledge that enable and encourage certain types of activities."[14] The novel genre was actively promoted by newspapers, and many of the writers I investigate here engaged in newspaper journalism. Through newspapers, native writers and translators attempted to reach a wider public with their novels, which in turn were heavily influenced by foreign literature. The novel was a contact zone; Mary Louise Pratt defines it as a "space of imperial encounters," where the colonized and the colonizers coexisted and interacted "within the radically asymmetrical relations of power."[15] The asymmetry of power is vividly represented in the selected novels analyzed in this book, which attempts to identify places of negotiation by comparing originals and translations, alterations of foreign ideas, and most important, descriptions of gender as a way to reinvent the past and envision the future of the national community.

The formation of the novel genre in Korea not only engineered the fiction of national community and modernity but also constructed an institution of literature that marginalized women from the male-dominant sphere of cultural productions. Thus this book argues that, from the turn of the twentieth century, gender became an important epistemological ground on which to define the Korean nation and modernity, and that the novel was one of the most effective technologies that mediated and popularized knowledge about gender. The novel, then, is a historical product that came out of the political, social, and economic conditions in early colonial Korea, where writers' and translators' negotiations with foreign powers are most clearly reflected in their ideological descriptions of men and women and their places in history and society.

THE PARADOX OF INVERSION: TRANSNATIONAL LITERARY FORCE AND FICTION OF NATION AND MODERNITY

The inversion of the novel, from "lowly" literature in Chosŏn to popular national literature at the turn of the century, can be read as a radical re-

---

14. Andre Schmid, *Korea between Empires, 1895–1919* (New York: Columbia University Press, 2002), 6.

15. Mary Louise Pratt, *Imperial Eyes: Travel Writing and Transculturation*, 2nd ed. (New York and London: Routledge, 2008), 8.

sponse to the changing global reality that pressured the native society to seek an alternative cultural form that could authenticate the nation. The inversion process involved the adoption and adaptation of foreign literary tradition and texts that ultimately reconstructed the existing literary tradition. This paradox of inversion, as I call it, meant something broader than the way the novel was reinvented in the national context. It also spoke to the dismantling of the traditional worldview that no longer functioned to maintain the shared intimacy among people. The literary practice of modifiying or even appropriating original fiction, which is often called adaptation (*pŏnan*) in Korea, influenced writers and readers significantly in their perception of the function and value of the novel in the transnational context.

Western texts arrived in Korea mainly through two routes: from China and from Japan, although the latter remained dominant, especially after Japan's annexation of Korea. Since Japan pioneered the translation of European and American texts before China and Korea, most foreign texts that arrived in Korea were based on the Japanese intermediary texts. At times they were based on multiple intermediaries, since texts from China written in Chinese script were generally translations of Japanese texts. Liang Qichao in particular was an inspirational figure for Korean reformers, who actively followed Liang's political vision for reforming China. Liang translated a number of Western fiction works from Japanese texts, and his reform project on literature as a tool to educate the masses in order to strengthen China also influenced Korean nationalist intellectuals in the first decade of the 1900s, a period during which they avidly read and translated Liang's translations.[16] Although this route was short-lived, it had a considerable impact on Korean nationalists such as Pak Ŭnsik, Sin Ch'aeho, and Chang Chiyŏn, who endeavored to reform the society by educating Koreans through the novel as a medium. As Japan's control of print media in Korea strengthened after the annexation and as nationalist intellectuals lost spaces in which to publish their works, Korean writers and translators of fiction, who had had direct contact with Japanese cul-

---

16. See the list of the translated works by Liang in Yi Manyŏl, "Kaehwagi ŏllon kwa Chungguk: Yang Kyech'o rŭl chungsim ŭro" (The Chinese influence on Korean journalism during the enlightenment period: Focusing on Liang Qichao), in *Han'guk kŭndae ŏllon ŭi chaejomyŏng* (Rethinking Korean modern journalism) (Seoul: Communication Books, 2001), 78–118.

ture through visiting and education, became prominent figures in the literary world throughout colonial Korea.

Newspapers played a significant role in mediating nationalist and colonialist discourses during this period. Unlike in the early 1900s, the only vernacular newspaper available to Koreans following the Japanese annexation was *Maeil sinbo* (The Daily News), which operated under the direct control of the Japanese colonial state. However, *The Daily*'s attempts to popularize fiction works were more vigorous than in the previous era, indicating that it regarded "the novel" as one of the most effective tools with which to disseminate its colonial policies. It serialized novels penned by creative writers such as Yi Injik and Yi Haejo in the first years after the annexation, but soon concentrated on translations of Japanese and Western novels via Japan from the early to mid-1910s.

Although writers and translators were under severe censorship in the suddenly narrowed publishing market from 1910, *The Daily* had to accommodate its readership by showing some level of flexibility as far as the novel was concerned. In its goal to reach a wider public, the newspaper used a dual approach to entertain and to educate the masses. The problem lay in balancing the two. The novel section in *The Daily* presented both great possibilities and challenges in maintaining this balance precisely because fictional representations of reality are open to multiple interpretations. Gauging the "real value" of the novel is always a daunting task since fiction can potentially blur the boundary between the real and the fictional. Further, *The Daily* faced increasing competition from native publishers, such as Sinmun'gwan, who were gaining considerable recognition for their publication of fiction works, both translated and original. This competition drove the newspaper to seek new ways to appeal to its readers; it began to occasionally allow native writers and translators room to imagine the colonial reality from critical perspectives. It is not a coincidence that the first modern novel in Korea was published in *The Daily*, a novel which was a product of the newspaper's editorial compromise rather than its interest in the literary value of Yi Kwangsu's work alone. Even though censorship posed limits on cultural expressions, it cannot be denied that the newspaper became an important channel for the development of the novel genre in colonial Korea.

Any form of imported culture goes through the process of meaning construction in the target culture, and its original ideas, customs, and aesthetics may be altered during this process. It is inevitable that translation creates a contextual difference between target and source culture since "the text in the target language has to be imagined in relation not just to the phonic and graphic elements of the source text, but to the audience and the broad literary system in which the translated text will be integrated."[17] The reception of a foreign culture by its colony carries with it the possibility of the colonized subjects' agency; as writing and reading subjects, Koreans' notions of selfhood and national identity were formed in their close engagement with foreign texts, mirroring the differences established through the translation process.

Existing scholarship in translation studies scrutinizes the relationship between translation and colonialism, identifying translation as part of an unequal cultural exchange between colonized worlds and colonizers, and exploring possibilities of a preserved and secured native culture through the acceptance, appropriation, and alteration of foreign culture in the form of translation.[18] In the case of colonial Korea, recent research has begun to examine the importance of translation in the formation and the development of modern Korean literature, viewing literature as a site of negotiation between the colonized and the colonizer where conflicting and competing narratives of colonialism and nationalism collide. While this book recognizes translation practice as a manifestation of the colonized's "desire to reconfirm his or her authorial and authoritarian voice";[19] as a medium that constructs and reinforces "the concept and the substance of national language and literature;[20] and as a process of extralinguistic

---

17. Jose Maria Rodriguez Garcia, "Introduction: Literary into Cultural Translation," *Diacritics* 34, no. 3/4 (Autumn/Winter 2004): 9.

18. See a collection of essays that investigates the relationship between translation and colonialism from theoretical and practical perspectives in *Post-Colonial Translation: Theory and Practice*, ed. Susan Bassnett and Harish Trived (New York: Routledge, 1999). See also a theoretical approach to translation as a site for perpetuating the unequal power relations among peoples, races, and languages in Tejaswini Niranjana, *Siting Translation: History, Post-Structuralism, and the Colonial Context* (Berkeley: University of California Press, 1992).

19. Serk-Bae Suh, *Treacherous Translation: Culture, Nationalism, and Colonialism in Korea and Japan from the 1910s to the 1960s* (Berkeley: University of California Press, 2013), xxvi.

20. Heekyoung Cho, *Translations' Forgotten History: Russian Literature, Japanese Mediation, and the Formation of Modern Korean Literature* (Cambridge, MA: Harvard University Press, 2016), 2.

and intralinguistc exploration of the modern concept, "the individual,"[21] it also views translation as a political act, encompassing the historical consciousness about and attitude toward culturally different "Others" formed within the transnational literary sphere.

The novel contributed to the process of imagining Korea as a national community by connecting people within the national boundary and culture as distinct from other nations.[22] In eighteenth- and nineteenth-century Europe, the formation of the novel was strongly affiliated with the establishment of the nation-state and the capitalist force.[23] This not only "set the tone of the new way of reading,"[24] but also grounded a new way of writing for Korean writers who did not yet have the notion of "authorship" or see their writing as an artistic endeavor. Rather, they viewed themselves as educators, reformers, and cultural mediators.

Even before its annexation of Korea in 1910, the Japanese colonial state also actively sought to utilize the novel. They did so for the same reason as the intellectuals did, recognizing its effectiveness in the dissemination of education for modernizing the Korean nation. What nationalist intellectuals tried to promote in their novels—that is, the modernization of Korea—was also the goal of the colonial state, though the political tension between nationalists and colonialists manifested to varying degrees in this fictional space. At times, it was explicit, especially right before the annexation. It was much more nuanced in the early colonial period, mainly due to the censorship. This historical tension gave a push to the development of modern Korean literature in terms of the variety of literary styles and characters.[25]

As the colonial government forced their presses to close down, nationalist writers found no place to advocate for Korea's political independence. But Korean writers and translators continued working with the colonial

21. Yoon Sun Yang, *From Domestic Women to Sensitive Young Men: Translating the Individual in Early Colonial Korea* (Cambridge, MA: Harvard University Asia Center, 2017), 4.

22. Benedict Anderson, *Imagined Communities: Reflections on the Origin and Spread of Nationalism* (New York: Verso, 2006).

23. Franco Moretti, *Atlas of the European Novel, 1800–1900* (New York: Verso, 1999), 17.

24. Moretti, "History of the Novel," 8.

25. Kwŏn Yŏngmin, *Han'guk hyŏndae munhaksa I* (A history of modern Korean literature I) (Seoul: Minŭmsa, 2002), 33.

newspaper, *The Daily*. And yet, this collaboration with the colonial media does not justify the national-versus-colonial binary prevalent in postcolonial scholarship on literary history. First, these writers viewed themselseves as something like cultural mediators whose sense of duty to modernize Korea happened to overlap with the colonial interest. They were able to work with and within the colonial power precisely because their civilizing mission was supported by the colonial state. Second, their fiction works, both creative and translated ones, reveal an ambivalent attitude toward modernity. This ambivalence often manifests itself in their construction of gender roles and relations where the suppressed position of colonized men, and by extension the Korean nation, is represented through descriptions of domestic affairs and of femininity and masculinity. The construction of gender hierarchy, female sexuality, and family in these works thus cannot be solely viewed as a manifestation of male anxiety over the control of patriarchal power in a colonial situation that systematically bars them from participating in the public sphere;[26] the handling of domestic issues could also articulate men's imagination of the nation and modernity under colonial domination.

In tandem with the formation of the novel was the male contest over nation and modernity, in which women were relegated to the margins of society and cultural productions yet were called upon as destined to support the nation by investing their intelligence, emotion, and physical energy into childrearing and housework. The nationalists' and the colonial state's emphasis on women's education in novels remained empty rhetoric, used to reinforce gender hierarchy in the service of the male-dominated reordering of the social sphere. The formation of the novel then signifies how gender became an important ground on which the fiction of the nation and modernity was constructed, and how the hegemonic language of gender resulted in a stringent gender hierarchy in the social and cultural spheres of colonial Korea.

GENDERED REPRESENTATION OF MODERNITY

The rhetoric of the transformation of women in premodern Korea into ideal national subjects in the modern colonized nation was widely used by

---

26. Ania Loomba, *Colonialism/Postcolonialism* (London: Routledge, 2001), 157–168.

the colonial state, and by *The Daily* in particular. Women's disadvantaged position as an uneducated and mistreated group was often criticized as a social malady in editorials, news reports, and novels. Yet pointing at women as a repository of feudalism did not lead the state to attempt to secure gender equality by institutional measures. Instead, the interplay of editorials, reports, and novels dealing with gender contributed to the establishment of the binary opposition of premodern Korea versus modern Japan through the blending of factual and fictional narratives of modernity.

In the early and mid-1910s, most Korean writers and translators concentrated on the issue of domesticity. Their novels dealt with women's education and conjugal and family relations, in which women gained greater mobility, crossing geographical boundaries and obtaining higher education overseas. Mobile women outside domestic and national boundaries, however, cannot be solely understood in terms of the colonial state's overall aim to promote its agenda of equality in the colony, since women's mobility is conditioned by domestic problems and determined by male guidance. Almost always, women return to their domestic space at the end of their extensive travels as wise mothers and good wives, committed to providing intellectual and emotional support for their families and husbands. However, it would be too simplistic to read the male-guided mobility of women as just a symbolic manifestation of the imperial enterprise of reorganizing the colonial order through gender dynamics.[27] Whereas the image of women is invariable in terms of the absence of subjectivity and complete submission to their husbands, male figures are more diverse, revealing the symbolic association of patriarchal power and nationalistic consciousness.

There are three distinctive narratives of men in these novels that reveal the ambiguity of imposed modernity: the self-criticism of feudalism through reduced patriarchal power, the attempt to restore this reduced masculinity by controlling the domestic sphere, and finally, the granting of transnational mobility to men as a way to fend off the exploitative nature of colonial capitalism. The works of Yi Injik and Yi Haejo, whose writing careers spanned the early 1900s to the early 1910s, contain good

---

27. Anne McClintock argues that "gender dynamics were fundamental to securing and maintenance of the imperial enterprise." See Anne McClintock, *Imperial Leather: Race, Gender and Sexuality in the Colonial Contest* (New York and London: Routledge, 1995), 7.

examples of the vehement criticism directed toward men, especially older generations of men who are depicted as immoral, corrupt, and greedy. These men, contrary to their mobile and educated daughters, represent the stagnation of Korea, as they lack the ability to rebuild the nation. These men are unwilling to educate themselves, unlike their female counterparts, and are punished for their shameful social behaviors by legal measures, criminalizing the moral flaws behind such behaviors.

The figures of elderly men in these novels functioned as a social criticism by native writers who believed that the former social elites, *yangban*, were to blame for Korea's lagging behind the new world order. Figures of young men, on the other hand, appear radically different from the previous generations. In Cho Chunghwan's translations of Japanese domestic fiction, these young men aspire to upward social mobility and display a strong commitment to serve society and support their families. The physical and emotional controlling of women by men illustrates how the colonial state's attempt to reorder society through gender in fact became an opportunity for male writers and translators to express through gender their anxiety over colonial control. This anxiety grew over time, and the politicization of emotion in the domestic space expanded to become global in novels produced in the mid-1910s. Men are not only given transnational mobility but also financial resources that enable them to restore their damaged masculinity in Korean translations of crime fiction, for example.

Besides the expression of male anxiety over colonial modernity through feminine roles and sexuality, the generational difference among men and the changing descriptions of their masculinity is noteworthy. Masculine voices expressing concern over modernization became more authoritative, and the desire to sever ties with the past was intensified over the period; male figures in these works evolved from incapable and immoral fathers to educated and responsible young men who willingly take on the heavy burden of changing the course of history. While the changing figures of patriarchy signified young Korean elites' political consciousness and intent to modernize the nation, this type of masculine voice of authority solidified the gender boundary in social and cultural spheres.

The deep-seated notion of gender distinction in cultural labor was enhanced in the following decades, especially in the 1920s, during which a greater number of Korean male elites engaged in cultural production more actively than ever as a way to modernize Korea, with the ultimate goal of actualizing national independence. In the literary sphere, the two most prolific modern novelists, Yi Kwangsu and Kim Tongin, made it clear that writing was a man's career, urging women to stay at home as good mothers and spiritual supporters for their husbands,[28] and denouncing them as readers who lacked esthetic sensibility and thus could never become writers.[29] Women were to receive guidance in their reading practice, and their intrusion into the male-specific cultural labor market came with a heavy cost that seriously endangered their livelihoods. This gendered notion of novel authorship not only confirms the homogenization of women in an ongoing ideology that buttressed male authority in the name of national progress and independence, but also reveals how it supported the rationality of modernity that is organized by masculine language.[30]

Chapter 1 discusses the process by which fiction (*sosŏl*) changed from the late Chosŏn to the turn of the century by focusing on authorship, readership, and the genre's connection to transnational literary practices and print media. Having been marginalized from the sphere of literature proper by Confucian elite culture, reformist intellectuals began promoting "the novel" publicly. Their approach to fiction work was pragmatic; it was seen as a tool to educate the populace to become national subjects for national progress while delivering the intellectuals' political vision of modern nationhood. Writers had a top-down approach to the novel, using female characters to disseminate their reformist agenda. These works were not necessarily directed to female readers; rather, stories about Korean women were meant to equate the masses with women, or with the uneducated who needed to be civilized. Women, in other words, were a single collective entity whose endeavors to educate themselves symbolized leveling up the status of the masses. I describe the process in which nationalists treated the masses as women through their novels as a "feminization process," in which the emphasis on women's roles in the national context and

---

28. Yi Kwangsu, *Sinyŏsŏng*, January 1925, 19–20.

29. Kim Tongin, "Sosŏl e taehan Chosŏn saram ŭi sasang ŭl" (Toward the embodiment of Koreans' thoughts in novels), in *Kim Tongin chŏnjip*, vol. 16 (Seoul: Chosŏn il-bosa, [1919] 1988), 138–141.

30. The language of reason and the techniques of domination have been organized around masculine norms and principles, leaving very little room for the discussion of feminine agency and desire or representations of femininity that consider women's experience of modernity. See Rita Felski, *The Gender of Modernity* (Cambridge, MA: Harvard University Press, 1995), 1–34.

gendered visions of the civilized world were the products of a nation-building project that dramatically changed the social status of authorship and the readership of fiction.

Chapter 2 focuses on historical novels by examining the impact of transnational literature on nationalist intellectuals at the turn of the century. The two most distinctive modes of constructing patriotic men and women embedded in the selected novels are political passion and public persuasion in the form of speeches and debates, which were intended to stimulate the masses to participate in the nation-building process by arming them with patriotic passion. While these modes of representation were not invented by Korean authors but borrowed from foreign texts, the textual differences between the translations and originals are the result of their negotiation with the invasive force of imperialism. The passion and persuasion directed toward the masses were more clearly delivered by the authors' gendering of national history and territory embodied in the altered figures of heroines. Special emphasis is placed on Confucianism-inspired reinterpretations of Western heroines such as Joan of Arc (1412–1431) and Marie-Jeanne Roland (1754–1793) who are transformed into national mothers. These women's nurturing motherly nature, rather than their political vision and acts, became inspiration for Koreans, illuminating how the reform program to turn the masses into national subjects was carried out through altering the femininity of these historical figures whose shining golden armor and heroic political acts could not compare to the maternal spirit of Mencius's mother.

Chapter 3 focuses on two novelists, Yi Injik and Yi Haejo, who concentrated on the production of creative fiction. These two writers are unique in this time period, first because of their professional attitude toward the novel and second because of their prevailing concern with women's issues. Although greater scholarly interest has been given to Yi Injik in postcolonial Korea for his fiction work *Tears of Blood* (*Hyŏl ŭi nu*), Yi Haejo is unique for his concentration on fiction writing; unlike other writers and translators who were also active in newspaper journalism, he remained a fiction writer until the end of his life. Yi Haejo's ongoing experiments with the novel form resulted in a diversification of themes and narratives.

The two writers' shared interest in reforming Korean society was often manifested in their description of mobile women. These women move from the domestic space to national and global space, usually by force, and by obtaining Western-inspired modern education, they are juxtaposed with morally corrupt and greedy Korean men. These men are elderly, pointing to the writers' criticism of former *yangban*, incurring shame for their inability to defend their nation against the external force and thus their loss of patriarchal authority. This deconstruction of traditional masculinity is spotted in a number of symbolic representations of home and family. Fathers are often absent at home at a time of familial or national crisis; men either lose or cannot father sons; and they are tricked and humiliated by their wives. These men can correct their character only through institutional measures; more specifically law enforcement, further demonstrating their impotent state where they have no choice but to accept the intervention of force to reorganize their domestic sphere.

Chapter 4 explores the emotional dimension of the colonial rule by analyzing Korean translations of Japanese domestic fiction in the early to mid-1910s. It scrutinizes the close relationship between the novel and the colonial newspaper, *The Daily*, in order to contextualize the popularization of the genre wherein romance and marriage by choice became the main topics. By comparing the reception of this genre in Japan and Korea, it aims to show how, what at first glance seemed to be a politically innocuous genre in fact, served dual purposes for the colonial state and the translator, namely Cho Chunghwan who greatly altered the original texts. For the colonial state, stories of romance and marriage by choice were an indicator of individuality and freedom guaranteed for the colonized; and women returning to their homes in these novels represent the social order in the domestic sphere, which the colonial government aimed to ensure.

However, writing about individuality and freedom in the absence of political rights, as well as romance and marriage by choice, provided an opportunity for Cho Chunghwan to express the ambiguity of modernity. The uneven experience of modernity and the anxiety over reduced masculinity in the public sphere caused him to alter the originals in ways that suggest the colonized men's discontent with the capitalist force and political suppression, especially in his emphasis on men's display of emotions such as love, hate, and faithfulness, all of which were often accompanied by their tears. Men's tears are juxtaposed with women's tears of remorse and atonement, signifying how the purity of men's tears is rewarded by women's commitment to becoming good wives. Behind the veil of the overflowing emotion expressed by young men and women, we see men's desire to sustain patriarchal power in the face of the colonial force that reduces their patriarchy by eliminating them from the public sphere.

The final chapter examines two works of crime fiction, *A Virtuous Woman's Resentment* and *Neptune*, produced in the mid-1910s. The former was a translation of *Diavola*, originally penned by Mary Elizabeth Braddon (1837–1915), and the latter was a translation of *The Count of Monte Cristo* by Alexandre Dumas (1802–1870). Whereas all the translations I examine in the previous chapters localized the imported texts by changing names and locations into Korean, these two unusually lengthy novels are differentiated by their foreign settings—Europe for the former and China for the latter. The translator Yi Sanghyŏp's strategic translations of the Japanese intermediary texts demonstrate how the increasingly exploitative nature of colonial rule stimulated Koreans to imagine transnational mobility and economic affluence. This is especially evident in *Neptune*, where the story of a vengeful Chinese man and his personal revenge on villains was a radical commentary on the colonial rule that seriously endangered Korean men's patriarchal authority.

This critical commentary on colonial rule was achieved through three distinctive features in these works. First, unlike the almost blind faith in law enforcement shown in previous novels, law and law enforcement are challenged here. The police or legal professionals are either incapable or are lacking morality and a work ethic, thus leaving protagonists to bring about justice by themselves. Second, Korea is invisible in these works: the only Korean presence is in the names of characters. This invisibility, however, actually reveals the colonial enterprise in Korea that produces numerous forms of injustice and discrimination; this is achieved through strategic alteration of the original texts. Third, the desire for transnational mobility and access to capital is evident: these are the two most crucial conditions that signify freedom for the colonized. Protagonists' free movement from one global city to another, together with the constant fabrication of their class and ethnic identities, represent the anxiety of the colonized about their experiences of the inconsistency of modernity.

The imagined Korean nation was built on the paradox of modernity that supposedly ensures freedom for all but in reality only justifies imperialists' exploitation of the colonized, thus enslaving them materialistically and spiritually.[31] This book tries to identify sites where that paradox reveals itself and investigate the way gender became an effective means to articulate that paradox. Thus, writers' and translators' grave concerns about nation and modernity were expressed most vividly in their handling of gender issues in novels. This kind of representation produced a rigid gender hierarchy in social and cultural spheres. Inasmuch as the male-dominated cultural sphere became an arena for expressing ambivalence toward the colonized masses, women, with their absence of representative power, were imagined as a single unified category whose role and sexuality served the purpose of embodying the ambiguous benefits of nation and modernity. The imagination of the Other by male writers and translators, in other words, produced woman as a perpetual Other during the colonial period.

---

31. See Susan Buck-Morris for a discussion of the paradox of the Hegelian notion of history in the Haitian context. Susan Buck-Morris, *Hegel, Haiti, and Universal History* (Pittsburgh, PA: University of Pittsburgh Press, 2009).

1

THE NOVEL IN TRANSITION

Fiction Authorship and Readership from Late Chosŏn to the Early Twentieth Century

THE TERM *SOSŎL* HAS EXISTED IN KOREA since premodern times, referring to various forms of fictional narratives, and yet its concept had changed significantly by the turn of the century. Consider the following excerpt from *Ch'ujae's Collection of Strange Stories (Ch'ujae kii)* that was published in the mid-nineteenth century.

> The old fiction narrator [*chŏn'gisu*] I talk about here lived outside Tong-daemun. He was especially good at reciting vulgar novels written in ver-nacular [*ŏnmun p'aesŏl*] before his audience, such as *The Tale of Sukhyang, The Tale of So Taesŏng, The Tale of Simch'ŏng* and *The Tale of the General Xue Rengui.* He recited these stories at different locations, traveling back and forth from Ch'ŏnggye stream to Chonggak area; and he repeated this sequence every month. People swarmed around him when he appeared because he was so talented in telling stories. At some point during the narration, he would shut his mouth all of a sudden especially when a story was moving toward a climax. Being so anxious to hear the next part of the story, people would throw coins toward him as a way to rush him to come back to the narration. This strategy is called the "technique of demanding money [*yojŏnpŏp*]."[1]

This scene shows a typical way of experiencing fictional narratives for people at the time who could expect to enjoy an approximately four-hour-long literary entertainment. From this passage, we can identify how our

---

1. Cho Susam, *Ch'ujae kii* (Ch'ujae's collection of strange stories), cited in Yi Sŭngwŏn, *Sarajin chigŏp ŭi yŏksa* (A history of jobs that disappeared) (Seoul: Irum, 2011), 103–104.

understanding of "the novel," which is also called *sosŏl*, is quite distant from how people perceived it then. First, fictional narratives were not always meant to be read. Oral performance was an integral part for both illiterate and literate people to experience the world of fiction. Fiction narrators were also invited to inner chambers at elite households in order to entertain women who were not free to go out of their houses. It seems that these narrators were mostly men who would disguise themselves as women or doctors to enter the inner chambers.[2] It is unlikely that women in elite households were illiterate in vernacular; inviting the narrators secretly to their inner chambers was more about the entertaining aspect of the performance, which involved acting. Second, fiction narrators relied on stories mostly written in vernacular—a trend with which literati, such as the author of *Ch'ujae's Collection*, were not familiar. Common folks had their own way of entertaining themselves with the aid of narrators such as the old man introduced above. Third, as the titles of the stories indicate, popular fiction works were drawn from tales and legends, with both native and Chinese origins. China in particular played a significant role, since fiction works from China were an important source for common folks and literati alike to imagine the world outside their domestic borders, especially from the late Chosŏn period.

The form, style, and content of the novel as well as reading practices would change at the turn of the twentieth century as a result of contact with external forces, a time that is often referred to as *Aeguk kyemonggi* (the period of the Patriotic Enlightenment Movement). In contrast to late Chosŏn, when fiction was subject to strict state censorship, vernacular fiction began to be promoted publicly from the turn of the twentieth century. Women who were excluded from the public sphere in Chosŏn were encouraged to read fiction as a way to be active members in the nation-building process. Reform-minded social elites promoted vernacular fiction enthusiastically, something Confucian literati in Chosŏn could not imagine doing. Women as well as low-class men, in fact, had been reading fiction all along in Chosŏn, as the aforementioned example shows. The popular written fiction and oral narratives they had consumed in the past, however, were not counted as "novels" proper now. Rather, these texts and

---

2. Ibid., 105.

the oral narratives were bad literary traditions to be eradicated in the minds of the nationalist social elites.

Unlike the Confucian literati's indifference to and disdainful attitude toward popular literature, a coterie of nationalist social elites at the turn of the century began to apply an entirely new perspective to fiction genres, though they still maintained an authoritative attitude when addressing readers. Sin Ch'aeho, for example, admonished his readers and writers about what kind of fiction they should read and produce. He criticized *sosŏl* that feature lewdness (*hoeŭm*), which he thought would eventually degrade the morality of national subjects. He believed "*Sosŏl* is the compass for patriotic national subjects" (*kungmin*), for it has the power to lead the masses to a "right place."[3] Sin's statement directs us to see writers' functional approach to the novel; many reform-minded intellectual writers such as Sin believed the novel to be study material for the ignorant masses so that they could be led to a "right place," that is, transformed into patriotic national subjects. In their eyes, traditional novels such as *The Tale of Ch'unhyang* or *The Tale of Unyŏng*—the two most popular novels in Chosŏn that were still widely read until the 1930s—were certainly not to be recommended, since they do not deal with national affairs but trivial and perhaps lewd matters, romantic encounters, and supernatural phenomena.

Although reform-minded social elites such as Sin promoted vernacular fiction, it would be premature to assume that these elites discovered aesthetic value in the popular fiction they had disregarded in the past. Their approach to fiction was instrumental, viewing it as a tool to educate the populace about the importance of modernizing their society for national progress. Fiction, in other words, became a conduit to deliver the reformists' political vision of modernity and nationhood. Nationalist intellectuals/writers' preoccupation with matters of nation and civilization would redefine the traditional notion of fiction. Their efforts to disseminate their fictional narratives through modern print media, newspapers in particular, would change the ways readers perceived the genre in the following decades.

---

3. Sin Ch'aeho, "Sosŏlga ŭi ch'use" (A trend among fiction writers), *Taehan maeil sinbo*, 2 December 1909.

Both fictional and nonfictional texts were preoccupied with ways to turn people into national subjects in gendered terms at the turn of the century. On the one hand, these works encouraged women to educate themselves to become wise mothers and good wives, and a large number of fictional narratives featured stories of Western and Korean women whose patriotic spirit was intended as a model for their fellow Korean women to follow. On the other hand, some female characters were portrayed as victims of the customs and manners of the past, such as domestic violence, concubinage, and class discrimination, all of which were to be eradicated in order for Korea to move forward. In other words, women became a barometer of civilization by playing their roles as exemplary mothers and wives as well as victims. These fictional narratives did not necessarily target female readers only. Even if they dealt with women's stories exclusively, emphasizing female characters' roles was a narrative strategy that could separate the present from the past. Having been excluded from public life in the past, the exposure of women's issues in public media was effective for stressing the horizontal social relations necessary for nation-building.

The masculine norms and principles articulated in both fictional and nonfictional texts resulted in the "feminization of the masses" at the time; writers used women to represent the masses while categorically dismissing their subjectivity and political agency. It is through this process that women became a homogenous category in colonial Korea, a subject to be disciplined and yet always remaining inferior. I use "feminization" in this chapter to mean a top-down process of indoctrinating the masses through the novel in which women played the central role in transforming the masses from ignorant and pitiful to educated and patriotic, "enlightened" individuals whose roles would be redefined in the national context.

THE STATUS OF FICTION IN LATE CHOSŎN

In Chosŏn, literature (*munhak*) was a broad term that referred to a wide range of intellectual and leisure activities, such as Confucian classics, poetry, calligraphy, music, and painting. The term was also used when referring to educational training, bureaucratic positions, and even culture itself.[4] Those categories of literature, however loosely defined, fell in line with the Confucian worldview: they were formed and practiced mostly by the literati class whose cultural activities were firmly rooted in Confucian-based principles of art and philosophy. The term *sosŏl*[5] was as broad as the term "literature" at the time, though it was placed in the periphery of literati culture.

In Chosŏn there was a strong tendency among literati to look down on forms of writing that dealt with sensual or fictional matters, although imported Chinese fiction—biographical fiction in particular—had been read by Chosŏn literati since the late seventeenth century.[6] Generally considered nonsense stories, the status of fictional narratives was especially low at this time. They were dismissed as a suitable pastime only for women and lower-class people. The status of fiction written in the Korean vernacular was even lower than that of fiction written in classical Chinese (*hanmun*). Fluency in classical Chinese was not only cultural capital for privileged people—more specifically *yangban*—demonstrating their social status, it was also a crucial condition for maintaining their authority.

Because a significant amount of Chosŏn literature originated in China, Korean fiction showed similarities to Chinese fiction. Scholars of premodern Chinese literature generally agree that *xiaoshuo* (fictional narratives, *sosŏl* in Korean) include some "historical writings, myths and legends, parables and allegories in philosophical writings, and records of extraordinary things and people in the Six Dynasties."[7] In premodern Korea, *sosŏl* meant both fictional and nonfictional narratives that dealt with a

---

4. Kwŏn Podŭre, *Han'guk kŭndae sosŏl ŭi kiwŏn* (The origin of modern Korean literature) (Seoul: Somyŏng, 2000), 20.

5. The term *sosŏl* was first mentioned by Zhuang Zi when he criticized people who gained bureaucratic positions by cozying up to authorities with the use of words. In this context, *sosŏl* is treated as a vulgar form of human interaction that utilizes spoken language to fulfill social and political ambitions.

6. The state played the central role in importing these novels and storing them in the palace. It was during the reign of King Chŏngjo when the import of these books was banned. Kwandong Min and Sŭnghyŏn Yu, "Chosŏn ŭi chungguk sosŏl suyong kwa chŏnp'a ŭi chuch'edŭl" (The acceptance of Chinese fiction and its agents in Chosŏn), *Chungguk sosŏl nonch'ong* (A treatise of Chinese fiction) 33 (2011): 175–205.

7. Ming Dong Gu, *Chinese Theories of Fiction: A Non-Western Narrative System* (Albany: State University of New York Press, 2006), 37.

wide variety of subject and thematic matters as well. What scholars commonly call premodern fiction (*kojŏn sosŏl*) in present-day Korea generally refers to works that were written in prose form, including legends, myths, and anecdotes.[8] In Japan, the term appears in the late seventeenth century when Ming phonology and linguistics drew the attention of Japanese Confucian scholars. It is generally referred to as "defective or dubious historical writings" (*haishi*: vulgar, unorthodox history) as opposed to "official history" (*seishi*).[9] In sum, fiction was generally perceived as an inferior category of narrative to "literature" in premodern East Asia.[10]

The seventeenth and eighteenth centuries saw a gradual change in terms of the authorship and readership of fiction. The amount of imported Chinese fiction increased dramatically. The sudden increase in Chinese books, including fiction, followed the loss of many texts that had been burned during the Japanese invasion (1592–1598) and the two Manchu invasions (in 1627 and 1636).[11] It must be noted that, in contrast to the Chosŏn government's reliance on the Qing court as a source to replenish texts, the content of a large amount of fiction from China displayed anti-Qing tendencies in its imagination of the restoration of the Ming. After the two Manchu invasions, an affiliation with and nostalgia for Ming China grew among Korean Ming loyalists who promoted "the theory of conquest of the northern areas" (*pukpŏllon*). The desire to revere the Ming was joined with the desire to restore national pride that had been damaged by the Manchus, and this was reflected in fictional narratives where militant heroes and heroines played important roles in the popular imagination of the lost era.[12]

---

8. Ji-Eun Lee, "Literary, Sosŏl, and Women in Book Culture in Late Chosŏn Korea," *East Asian Publishing and Society* 4 (2014): 44.

9. See Tomi Suzuki, *Narrating the Self* (Stanford, CA: Stanford University Press, 1996), 15–32, for the status of *shōsetsu* between the late seventeenth century and the early twentieth century.

10. In China, the status of the novel began to be elevated in the eighteenth century through the publication of *The Dream of Red Chamber*. Ming Dong Gu, *Chinese Theories of Fiction*, 20.

11. As a way to restock books in state institutions, the Chosŏn government imported large quantities of books from China shortly after these two national disasters; Chinese fiction was also brought to the peninsula during this time, mostly by interpreters who accompanied envoys to China. Ibid., 187. Min Kwandong and Sŭnghyŏn Yu, *Chosŏn ŭi chungguk sosŏl*, 187.

12. The texts that are currently available were mostly written in the nineteenth century, and attempts to identify the Chinese influence in Korean literature are pursued by

Korean readers' interest in Chinese fiction perhaps had partly to do with the emergence of the aesthetically refined late Ming novels such as *The Dream of Red Chamber* (*Hongloumeng*) and *The Golden Lotus* (*Jin Ping Mei*). As Ming Dong Gu points out, these novels were noteworthy in the history of Chinese fiction for their exploration of the inner worlds of characters, which, he argues, was a trend that was rooted in Tang fiction such as *The Story of Ying Ying*.[13] This new literary development in Chinese fiction did not go unnoticed by Chosŏn literati who read *The Dream of Red Chamber* and *The Golden Lotus,* and vernacular translations of these novels were widely read by elite and nonelite women, doctors, technicians, and scientists until the turn of the twentieth century.[14] Despite the burgeoning interest in fiction, fictional works were still not fully recognized as a "legitimate" literary genre by the Chosŏn literati and the state, especially during the reign of King Chŏngjo (1752–1800), who imposed tougher censorship than had existed in the previous era. The state's tight control of reading materials derived from some of the imported books that questioned the legitimacy of the Chosŏn state; and the punishment for those who violated the state rule was severe at times.[15] However, the number of imported books did not decrease, since booksellers, brokers, and readers alike found ways to circumvent the state regulation, going underground to circulate books.[16]

Despite his strict rule on the import and circulation of some books from Qing, especially fiction, King Chŏngjo (1752–1800) is well known for

---

examining secondary sources. Im Sŏngnae, *Chosŏn hugi ŭi taejung sosŏl* (Popular fiction in late Chosŏn) (Seoul: Pogosa, 2008), 23.

13. Ming Dong Gu, *Chinese Theories of Fiction,* 80.

14. Im Sŏngnae, *Chosŏn hugi ŭi taejung sosŏl,* 48. It should also be noted that even some well-recognized literati started to pay serious attention to Chinese fiction at this point, exchanging ideas about and criticism of the literary form and its content within their literati circles. Chŏng Sŏnhi, "18 segi Chosŏn munindŭl ŭi chungguk sosŏl toksŏ silt'ae wa toksŏ tamnon" (Reading patterns and literary discourses among Choson literati in the eighteenth century), in *17/8 segi Chosŏn ŭi oeguk sŏjŏk suyong kwa toksŏ munhwa* (The reception of foreign texts and the reading culture in seventeenth and eighteenth-century Chosŏn), ed. Hong Sŏnp'yo et al. (Seoul: Hyean, 2006), 53.

15. At one point, more than one hundred booksellers and brokers were imprisoned, tortured and executed. Jamie Jungmin Yoo, "Networks of Disquiet: Censorship and the Production of Literature in Eighteenth-Century Korea," *Acta Koreana* 20, no. 1 (2017): 249–250.

16. Ibid., 272.

his passion for books from Qing; Chinese sources were crucial to enrich and enlarge his famous private library, *Hongjae*. The king's practice of avidly collecting books derived from his emphasis on transnational cultural and economic exchanges with Qing, which he thought tremendously important for national development in many areas of society. Many other elites followed suit in various ways, such as joining the official delegation to the Qing court or asking the delegates to purchase books, though their interest in books went beyond scholarly, including something that would annoy the king: fiction.[17]

Given the disdainful view of fiction and the tightened censorship of the time, authors would generally conceal their true names when publishing fiction works. Some literati's engagement with vernacular fiction, if known to the public, was harshly criticized by their peers. When one of the most celebrated calligraphers and scholars of late Chosŏn, Kim Chŏnghŭi (1786–1856), translated the famous Chinese love story *Sŏsanggi* (*Romance of the West Chamber*)[18] into the Korean vernacular, his friend showed deep concern over his engagement with this "lowly" form of culture: "A virtuous gentleman [*kunja*] should not read anything but words of sages. It is inappropriate to turn your head to a trivial and sensual fiction like *Sŏsanggi*, but you are even translating it!"[19] Kim Chŏnghŭi's translation of the story may have been alarming to Confucian literati like his friend at the time. Reading fictional narratives was often perceived as a woman's pastime; the Korean vernacular *ŏnmun* (vulgar script) was the script for women and the lower class that literati avoided using, since doing so could diminish their status and authority that was maintained by their knowledge of Chinese script and Confucian texts.

---

17. Nineteenth-century Chosŏn, unlike the conventional view of it as a period of waning culture (including popular culture), was a culturally dynamic era for the transcultural literary flow that reached even common folks and the circulation of court culture of Chosŏn outside the palace. Pak Ch'ŏlsang, *Sŏjae e salda: Chosŏn chisigin 24in ŭi sŏjae iyagi* (Stories of private libraries of 24 intellectuals in Chosŏn) (Seoul: Munhak tongnae, 2014), 196–197.

18. *Xīxiāngjì*. It is a tragic love story set in the Tang dynasty, written by Wang Shifu of the Yuan dynasty.

19. Cited in Ōtani Morishige, *Chosŏn hugi sosŏl tokja yŏn'gu* (A study of fiction readership in the late Chosŏn) (Seoul: Korea University, [1985] 1995), 116.

As Kim's case shows, it would be simplistic to view the readership of fiction written in classical Chinese (*hanmun sosŏl*) and that of fiction written in the Korean vernacular as categories of readers that were firmly separated by gender and status based on the script they read. The attributes of popular appeal (*t'ongsoksŏng*) in vernacular fiction—such as sensual and nonrealistic handlings of human affairs, considered a prominent feature of vernacular fiction in the scholarship of modern Korean literature—are also seen in *hanmun sosŏl*, especially since the seventeenth century, such as *The Tale of Unyŏng* (*Unyŏngjŏn*) or *The Tale of Sangsa-dong* (*Sangsa donggi*).[20] As Janet Yoon-sun Lee points out, the image of emotionally vulnerable elite men, who become victims of love in these two fiction works, defies the ideal of the Confucian gentleman portrayed in Chosŏn, who cultivates his morality and knowledge to serve the state and the society. Lee argues that this image of men demonstrates how social expectations of the elite masculinity are negotiated in these works by allowing men to speak frankly about their passion for romance.[21] In other words, there were particular fictional narratives with appeal for nonelites that also interested male elites.

Further, many male elites either translated Chinese fiction into vernacular or authored vernacular fiction. Some notable translators and authors are Kim Chŏnghŭi, Hong Hŭibok (1794–1859), Hŏ Kyun (1569–1618), and Kim Manjung (1637–1692). Hong mentioned that he translated *The Most Admirable Stories* (*Cheil kiŏn*,[22] c. 1840) in vernacular in order for his "family to share the joy of reading fiction,"[23] while Kim Manjung wrote *The Cloud Dream of the Nine* (*Kuunmong*, 1789) to entertain his mother. It seems that Hong was not a rare case, since he reported that literati with no official positions like Hong himself, as well as learned women, also translated fiction during his time.[24] So it seems that reading fiction was one of the most popular leisure activities for a wide spectrum

20. Yang Sŭngin, *Hanmun sosŏl ŭi t'ongsoksŏng* (The popular appeal in fiction written in Chinese script) (Seoul: Pogosa, 2008).

21. Janet Yoon-sun Lee, "Dilemma of the Lovesick Hero: Masculine Images and Politics of the Body in Seventeenth-Century Korean Love Tales," *Journal of Korean Studies* 21, no. 1 (2016): 45–69.

22. The Chinese original is *Flowers in the Mirror, Kyŏnghwarok*, a fantasy novel written by Li Ruzhen (1763–1830) in 1827.

23. Ōtani Morishige, *Chosŏn hugi sosŏl tokja yŏn'gu*, 124.

24. Cited in Min Kwandong and Yu Sŭnghyŏn, *Chosŏn ŭi chungguk sosŏl*, 189.

of people during the eighteenth century.[25] And it played a role beyond entertaining readers. It also challenged the strict social values and hierarchy in their society. Fiction written by Hŏ Kyun, Kim Manjung, and Pak Chiwŏn (1737–1805), for example, includes the social criticism of class hierarchy and political corruption as well as the state's economic policies and practices.

Some popular vernacular fiction that circulated among women featured women's desire to demonstrate their intellectual and physical strengths to stand on equal footing with men.[26] Nineteenth-century vernacular fiction such as *The Story of Yi Taebong* (*Yi Taebongjŏn*), *The Story of Hwang Un* (*Hwang Unjŏn*), and *The Story of Chŏng Sujŏng* (*Chŏng Sujŏngjŏn*) all portray heroines whose intellectual and militaristic abilities surpass those of their male counterparts. These examples illustrate that authors were well aware of their intended readers' discontent with the draconian social structure and values so deeply rooted in neo-Confucian orthodoxy. Reading, in other words, was a social act by which underprivileged men and women could identify social problems. The popular appeal of fiction, then, can tell us about people's attitudes toward their society in a way that official literature and history do not. Thus it should be questioned whether the Chosŏn literati's vehement attacks on vernacular fiction, in which they positioned this fiction as a cause for the degradation of literature and deterioration of people's morality,[27] were in fact a way of recognizing social unrest and disorder that was manifest in the act of reading.

The claim by existing scholarship that reading fiction was a predominantly female activity, and its presumption that readership was divided along gender lines according to script, have not been sufficiently supported.[28] As Ji-Eun Lee rightly points out, the male-dominant arena of cultural

---

25. Ibid., 20.

26. It must be noted, however, it is challenging to generalize the characteristics of fiction works produced in late Chosŏn that emphasize women's roles because of the inconsistency of narrative structures as well as the diversity of female characters in them. Ha Kyŏngsim, "Chosŏn yŏsŏng yŏngung sosŏl ŭi ch'urhyŏn paekyŏng e kwanhan siron" (An essay on the emergence of heroines in Chosŏn fiction), *Chungguk munhak nonjip* 69 (2011): 306.

27. Chŏng Yakyong, cited in Yi Minhi, *Chosŏn ŭi pest'ŭssellŏ* (Bestsellers in Chosŏn) (Seoul: Pŭronesis, 2010), 27.

28. Ji-Eun Lee, "Literary, Sosŏl, and Women in Book Culture," 39.

production during Chosŏn, as well as during the colonial period, contributed to the common assumption that women were readers of fiction, rather than producers—notions that have been uncritically accepted in the existing scholarship in Korea.[29] Lee's argument forces us to challenge the gendered notion of fiction readership that has been prevalent in the writing of the history of literature. This problem was present in colonial Korea when male writers denounced women's reading of romance fiction as an inferior cultural activity. The very act of judging the value of literature is bound up with social power that legitimizes and reproduces the culture of the socially privileged.[30]

THE BOOK CULTURE AND READING AS
A SOCIAL ACT IN LATE CHOSŎN

A young maiden knocks on a wooden door of a modest-looking house at night and the master of the house peeps into a small hole in the door to identify the night visitor. Upon recognizing the familiar face, the master opens the door and quickly hands over a book to her. She then puts the book under her sleeve and disappears into the night by covering her head and face with a long hood.

Who is this young maiden? What kind of book is she getting from the man and most of all, why should they be so secretive about the book? Although this scene is borrowed from a contemporary film, *Forbidden Quest* (2006), its portrayal of a bookseller/lender in action in a late Chosŏn setting perhaps captures the atmosphere of the book industry and readership reasonably well. The book the maiden was borrowing was a popular romance fiction with obscene drawings in it. She is a maid sent by a woman in an elite household who takes the risk of being criticized or even pun-

---

29. Ji-Eun Lee argues that the social conditions in which women produced and consumed novels as well as their literary encounters outside these rigid social boundaries have been ignored in the existing scholarship. For a discussion of the relationship between female readership, book culture, and the constructive evaluation of the existing scholarship on the gendered notion of fiction reading, see Ji-Eun Lee, "Women in Book Culture," in *Women Pre-scripted: Forging Modern Roles through Korean Print* (Honolulu: University of Hawai'i Press, 2016), 16–35.

30. Terry Eagleton, "An Introduction: What is Literature?" in *Literary Theory* (Minneapolis: The University of Minnesota Press, 1996), 13.

ished for reading such a vulgar book. The risk for the bookseller/lender was even higher, as they were subject to rigid regulations on circulating unorthodox texts. Collecting works of fiction was extremely challenging in this circumstance not only because book collecting was very costly but also because shelving fiction in a library was considered blasphemous. Thus, it was unimaginable for elite men to house unorthodox texts such as fiction in their libraries in plain view. Common folks and women therefore had to find other ways to obtain fiction. By the eighteenth century, they took great advantage of book rental depots or commercial libraries called *sech'aekka*. These depots were concentrated in Seoul, though some popular romance fiction was also circulated in other commercial cities such as Ansŏng and Chŏnju. According to Maurice Courant (1865–1935), a secretary to the French ambassador in Seoul in the 1890s, much of the romance fiction was written in vernacular script, and the book depots that distributed them remained popular in the Seoul area until the turn of the twentieth century.[31] The depots seem to have existed into the 1910s, as one of the leading female writers of the 1930s, Pak Hwasŏng, recalls her mother frequently borrowing books—both traditional and contemporary fiction—from depots when Pak was a child.[32]

The distribution of vernacular fiction was enhanced from the mid-nineteenth century through the emergence of *panggakpon* editions, or woodblock-print texts. Ōtani Morishige observes that the emergence of the new book format could mean that a new kind of readership increased, possibly people who were literate in *han'gŭl* only. *Panggakpon* arose to supply this group's high demand for fiction.[33] The commercialization of vernacular fiction and the increase in its readership were worrisome for some literati whose criticism of this consumption pattern was directed at women. A prolific Confucian scholar and official during the reign of King Chŏngjo, Ch'ae Chegong (1720–1799), observed women's practice:

---

31. Maurice Courant, *Han'guk sŏji* (Biliographic Coréenne), trans. Lee Heejae (Seoul: Iljogak, [1894] 1994), 3.

32. Sŏ Chŏngja, *Han'guk kŭndae yŏsŏng sosŏl yŏn'gu* (A study of modern Korean novels written by women writers) (Seoul: Kukgak charyowon, 1999), 21–22.

33. Ōtani Morishige, *Chosŏn hugi sosŏl tokja yŏn'gu*, 109.

> Women are so infatuated with fiction, the only thing they consider as work these days. The number of fiction increases each day, reaching more than one thousand. Merchants hand-copy the fiction works and make a profit from lending them out. Because women do not have economic sense, they sell their hairpins and bracelets, and even make a loan to borrow fiction. These women spend their entire day (reading novels) while forgetting their household duty.[34]

Ch'ae left this record in the late eighteenth century, even before *panggak-pon* started to appear. Perhaps he was exaggerating the phenomenon of women's "infatuation with fiction," since the possibility that he could observe women outside elite households was slim. However, this statement allows us to see interesting aspects of book culture at that time when women even took out loans to borrow books they desired to read. First, women comprised a large portion of the book market, though not all had the option to go to the depots by themselves. Despite their limited access to fiction, unlike commoners who were freer to frequent the book depot, wives and daughters of elite men had to be resourceful enough to acquire books they wanted to read. Second, there seems to have been ample opportunity for women to read entertainment-focused texts in addition to Confucian texts that instruct them on womanly conduct and virtues. Third, women had their own reading spaces where they could express their social and personal desires, and also recognize other people's opinions about matters that concerned their reading materials. The only people who kept records of borrowers were the owners of the book depots, thus readers' individual identities remained anonymous. However, some readers scribbled comments on the pages of their borrowed books—complaints about the quality of narratives, impressions of books after reading them, discontent with other people's scribbling on the books—and, at times, they would draw obscene pictures on the pages.[35] We can detect the sense of liberty in readers' scribbling, comments that touched on personal and public issues, such as sexual desire and discontent with the book-borrowing market. The act of reading popular fiction was considered unproductive and uncultured behavior by Confucian standards, and leaving

---

34. This line is written in a "foreword" of a book, *Yŏsasŏ* (Four books for women), left by Ch'ae's late wife. Cited in Im Sŏngnae, *Chosŏn hugi ŭi taejung sosŏl*, 43.

35. Yi Minhi, *Chosŏn ŭi pest'ŭssellŏ*, 64–67.

obscene drawings and words might have been viewed as deviant, especially when women were involved. In other words, the fiction-reading public not only enjoyed the freedom of putting their hands on prohibited materials but also had the freedom of expressing their private desires in them. This kind of autonomy, no matter how slight, was secured by the anonymous status of readers in the book market.

Fiction-reading practices in late Chosŏn appear to have been flexible, since the way in which vernacular fiction was mediated was not limited to texts only—a fact that has been largely dismissed in the established scholarship on premodern Korean literature.[36] Oral narrative performances were popular in rural areas as well as in Seoul. Professional storytellers, people who narrated stories in speech style (*kangdamsa/chŏn'gisu*) or in singing style (*ch'ang kwangdae*), emerged in the eighteenth century and performed popular narratives for audiences who gathered in community spaces such as inner chambers, pharmacies, archery ranges, and so on.[37] Some storytellers were so skilled that they could immerse their audiences in fictional worlds. In the early nineteenth century, for example, an audience member was so absorbed in a performer's narration of a murder scene that he ended up stabbing the performer with a knife. The performer's acting as a villain was so skillful, we are told, that the audience member lost the ability to distinguish reality from fiction, thus motivating him to punish the villain.[38]

The oral narrative performance seems to have enjoyed wide popularity even at the turn of the century, as mentioned by the American missionary George W. Gilmore (1857–1933) who stayed in Seoul between 1886 and 1889:

> While promiscuous social gatherings are, from the nature of things, not permitted in Korea, there are usually little assemblies of men after night, and groups may be seen in the little anteroom or entrance, seated around

---

36. This is also the case in the scholarship on premodern Chinese-Korean literary interactions, which gives little consideration to the influence of Chinese literature on orally transmitted texts, such as the localization of the Liang-Zhu tale in Korean shamanistic ritual, for example. Sook Ja Cho, "Within and between Cultures: The Liang-Zhu Narrative in Korean Local Culture," *Harvard Journal of Asiatic Studies* 74, no. 2 (2014): 207–248.

37. Im Sŏngnae, *Chosŏn hugi ŭi taejung sosŏl*, 25–27.

38. Ibid., 30.

the hibachi if it is cold, chattering or singing songs or telling tales or listening while one reads a book. One thing which strikes a newcomer as particularly strange is that a Korean when reading, no matter what it is—song, letter, book or prayer even—sings or rather intones it.[39]

According to records by a number of Western missionaries, the practice of oral performance (or simply reading texts aloud in gatherings) was frequently seen, indicating that reading fiction was a popular form of culture at least until the early twentieth century. The popularization of oral storytelling points to the obvious fact that literacy was not an indispensable condition for experiencing the literary culture. Storytellers' performances helped illiterate audiences to participate in the popular culture. A more significant element of the performance is that "reading" was also a community-based activity that embodied visual and sonic elements familiar to the audiences through gestures, dialogues, impersonation, laughter, and possibly dialects. The vernacular script—or the visual and sonic narrations associated with vernacular fiction, which were considered a low form of "languages"—were heteroglossial because they were placed outside the periphery of the "official" language defined by the state and the authorities, and yet they embodied the potential of countering the language of the center.[40] One of the most popular *p'ansori* narratives, *The Tale of Ch'unhyang*, is just one example that took a critical view of class structure and corruption in the government.

The book culture in late Chosŏn tells us that fiction readership was heterogeneous, and the choice of readings for women was diverse. At the same time, the contents of some of the popular vernacular fiction indicate that fiction served a social function, implicitly expressing social criticism of the class structure as well as gender discrimination. The illegitimate status of fiction—that is, its placement squarely outside the official literature in the Confucian political order—in fact served its political purpose by challenging the dominant state power that was associated with literati culture. The sustainability of fiction's circulation channels proves this point. Even though the state tried to suppress these channels at times, the

---

39. Cited in Michael Kim, "Literary Production, Circulating Libraries, and Private Publishing," *Journal of Korean Studies* 9, no. 1 (2004): 13.

40. M.M. Bakhtin, "Discourse in the Novel," in *The Dialogic Imagination*, ed. M. Holquist (Austin: University of Texas Press, [1934] 1981), 269–273.

readership of popular fiction did not diminish. Likewise, women's reading of fiction in inner chambers meant that they were not limited to the private sphere exclusively. Reading connected them to the outside world and enabled them to participate in the reading culture experienced by their fellow women and men.

As shown by the literati's attacks on women for reading fiction, domestic space was not outside state power. The state did not deal with women's domain directly,[41] yet it was a space that concerned the state in terms of maintaining Confucian moral order. As Betty Joseph argues, "women can posit new forms of subjectivity that do not define political power simply in terms of access to public space," especially when home is placed both inside and outside the system of power, an "in-between space" where the personal becomes the political.[42] Even though women were physically confined to domestic space (particularly women in elite households), fiction was a medium that they identified with, one that allowed them to imagine their social selves.

FUNCTIONAL APPROACH TO FICTION
IN THE EARLY 1900S

At the turn of the century there was renewed interest in the political arena in the previously ignored cultural activity of reading fiction. Korea's geopolitical position had been shifting since the last quarter of the nineteenth century. It became clear that China's power was declining, and the aftermath of the first Sino-Japanese War (1894–1895) increased Koreans' fear that they, too, would soon become a victim of newly advancing global powers. This period is often referred to as *Kaewhagi* (the Enlightenment Period) or *Aeguk kyemonggi*—a time in which "a disparate group of intellectuals, reformers, and publicists made the nation the premier subject of intellectual exchange for the first time in the peninsula's history,"[43] between 1895 and 1910. Intellectuals, reformers, and publicists sought to se-

---

41. Martina Deuchler, *The Confucian Transformation of Korea: A Study of Society and Ideology* (Cambridge, MA: Harvard University Press, 1992), 280.

42. Betty Joseph, *Reading the East India Company, 1720–1840: Colonial Currencies of Gender* (Chicago: University of Chicago Press, 2004), 95.

43. Schmid, *Korea between Empires*, 3.

cure Korea's independence against foreign powers through their writings about the national culture and history. While these writings shared a common nationalistic impulse, their political vision of how to "enlighten and civilize" Korea was varied; some turned their eyes to the West to obtain advanced science and technologies while others considered Japan as a model to civilize Korea. As Japanese imperial force was manifest in 1905, when Korea became Japan's protectorate, the urgency of restoring Korea's independence was expressed in fictional narratives.

Many nationalist elites chose to work in journalism and fiction writing in order to reach a larger audience, especially women and less-educated men. Fiction writing was strategically employed to help educate the general public about the meaning and importance of nation and civilization. In these writings, "civilization" generally meant the promotion of education, domestic and public hygiene, and a number of social reforms, such as the ban on early marriage, the remarriage of widows, and the ending of *yangban* privilege, to name just a few. In contrast to the general view of fiction as a low form of culture in Chosŏn, the promotion of fiction in this period can be seen as radical. This does not mean that all previously circulated fiction was now considered proper for readers, however. Considering the fact that most writers came from a Confucian background, subject matter that did not fit their Confucian tastes (such as love affairs and supernatural phenomena) were generally avoided. Even when these matters were discussed they remained sub-themes supporting the main narrative on the nation and civilization, devoid of a sensual dimension. Furthermore, having positioned themselves on the frontiers of social reformation projects, some intellectuals criticized the authorship and readership of both traditional and contemporary fiction because of its impractical content.

Sin Ch'aeho was particularly critical of fiction writers who wrote about subjects outside national matters and believed that the novel could be a means to inspire Korean readers with patriotism. Sin's literary production concentrated on the reinterpretation of heroes in premodern Korea and the West, such as General Ŭlchi, General Yi Sunsin, Napoleon the Great, George Washington, and Peter the Great, for example. Their extraordinary intellectual and military skills and superior morality would inspire Koreans to succeed in their struggle to survive in a competitive world.

Sin's idea of fiction was influenced by Liang Qichao, whose political views and enthusiasm for reforming China significantly influenced progressive Korean intellectuals.[44] Liang's works were avidly read in Korea, especially between 1906 and 1909, when forty-five different articles and a year-long series of his essays were translated and introduced in various Korean newspapers and journals.[45] As well, a collection of Liang's written works produced in Japan between 1902 and 1908 was compiled and translated into Korean. Entitled *Ŭmbingsil munjip* (A collection of the works of Ŭmbingsil,[46] translated by Chŏn Hanggi), it became "like a textbook"[47] for Korean reformists seeking methods and strategies for building a stronger modern nation.[48]

Besides his promotion of education for national growth, Liang inspired Korean intellectuals with his innovative ideas about literature. Liang focused on three genres—poetry, prose, and fiction—but his emphasis was on fictional narrative because of its potential to "awaken" people to the need for government reform.[49] In his "On the Relationship between Fiction and the Government of People," he states, "If one intends to renovate people of a nation, one must first renovate its fiction. Therefore, to renovate morality, one must renovate fiction."[50] The power of fiction, he continues, rests in its capability to "mold the human into more intelligent or duller beings," and to "move men's minds profoundly" through the "subtlety and

---

44. See the list of the translated works by Liang in Yi Manyŏl, "Kaehwagi ŏllon kwa chungguk," 78–118.

45. Ibid., 102.

46. Ŭmbingsil is Liang's pen name. Its literal meaning is "cooling the heat by swallowing ice."

47. In fact, apart from *Ŭmbingsil munjip*, some of Liang's texts, such as *Wŏlnammangguksa* (The fall of Vietnam), were used in classrooms in private schools. This book in particular was translated into three different scripts: Chinese, a mixture of Chinese and *han'gŭl*, and just *han'gŭl*. These versions were intended to reach people with diverse levels of education. Chŏng Sŏnt'ae, *Han'guk kŭndae munhak ŭi suryŏm kwa palsan* (Essays on modern Korean literature and thought) (Seoul: Somyŏng, 2008), 124.

48. Chŏng Chinsŏk, *Ŏllon kwa han'guk hyŏndaesa* (Journalism and modern Korean history) (Seoul: K'ŏmunik'eisyŏn Books, 2001), 102.

49. Theresa Hyun, *Writing Women in Korea* (Honolulu: University of Hawai'i Press, 2004), 30.

50. Liang Qichao, "On the Relationship between Fiction and the Government of People" (Lun xiaoshuo yu qunzhi zhi guanxi), in *Modern Chinese Literary Thought: Writings on Literature 1893–1945*, ed. Kirk Denton (Stanford, CA: Stanford University Press, 1996), 74.

technique" that is intrinsic to fiction.[51] Liang's pragmatic approach to fiction is reflected in his translation of biographical works that deal largely with patriotic heroes and heroines in Europe. Korean nationalist intellectuals, especially Sin Ch'aeho, Pak Ŭnsik, Chang Chiyŏn, Hyŏn Ch'ae, and Chu Sigyŏng, were especially enthusiastic about translating Liang's historical fiction that dealt with lives of Western heroes and heroines such as Lajos Kossuth, Madame Roland, and Oliver Cromwell, among others.

While Korea saw the development of new narratives and the book market's interest in promoting them, traditional fiction was still popular despite being discredited by some social elites who viewed its popularity as a bad habit that seriously undermined the Korean national character. Pak Sŭngjo, a former official at the Police Bureau (*kyŏngmuch'ŏng*), stated:

> I believe the most detestable and wretched individuals in the world are those who at weddings, residences, markets, and atop straw mats in the alleys read in a loud voice copies of what are called "rented vernacular fiction" like *The Life of Hong Kilttong* (*Hong Giltongjŏn*), and *The Life of So Daesŏng* (*Sodaesŏngjŏn*), etc. They waste away the entire day and pass meaningless lives. What possible benefit can these rented vernacular stories have for the people in their daily livelihoods? That is why I am determined to ban this practice entirely.[52]

Pak's statement demonstrates that popular fiction was still an essential part of people's daily lives and illiteracy did not bar people from experiencing the joy of "reading."[53] In addition, it shows what elements of traditional fiction were criticized in light of nationalist discourses. Besides Sin Ch'aeho and others' discontent with the "lewdness" of traditional fiction, the mythical and supernatural elements of these works were also an object of criticism for nationalist thinkers. Some of the most frequently criticized works of fiction were *The Tale of Ch'unhyang*, *The Cloud Dream of the Nine*, *The Life of Hong Kilttong*, and *The Life of So Daesŏng*, all of which were disparaged by nationalist writers for their lewdness and absurdity. However, these were the most popular fiction of the day and were not likely to be put away to the attic, in spite of Pak Ŭnsik's (1859–1925) wishes.

---

51. Ibid., 75–76.
52. Cited in Michael Kim, "Literary Production," 11–12.
53. Ibid., 12.

What people ought to read, Pak argued, are stories of heroes from the past so that people will emulate their lives for their nations.[54]

By no means did the nationalist writers ignore the entertaining quality of fiction, however. As Liang Qichao emphasized, storytelling techniques were an important element that writers must keep in mind in order to enhance their works' accessibility. The entertaining aspect of the storytelling was usually emphasized in any advertisement of "the novel." The advertisement for Chang Chiyŏn's translation of a fictional biography of Marie-Jeanne P. Roland, *The Story of Madame Roland* (*Raran puinjŏn*), states: "In order to nourish ordinary people's [*ilban kungmin*] patriotic spirit, this novel [*sosŏl*] is written entirely in the national script [*kungmun*] and in a highly entertaining way. Those men and women who are patriotic and educated are highly encouraged to read this novel."[55] Another advertisement for Chang's translation of a fictional biography of Joan of Arc, *The Story of a Patriotic Lady* (*Aeguk puinjŏn*), also emphasizes the entertaining aspect of the novel, and it stresses that *The Story* is a must-read item for "patriotic men and women."[56]

Certainly, the newspaper where these advertisements appeared, *Taehan maeil sinbo* (*The Korea Daily News*), reflected the editorial team's wishful thinking in their attempt to turn ordinary people into educated men and women. This top-down elitist view of the novel resulted in the creation of a hierarchy, a distinction between traditional novels (*ku sosŏl*) and new novels (*sin sosŏl*), characterizing the former as inferior to the latter, and, by extension, written for the unenlightened. Nationalist newspapers in particular contributed to the wide spread of the rigid boundary between the old/the unenlightened and the new/the enlightened through the fictional narratives they published.

---

54. Pak, "Kisŏ" (Foreword), *Taehan maeil sinbo*, 8 February 1907.

55. "Kŭnse cheil nyŏjung yŏngung" (The Most Courageous Modern Heroine), *Taehan maeil sinbo*, 20 November 1907.

56. "Sin sosŏl *Aeguk puinjŏn*" (New Novel, *The Story of a Patriotic Lady*), *Taehan maeil sinbo*, 9 October 1907.

THE NOVEL AND NEWSPAPERS

The transformation of the novel in the early 1900s and 1910s was in tandem with the development of newspapers, though it was not the Korean reformist writers who initiated newspaper-serialized fiction for Korean readers, but rather Japanese residents in the Korean peninsula. The first modern newspaper on the Korean peninsula, *Chōsen shinpō*, was published in 1881 in Pusan.[57] It was two years later, in 1883, when the first modern Korean newspaper, *Hansŏng sunbo*, was established by the Chosŏn government.[58] Shortly after, the newspaper business began to thrive. About 130 different newspapers were established between 1881 and 1910, most between 1905 and 1910, a time when the nationalist movement was growing in intensity.[59] Thus newspapers were generally divided into two opposing groups: Japanese-run papers and nationalist papers. The former group was greater in number,[60] and these papers were circulated among Japanese residents and Koreans alike, but the latter reached a larger readership.[61]

---

57. The Japanese population grew substantially in Pusan shortly after the Kanghwa Treaty was signed, from 100 in 1875 to around 1,800 in 1882. Articles were published in Chinese and Japanese. Chinese-language articles were intended to reach educated Koreans. Although there were some exceptions, such as one Korean-Confucian scholar's strongly anti-Japan, antiforeign memorial, most Chinese-language articles emphasized the benefit of economic and political collaboration between Japan and Korea, whereas Japanese-language articles were written for Japanese readers, publishing items that served their economic, and political interests. Albert A. Altman, "Korea's First Newspaper: The Japanese *Chōsen shinpō*," *The Journal of Asian Studies* 43, no. 4 (Aug. 1984): 685–696.

58. This was part of the government's attempt to adapt to the changing world; the aim was to "enlighten" (*kyemong*) the country's people and open its door to the West, which meant adopting Western knowledge and interacting with the West. Yi Haech'ang, *Han'guk sinmunsa yŏn'gu* (A study of the history of Korean newspapers) (Seoul: Sŏngmungak, 1971), 19.

59. The total number of newspapers was 136, and thirty-seven of them were published between 1881 and 1904. See the list of newspapers that existed during the period in Han Wŏnyŏng, *Han'guk kaehwagi sinmun yŏnjae sosŏl yŏn'gu* (A study of serialized newspaper fiction works in the enlightenment period) (Seoul: Ilchisa, 1990), 20–25.

60. Based on the list of newspapers compiled by Han, forty newspapers out of ninety-nine published between 1905 and 1910 were Japanese-run papers. Ibid., 20–25.

61. The exact figure of each paper's readership has not been identified; however, the most popular nationalist paper, *Taehan maeil sinbo* (*The Korea Daily News*), obtained almost 13,000 readers in 1908 alone. Ibid., 47.

Religious papers were also increasing in number,[62] but they were by no means politically neutral since they frequently dealt with national issues.

It was also in the Japanese-established newspaper *Hansŏng sinbo* (1895–1906), which would become *Kyŏngsŏng ilbo* in 1906, where "the novel" section first appeared. *Hansŏng sinbo* was published in Japanese and in the Korean vernacular. The newspaper published forty fictional works between 1895 and 1906, all of them written in Korean. Although fiction was treated independently from nonfictional works such as editorials and news reports, the concept of "the novel" does not seem to have been clearly defined by the paper's editors. Narratives published under the broad category of "the novel" (*sosŏl*) came in all varieties: traditional fiction, contemporary fiction, translated fiction, and unofficial histories.[63] Furthermore, individual fiction was serialized over just a few days, making it significantly shorter than what might be considered a novel today.

The mixed bag of fiction works in *Hansŏng sinbo* rather reflects the paper's editorial policy; that is, to present Korean readers with familiar stories, and with new fictional narratives written in a manner that would be received without cultural resistance from Koreans. The paper's cultural assimilationist policy was designed by influential politicians such as the Japanese diplomatic ministers to Korea, Inoue Kaoru (1836–1915) and Miura Koro (1876–1910).[64] Although the paper criticized the pro-Chinese Korean conservatives (*sugup'a*) for their rejection of social reforms at times, in general, political affairs were not the paper's editorial focus since it intended to influence the public opinion mainly through cultural means.

It is interesting to note that women were central figures in many of the paper's fictional narratives. Overall, these women struggled to uphold traditional virtues such as chastity and loyalty to their husbands; and they were rewarded for their struggles at the end by gaining economic independence or reuniting with their spouses. The motifs and plots were nothing

---

62. There were three Christian-focused newspapers published between 1889 and 1904, and seven between 1905 and 1910. Ibid., 20–26.

63. Kim Yŏngmin, "1910 nyŏndae sinmun ŭi yŏkhal kwa kŭndae sosŏl ŭi chŏngch'ak kwajŏng" (The role of newspapers in the 1910s and the formation of modern fiction), *Hyŏndae munhak ŭi yŏn'gu* 25 (2005): 261–300.

64. Lee Yumi, "Kŭndae ch'ogi sinmun sosŏl ŭi yŏsŏng inmul chaehyŏn yangsang yŏn'gu" (A study of the image of women in fiction in modern Korean newspaper), *Han'guk kŭndae munhak yŏn'gu* 16 (2007): 78–79.

new to readers, and yet a significant feature in these stories is the sense of gender equality. The paper introduced gender interactions in an "enlightened country" (*munmyŏngguk*), Japan, where married couples enjoyed the freedom to express affection in both public and domestic spaces, and women received respect for obtaining education.[65] Images of women played a central role in Japan's attempt to civilize Korean society by juxtaposing "advanced Japan" and "backward Korea"; the remnants of Confucian feminine virtues such as chastity and frugality were strategically deployed to influence Korean readers. The paper downplayed its political agenda in fiction works, and yet it mediated the feminine position of Korea through the construction of women as objects of reform, homogenizing them as a single category that paralleled Koreans as a whole.

Not unlike the editors of *Hansŏng sinbo*, nationalist intellectuals such as Sin Ch'aeho and Pak Ŭnsik in *The Korea Daily* (*Taehan maeil sinbo*) approached fictional narratives from a functionalist point of view—and their idea of fiction, too, was not consistent in terms of forms and styles. *The Korea Daily* was able to maintain its anti-Japanese stance even as nationalist presses gradually succumbed to the tightening noose of Japanese censorship toward the end of the first decade of the twentieth century. The fact that the owner of the paper was an Englishman (Ernest Bethel [1872–1909]), worked in its favor, helping the nationalist writers and journalists circumvent censorship. As the most popular paper at the time,[66] the paper also played a significant part in the development of fictional genres.

Unlike *Hansŏng sinbo*, however, fictional narratives were characterized by their contemporariness, delivering what Kim Yŏngmin calls storylike editorials (*sŏsajŏk nonsŏl*), which appeared for the first time in 1905 in *The Korea Daily*. Although short-lived, the "storylike editorial" provides us with an example of how nationalist writers used fictional genres as tools for social reform and how they perceived the notion of authorship. *The Korea Daily* serialized *Travellers' Stories* (*Hyanggaek tamhwa*) for two days, on October 29 and 31, on the third page under "International News" (*oebo*) and "A Brief History of Foreign Countries" (*yŏksa kaeyo*). In the story a journalist who identifies himself as "Usisaeng" reports stories he

---

65. Ibid., 86–87.

66. *Taehan maeil sinbo* enjoyed great popularity, obtaining almost 13,000 subscribers in 1908 alone—the highest number among all the papers in Korea. Han Wŏnyŏng, *Han'guk kaehwagi sinmun yŏnjae sosŏl yŏn'gu*, 47.

hears from travelers criticizing corrupt government officials. As Kim Yŏngmin points out, works like *Travellers' Stories* served a similar purpose to editorials (*nonsŏl*), in that both delivered stories in real time, framing contemporary concerns within the dialogue among travelers. The only difference between fiction and editorial, he argues, is the fictional narratives' occasional recycling of traditional narrative strategies such as the use of dreams, legends, and myths.[67]

Three particular aspects of the storylike editorials (*sŏsajŏk nonsŏl*) may be singled out to show how the novel was perceived from 1900–1910.[68] First, real authors' names were not revealed in these editorials; the authors may not have felt it was necessary to claim authorship. The sense of creativity we associate with modern novels is absent in this context. In their nascent stage, novels published in the paper were very short in length. With few exceptions, they hardly ran for more than three days. Furthermore, these short novels often ended "incomplete" (*miwan*), indicating that writers favored this form of writing for mediating their social criticism and political thoughts immediately; they saw their position as reformists first, not as creative writers.

Second, the storylike editorials were published in pure *han'gŭl* whereas the rest of the newspaper was written in the mixture of *hanmun* and *han'gŭl*, though the former was used predominantly. This pattern was commonly seen in other papers and persisted even after *The Korea Daily* was taken over by the colonial newspaper, *The Daily News* (*Maeil sinbo*), in 1910. These works, unlike other sections in the newspapers, catered to women, youths, and less educated men, thus the use of *han'gŭl* was imperative. The consequence of using *han'gŭl* went beyond the possibility of reaching the masses: it also fostered the development of a prose style. A common feature of this type of narrative was the insertion of public speeches and debates, which conveyed the liveliness of everyday language.

Third, even though writers used traditional narrative frames such as dreams, legends, and myths, their fiction was preoccupied with civilization and enlightenment discourses. *The Korea Daily*, despite its anti-Japanese stance, and the Japanese newspaper *Hansŏng sinbo*, shared many

---

67. Kim Yŏngmin, *Han'guk kŭndae sosŏlsa* (A history of modern Korean fiction) (Seoul: Sol, 1997).

68. The following points are articulated further in Kim Yŏngmin's book, *Han'guk kŭndae sosŏlsa*.

ideas: both promoted Western-inspired education, gender equality, and the prohibition of old customs and manners. As Andre Schmid demonstrates, "Korean nationalists and Japanese colonialists shared much in the way of conceptual vocabulary, themes in cultural representation, and narrative strategies" when endorsing "capitalist modernity."[69] Although the political agencies and goals were different, fiction writing was an extension of these two groups' political efforts to reform Korean society beyond the economic sector; they tried to cast the political consciousness of the people and redirect their social behavior as essential to the mythmaking of the modern nation-state.

Shortly after *The Korea Daily*'s establishment of "the novel section," other newspapers followed the suit. The *Capital Gazette* (*Hwangsŏng sinmun*) and the *Independence News* (*Mansebo*) began to publish novels from 1906, and the Christian newspaper the *Kyŏnghyang Daily*, which had used *han'gŭl* only since its inception, began to publish novels as well. Just a few months after *The Korea Daily* published the storylike editorials, "novels" in a longer form were serialized in the same newspaper. Other papers also began to serialize longer novels, and included the authors' names. Writers of these longer novels, even though they were engrossed with the civilization and enlightenment discourse, tried to make the best use of the entertaining elements of fiction such as romance and marriage. Independent publishers also jumped on the bandwagon by republishing and selling the serialized newspaper novels in separate volumes, and by publishing creative works and Korean-translated Japanese novels. The transition from the storylike editorial to longer novels, however inconsistent the writers' conceptualization of the novel in the literary sense was, demonstrates the decisive role newspapers played in the general perception of the novel as an independent genre quite separate from nonfiction writings.

TRANSNATIONAL LITERARY FORCES AND TRANSLATION

The development of Korean literature during the *Aeguk kyemong* period occurred in a transnational context in which print capitalism contributed to the enhancement of the intellectual exchange between Korea and Euro-

---

69. Schmid, *Korea between Empires*, 102.

American, Chinese, and Japanese texts. Nationalist writers relied heavily on Liang Qichao's works in the early 1900s, as discussed earlier. And yet the import of Japanese texts by Japanese writers outnumbered Liang's texts. Although writers published "their" novels with their names, most of their works were in fact translations of novels imported from Japan. Liang Qichao was also influenced by Japanese novels from the time he was exiled to Japan in 1898, and his translations of Japanese novels became intermediary texts for Korean nationalist intellectuals. Therefore, it is reasonable to conclude that it was first through the translation of Japanese fiction that Korean intellectuals discovered the didactic value of novels that would serve their political interests.

It must be also noted that a majority of novels produced during this time were Korean translations of Japanese *political* novels. Translations of Japanese political novels (*seiji shōsetsu*) were especially dominant. *Seiji shōsetsu* coincided with the development of liberal thought in Japan, when intellectuals believed that the novel was the best means to inspire patriotism and enlighten society. They believed this would be accomplished by embodying in the novel the political views put forward by the leaders of the Liberty and People's Rights Movement.[70] Many writers of political novels in Japan were former samurai who later became parliament members. As Atsuko Sakaki points out, it was thus "natural" for the "samurai-turned-statesmen" to write novels in the classical Chinese writing style (*kanbun*) that was traditionally used when discussing government affairs and social issues among government officials.[71] In other words, the intended readers of political novels were current and upcoming social elites, in keeping with the Meiji government's attempts to educate young intellectuals for their future political participation.[72] By contrast, although

---

70. Translations of Western political philosophy influenced political novelists in their development of liberalism, particularly among those who were involved in the Liberty and People's Rights Movement (*jiyū minken undō*). The movement was quelled in 1890, its initial philosophy of freedom and equality replaced with success stories of young Japanese people who dedicated their lives to their country's welfare. Donald Keene, *Dawn to the West: Japanese Literature in the Modern Era* (New York: Holt, Rinehart and Winston, 1984), 76–95.

71. Atsuko Sakaki, "Kajin no Kigū: The Meiji Political Novel and the Boundaries of Literature," *Monumenta Nipponica* 55, no. 1 (2000): 95.

72. Douglas R. Howland, *Translating the West: Language and Political Reason in Nineteenth-Century Japan* (Honolulu: University of Hawai'i Press, 2002), 31–60.

most Korean authors were former *yangban*, their intended readership was broader than that of the Japanese authors—the general public or the masses (*inmin*). Thus most of them wrote their novels in pure *han'gŭl*, first to reach the masses and second to build national character by elevating the status of *han'gŭl* as the national script. Even though some writers, such as Sin Ch'aeho and Pak Ŭnsik, predominantly used Chinese characters in their novels, their conscious effort to deploy *han'gŭl* was evident; they wrote novels in the fashion of spoken Korean. What concerned both Japanese and Korean writers was the emphasis on "civilization and enlightenment" (*munmyŏng kaehwa* in Korean and *bunmei kaika* in Japanese) deeply embedded in political novels, which was deemed essential for making a strong nation.

During the 1880s and 1890s, *bunmei kaika*, a translation for the English and French term "civilization," was one of the key concepts concerning the Meiji social ideologues in their vision for national progress.[73] The concept of *bunmei kaika*, which was translated as "civilization and enlightenment," was under constant development until the 1890s, though in general it had a double meaning at the time of its usage: "universal civilization" and "Westernization."[74] Yu Kilchun first borrowed the Japanese neologisms *munmyŏng kaehwa* in his book, *Travels in the West*, in the 1880s (though it was only available to the public starting in 1895), his usage of the terms was not too different from the Japanese version since the book, despite some observations on the West, was mostly based on his experience in Japan. In fact, its model was Fukuzawa Yukichi's *Conditions in the West* (*Seiyō jijō*, 1867), to which it was remarkably similar in form and content. Yu Kilchun's book, together with Japanese dictionaries available at the time, became a reference point for the spread of new concepts from Japan, including *bunmei kaika*, which in turn would be used frequently in political essays, editorials, and works of fiction in early twentieth-century Korea.[75]

Almost all translators before 1910 were trained in Confucianism, and some were highly regarded for their scholarly achievements in neo-Confucian philology and philosophy: Sin Ch'aeho was awarded with an

---

73. Howland, *Translating the West*, 33.
74. Ibid., 5, 33.
75. Schmid, *Korea between Empires*, 111.

honorary title at Sŏnggyun'gwan in 1905, and Pak Ŭnsik had started his new career as a journalist in 1898 at the age of thirty-nine while still serving the government as a scholar-official. Most of these intellectuals had never traveled outside Korea prior to 1910 and had no knowledge of foreign languages other than their expertise in classical Chinese. While their reliance on Chinese intermediary texts explains their affiliation with Liang's works in terms of the linguistic familiarity, it is important to note that these writers by no means followed Liang's texts faithfully. Translators, who were mostly nationalist intellectuals, prioritized national interests, incorporating domestic affairs into Liang's versions. The prioritization of domestic issues often resulted in severe alterations and distortions of the originals. These altered passages, more often than not, criticize the invasive nature of Japanese imperialism and promote patriotism among Koreans. Texts from Japan, in other words, were used to challenge Japanese imperialism, demonstrating how translation became an act of resistance against Japan while adopting Western knowledge and ideas about nation and civilization via Japan at the same time.

Translation practice in a colonial society is by no means an ideology-free act. On the contrary, it is destined to involve itself in the cultural hierarchy already embedded in the very texts being translated, and it operates within a cultural system in which translators' texts and their intended target readers are regulated by colonial power. As Tejaswini Niranjana demonstrates, translation "as a practice shapes, and takes shape within, the asymmetrical relations of power that operate under colonialism,"[76] and it functioned as a "significant technology of colonial domination."[77] In fact, most of Liang's works came under severe censorship from 1907 when the Korea Newspaper Law (*shimbunshihō*, 1907) and the Publication Law (*shuppanhō*, 1909) were promulgated by the state, suppressing the circulation of nationalistic texts that encouraged Korea's independence from foreign power. By 1909 the publication of Liang's works ceased altogether.[78]

---

76. Niranjana, *Siting Translation*, 2.

77. Ibid., 21.

78. Yi Soyŏn, "Ilche kangtchŏmgi yŏsŏng chapchi yŏn'gu" (A study of women's journals in colonial Korea), *Ehwa sahak yŏn'gu* 29 (2002): 219.

However, translation practice in the Korean colonial context was not entirely subordinate to the power structure. For one thing, the fidelity of translation was understood quite differently than it is today. More often than not, original texts were abbreviated, distorted, and altered in order to enhance the communicability of foreign culture in the domestic context and to reflect the translators' political vision.[79]

Korean translators' attitude toward foreign texts at the time is characterized by their conscious attempt to domesticate the Japanese texts to serve their domestic interests while circumventing the state censorship. Relations of power certainly underpinned the translation practice at the time. Translation was used by the colonizer as a hegemonic tool to colonize natives culturally.[80] However, translators' exposure to the colonial force also reshaped their subjectivity, making them more conscious of their roles as social reformers; their position was not ideology-free or neutral.[81] Korean nationalist intellectuals who were also translating foreign texts in the early 1900s as well as in the 1910s attempted to negotiate with the imperial force through various translation strategies. The negotiation process, as Karen L. Thornber argues, is another modality of integrating foreign systems into the native society besides dominance and resistance.

Korean translations of Euro-American, Japanese, and Chinese texts altered original narratives at the time; thus scholars of Korean literature often call the translations of foreign texts "adaptations." The gap between translation and adaptation can be explained by the many factors that were conditioned by local contexts, yet the primary reason for the translators' infidelity to the originals was their desire to communicate and legitimate

---

79. Lawrence Venuti, "Translation, Community, Utopia," in *The Translation Studies Reader*, 2nd edition, ed. Lawrence Venuti (New York: Routledge, 2000), 498.

80. Niranjana, *Siting Translation*.

81. I follow Maria Tymoczko's argument that translators can never be placed in the "in-between" space—i.e., between cultures and cultural loyalties—since they inevitably engage in divergent social changes and ideologies, operating in one system of language to another: translation is rather a political action that requires affiliations with ideologies, institutions, and programs of change and directs translators to act collectively at times. Maria Tymoczko, "Ideology and the Position of the Translator: In What Sense is a Translator 'In Between'?" in *Apropos of Ideology: Translation Studies on Ideologies in Translation Studies*, ed. Maria Calzada Perez (Manchester, UK: St. Jerome Publishing, 2003), 181–201.

views on politics and society in their works, thus making sense of the foreign figures and their symbolic power in the native context. Imported texts also helped nationalist translators in their reworking of Korean history by identifying certain moments in Korean history with those in mainly European history. Translation functioned as a vehicle not only to shape and reflect writers' political subjectivity but also to help Korean readers imagine nation and modernity.

ENTERING THE NEW WORLD OF FICTION

The reading culture in Chosŏn involved more than literary texts. Oral performance was an integral part of how people experienced fictional genres; thus literacy was not mandatory for ordinary people to experience literary culture. In traditional narratives, especially in vernacular fiction, the voice of social criticism was often embedded both inside and outside the texts. It was expressed in narratives, and readers also participated by circulating their observations of matters that concerned their social lives. The state's strict neo-Confucian stance meant that popular fiction writers had to remain anonymous and the circulation of vernacular fiction was prohibited yet both still managed to function, rather well, providing readers with critical views on class and gender hierarchy.

The competition among Euro-American and Japanese imperialists over Korea not only brought with it a series of political upheavals but also ideological and practical tools that would shape Korean intellectuals' ideas about the Korean nation and national identity. Their authoring and translating of fiction works, as "the novel" was called, was one of the most palpable changes made in the history of Korean literature. Even though they maintained an instrumentalist attitude toward literary works, the promotion of vernacular script, the experimentation with narrative structures, and the active deployment of modern media show that their role as authors and translators cannot be separated from the production of knowledge about the nation-state, a historical space where significant changes in Korean literature were made.

The ways in which these nationalist writers nationalized masculinity and femininity in the novel is the central point where the ideas of nation and civilization coalesce, further producing divergent visions for national progress, and mediating gender roles that were considered crucial for this progress. The transforming process of the novel and its emphasis on women's roles in the early 1900s must therefore be approached by considering the material conditions—imported foreign texts and the adoption of modern media in particular—together with the intellectual labor the nationalist intellectuals put into the writing and translating of novels, which was their conscious response to the problems of nation and modernity. These writers' translations of Japanese novels carry their emotional and intellectual investment in negotiation with the imperial power by domesticating the images of Western and Japanese heroes and heroines, thus constructing their cultural differences. The process of making the novel thus intersects with the process of constructing nationhood, and through this process gender became the central element in shaping modern Korean literature.

2

GENDERED REPRESENTATION
OF THE NATION

Constructing National Heroes and Heroines

ONE OF THE MOST BELOVED AND IMMORTAL HEROES in Korea is Admiral Yi Sunsin (1545–1598), celebrated for his resistence to Toyotomi Hideyoshi's invasion of Chosŏn (1592–1598). Admiral Yi did not enjoy the same level of public admiration when he was alive. It was only after the Chosŏn state was humiliated by the Qing force that Yi became the icon of a loyal vassal to the king and a symbol of Chosŏn's Sinocentric stance within the ruling class.[1] Spearheaded by a coterie of nationalist intellectuals, the elevation of Admiral Yi to national hero only began at the turn of the century when Chosŏn was in difficulty.

Ironically, the rebirth of the admiral was inspired by Korean writers' and translators' exposure to biographies of heroes and heroines from the West. These works functioned as more than just biographies; they were stories of nation-building and national identity embodied in the figures of the past. A list of biographies from the West via Japan and China shows that Korean writers and translators were especially keen on stories of exemplary heroes and heroines who dedicated their skills and knowledge to, and even sacrificed their lives for, their nations. By altering the form and the style of such biographies of heroes and heroines from the West, and by authenticating the exemplary people who made some Western nations strong, nationalist intellectuals aimed to inspire the Korean people to be patriotic and diligent in civilizing their society. Through this transna-

---

1. No Yŏnggu, "'Yŏngung mandŭlgi' yŏksa sok ŭi Yi Sunsin insik" (The reception of Yi Sunsin in the history of 'making heroes'), *Yŏksa pip'yŏng* (2004): 340–348.

tional literary flow, not only did figures like Joan of Arc become universal models for citizens, but figures from Korean history were also appropriated to serve the mission of civilizing and enlightening the nation.

The nationalist intellectuals' construction of national heroes and heroines at the turn of the century can be described as a collective fantasy about shaping national identity when such a thing did not exist yet. The "biographical novel," as they were called, was the literary genre that represented their idea of the novel in terms of its political function. And yet, their gendered positions on ideas of the nation were presented with little ambiguity. More often than not, their patriarchal stance was voiced in their construction of heroes and heroines in their works, both translated and original, which aimed to persuade the public to be patriotic citizens through performing their newly assigned gender roles.

Some of the progressive Chinese thinkers of the time, such as Liang Qichao and Kang Youwei, became inspiring figures for Korean nationalist intellectuals because of their leading role in the reform movement in China, and their conservative views on political and social changes. Liang's works were especially popular among Korean reformers, though many of his works, political novels (*chŏngch'i sosŏl*) in particular, were translations of Japanese political novels (*seiji shōsetsu*).[2] Liang's works in turn became intermediary texts for Korean translators. It is noteworthy that Liang prioritized "translating the meaning over the word," paraphrasing the Japanese novels, changing names and places into Chinese equivalents, and abbreviating texts—a common practice among Chinese translators at the time.[3] This trend was followed by Korean translators and translators of biographical novels in particular who had to rely on Chinese intermediary texts rather than Japanese originals. Korean translators' domestication of texts, in other words, cannot solely be understood as a feature unique to Korea. In the act of the ideological translation, the original loses its originality, but what matters to the translator is re-creating the past through the eyes of the Other. The originality of the past thus was

---

2. Luo Xuanmin, "Ideology and Literary Translation: Liang Qichao," *Perspectives* 13, no. 3 (2005): 183.

3. Ibid., 182–183.

created through translation, an ironical act that was completely justified in the name of nation.

Korean nationalist intellectuals such as Pak Ŭnsik, Sin Ch'aeho, and Chang Chiyŏn were inspired by Liang's idea of the value of fictional narratives, or "the novel" (*xiaoshuo* in Chinese and *sosŏl* in Korean) as it was termed by Liang as well as the intellectuals, giving priority to political over aesthetic value. Although they did not write as extensively as Liang did on the merit of the novel, they tended to agree with his emphasis on the political value of the novel for reform purposes. Transfer of Chinese and Japanese texts via China would last little more than a decade. As Korea was fully annexed by Japan, the Japanese route—transfer of Japanese texts and Euro-American texts via Japan—dominated the publishing industry from 1910 onward. However, the short-lived Chinese connection created an important literary space in Korea by enabling Korean nationalist writers to experiment with the novel, reimagining Korea's place in a global context.

Pak Ŭnsik, Sin Ch'aeho, and Chang Chiyŏn were hard-nosed nationalists who were at the front lines of the promotion of national independence, education for the masses, and class and gender equality in their authoring and translations of biographical novels. In their stories of exemplary men, the masculine power of male literati in terms of their possession of Confucian knowledge is challenged. The image of the Confucian gentleman is transformed into that of both intellectually and physically outstanding humans,[4] reshaping traditional virtues associated with men in the nationalistic ideological framework.[5] Sin was especially critical of male elites for failing to ensure national independence by deserting their Confucianism-based moral principles. The morally weakened men thus had to be renewed as national subjects, armed with a rekindled sense of national duty in body and spirit.

While Pak and Sin concentrated on the construction of ideal men, Chang Chiyŏn paid great attention to translating heroines from the West.

---

4. Vladimir Tikohnov and Yi Hye Gyung, "The Confucian Background of Modern 'Heroes' in the Writings of Sin Ch'aeho: In Comparison with Those of Liang Qichao," *Acta Koreana* 17, no. 1 (2014): 339–374.

5. Vladimir Tikhonov, "Masculinizing the Nation: Gender Ideologies in Traditional Korea and in the 1890s–1900s Korean Enlightenment Discourse," *The Journal of Asian Studies* 66, no. 4 (2007): 1029–1037.

Chang also altered social norms when translating these heroines: they
went from traditional Confucian, passive, and reticent figures to active
and outspoken social agents, re-creating the Confucian virtuous woman
in a national context. This is not to say that the heroines spoke specifically
about equal rights and equal participation in nation-building; rather, their
voice was masculine, mirroring male nationalists' top-down attitude toward the masses, which they viewed as objects of reform. In addition,
translations of biographies of exemplary women such as Joan of Arc and
Marie-Jeanne Roland were not necessarily directed only to female readership. The intended readership included men who would be moved by
women's self-sacrificing motherly spirit and actions. The construction of
national heroes and heroines, both originals and translations, created gendered boundaries for private and public spheres by reappropriating
Confucianism-based gender roles and adopting narrative tools such as
public speeches (*yŏnsŏl*) and public debates (*t'oron*). Through these figures
of national heroes and heroines, not only did writers present their ideas
about the nation, but they also conveyed their political passion for the nation by having their characters speak with rage, vigor, and provocation in
speeches and debates.

HYBRID MASCULINITIES IN SIN CH'AEHO'S BIOGRAPHICAL NOVELS

There had been heroic fiction in Chosŏn, and until the turn of the century
some of the most popular works were about fictional heroes who possessed physical strength—often in their mastery of martial arts—and supernatural power. Stories of these heroes were widely read and recited, and
their storylines reflected the popular imagination of Chosŏn's relationship
with China. The desire to maintain Chosŏn's independent status is evident
in *The Story of So Daesŏng* and *The Story of Yu Ch'ungnyŏl*, though this
independence is expressed more as anti-Qing sentiment, while criticism
of gender and class inequality is strongly reflected in *The Story of Hong
Kilttong* and *The Story of Princess Pari*. For Korean nationalist writers,
these fictional characters were not qualified to become models for their
heroes, since historical reality was the defining feature of their heroic fiction. The rewriting of these characters was a way to reconstruct national

identity away from China, legitimizing the unbroken continuity of Korea's independent status. Korea's national heroes thus had to be reborn as independent human beings whose fate was not determined by aggressors external to them and by supernatural influences.

Heroes in European histories were frequently used as examples to authenticate heroes in Korean history. A number of biographical novels about heroes in the West was introduced through Japanese political novels via Chinese intermediary texts. The first Japanese political novel that was translated in Korea was *The Founding of the Swiss Republic* (*Sŏsa kŏn'gukchi*, 1907) by Pak Ŭnsik,[6] based on *Wilhelm Tell* originally written by Friedrich von Schiller (1759–1805) in 1804.[7] Korean translators were attentive to reflecting the domestic situation in their works. *The Founding* is one example out of many in which references to China were consciously deleted or replaced with references to Korea.[8] Besides the paralleling of other nations' historical circumstances with Korea's, nationalist intellectuals constructed national heroes by modeling military leaders from the West. These included Giuseppe Mazzini (1805–1872), Camillo di Cavour (1810–1861), Giuseppe Garibaldi (1807–1882), Peter the Great, Napoleon, and so on, whose contributions to the founding of their modern nations were introduced to Koreans through Liang Qichao's texts, even though most of his texts were intermediary texts of Japanese originals. As these examples demonstrate, most heroes of the West whose biographies were translated in Japan at the time were known for their extraordinary leadership in politics and military, reflecting Meiji Japan's active promotion of the slogan, *fukoku kyōhei* (rich country, strong army). Political reformers

---

6. It was first serialized by *Taehan maeil sinbo* (*The Korea Daily News*) in July 1907 and later published in a book volume by Taehan maeil sinbosa in the same year. The Korean title is directly borrowed from the Chinese intermediary text.

7. It is translated in a combination of *han'gŭl* and Chinese script but the latter is predominant. Pak used a Chinese intermediary text, translated by Zheng Zhe (1880–1906), more commonly known as Zheng Guangong) in 1902, which was based on a Japanese translation of Schiller's work. It is not clear what Japanese text Zheng Zhe used since there are more than seven different Japanese translations of *Wilhelm Tell* that were produced between 1880 and 1905. See the list of the translations in Youn Young-Shil's "Tong asia chŏngch'i sosŏl ŭi han yangsang" (A case of political novel in East Asia), *Sanghŏ hakpo* 31 (Feb. 2011): 20–26.

8. For example, Pak prioritized "self-directed independence" (*tongnip chaju*) and "freedom" (*jayu*) rather than "competing with the global powers" as expressed by the Chinese translator of the Japanese version of *Wilhelm Tell*, Zheng Zhe in Youn Young-shil, 35..

in China and Korea shared the Japanese idea of strengthening the national economy and military force as a way to make their nations competitive.

Although Sin Ch'aeho also translated historical biographies of Western heroes, such as *The Three Heroes Who Founded Italy* (*It'aeri kŏn'guk samgŏljŏn*, 1907)[9] based on Liang's text,[10] he was more interested in reconstructing military heroes in Korean history, such as Ch'oe Yŏng, Yi Sunsin, and Ŭlchi Mundŏk. These exemplary figures were depicted as fearless warriors who demonstrated patriotic passion and a self-sacrificial spirit. Sin's emphasis on the military leadership of these generals challenged the moral superiority of the literati class in Chosŏn, where physical prowess was not upheld as a trait of wise men (*kunja*) by Confucian standards. However, Sin argued that a hero's military ability alone does not guarantee a nation's survival in the competitive global environment of his time. He also emphasized the role of professionals, such as politicians, philosophers, and literary figures whose great achievements in their professions would strengthen national character.[11] For example, the general Ŭlchi, in Sin's biographical novel, is not only talented in his military skills but also possesses knowledge of internal political affairs (*munmu kyŏmbi*).[12] A nation without a hero like the general is doomed to fall, and "because of Ŭlchi," Sin continues, Koguryŏ alone was able to compete with the emperor Yang of Sui in East Asia. Sin emphasized the importance of a man's intellectual ability, which, in his thinking, would ground one's moral character.

Despite his attempt to authenticate Korean history apart from China,

---

9. Sin's translation was first serialized in *Capital Gazette* from December 18 to December 28 in 1906 and published in book volume in 1907 by Kwanghak sŏp'o. Kim Chuhyŏn, "Wŏlnam mangguksa wa it'aeri kŏn'guk samgŏljŏn ŭi ch'ŏt pŏnyŏkja" (The first translator of *The History of the Fallen Vietnam* and *The Three Heroes Who Found Italy*), Haksul palp'yo charyojip (conference proceedings) in *Han'guk hyŏndae munhakhoe* (2009): 167–178.

10. Liang's intermediary text is based on a Japanese novel, *Itaari kenkoku sanketsu* (1892), by Hirata Hisashi, which was a translation of *The Makers of Modern Italy* (1889) by J.A.R. Marriott. Son Sŏngjun, "Yŏngung sŏsa tong asia suyong kwa chungyŏk ŭi wŏnbonssŏng: sŏgu t'eksŭt'ŭ ŭi han'gukjŏk chae maengnakhwa rŭl chungsim ŭro" (Second-hand translations of Western biographical fictions and their originality), PhD diss., Sungkyunkwan University, 2012.

11. Sin Ch'aeho, "Yŏngung kwa segye" (Heroes and the world), *Taehan maeil sinbo*, 16 September 1908, reprinted in *Tanjae Sin Ch'aeho chŏnjip: pyŏlchip*, 4th edition (Seoul: Tanjae Sin Ch'aeho kinyŏm saŏphoe, 1977), 111–113.

12. Sin Ch'aeho, *Ŭlchi Mundŏkjŏn*, reprinted in *Sin Ch'aeho chŏnjip: pyŏlchip*, 179.

Sin Ch'aeho always valued Confucian tradition, especially for its moral instructions. He claimed that the spirit of Confucianism must be renewed: "revering Confucianism" (*yugyo sungsang*) was not the cause for the weakened state of the Confucian nation, Korea. Rather, he argued, those who failed to observe the Confucian way of living were to blame.[13] Sin believed that observing the "way" is one of the most important elements that make people patriotic and sacrificial, and he stressed Confucian virtues in his novel, especially in *The Greatest Hero of the Chosŏn Navy Yi Sunsin* (*Sugun cheil wiin Yi Sunsin*, 1908).[14] Sin begins the novel by describing Yi Sunsin's family as made up of Confucian scholars (*yurim*), which provided Yi with intellectual and moral nourishment. Even though Heaven determined his path as a soldier, Yi studied Confucianism until the age of twenty.[15] In the work, Sin criticized those political elites in the royal court who prioritized their personal interests over public affairs, even at the expense of sacrificing a loyal vassal such as Yi Sunsin. In contrast to those petty elites in the novel, Yi stood out for his upholding of moral principles as taught by Confucianism.

While Sin called for a renewal of Confucianism, he maintained a critical attitude toward China in the novel, which minimizes Ming's involvement in the Korea-Japan war. Ming soldiers dispatched to Chosŏn are depicted as ruthless bandits, "looting properties and damaging fields."[16] The Ming admiral, Chin Lin, is depicted as "violent and unrefined," and thus is not respected by his own soldiers.[17] The work credits Yi's excellent commandership and his moral superiority for turning those "arrogant and disorderly" Ming soldiers and the general into a useful force against the Japanese. The negative portrayal of the Chinese was a way of representing the fate of China, which had fallen behind the global competition and failed to observe Confucian virtues. In Sin's fictional works, heroes in Korean history were reborn as "Confucian social Darwinists," to borrow Tikhonov's words, who do not lose their Eastern spirit (*tongdo*) while

---

13. Sin, "Yugyogye e taehan illon" (A view on the Confucian communities), *Taehan maeil sinbo*, 28 February 1909.

14. This work was serialized in *Taehan maeil sinbo* from 2 May 1908 to 8 August 1908.

15. "Sugun cheil wiin Yi Sunsin," *Taehan maeil sinbo*, 3 May 1908.

16. Ibid., 24 May 1908.

17. Ibid., 11 June 1908.

adopting Western technologies (*sŏgi*),[18] and who will have to survive in the new global order.

In Sin's and Pak's essays and other works, moral superiority and physical strength are constitutive of national masculinity, and this image of national masculinity was not only confined to their works. Other young intellectuals, such as Ch'oe Namsŏn, also presented an ideal image of young Korean men, by blending these two qualities in his literary magazine, *Sonyŏn* (*Boy*), published in Japan during the early 1900s. The blending of the traditional and the Western—the revering of Confucian virtues and the celebration of physically strong bodies, respectively—characterizes the national masculinity embodied in Sin's heroes.[19]

Like his Chinese counterpart Kang Youwei (1858–1927), Sin Ch'aeho maintained his faith in Confucianism, viewing Confucianism as a religion that provided people with spiritual guidance that united them as national subjects. In his essay "New Citizens of the Twentieth Century" (*Isip segi sin kungmin*), Sin criticized both old and new religions that failed to serve national purposes. And yet, he wrote, only two religions—Confucianism and Christianity—had the potential to strengthen the nation and the people's spirit. Confucianism had great power to influence Korean people; thus it was desirable to make it the national religion, while Christianity must also be widely encouraged.[20] Although he did not discuss the merits of Christianity extensively compared to his in-depth discussion of Confucianism in the essay and elsewhere, he perceived the growing influence of Christianity as a positive force as long as people were aware of the intrusive motivations that often came with it. Sin privileged Confucianism over Christianity, and his "means to an end" attitude toward religion indicates that the Western religion was considered useful insofar as it was a remodeling of Confucian values, thus "correcting" people's morality.

Sin's articulation of heroes in his essays and fiction works was a step toward his conceptualization of *minjok*, one ethnic nation where all the people must act the way heroes in their history did. Based on evolutionary theory (*chinhwa*), Sin argues that Korean *minjok* "would have been leading the world by now" considering how great they were in premodern

---

18. Vladimir Tikhonov, "Masculinizing the Nation," 1035.

19. Ibid., 1029–1065.

20. *Taehan maeil sinbo*, 22 February–3 March 1910, cited in *Sin Ch'aeho chŏnjip: pyŏlchip*, 227–228.

times. General Ŭlchi and his men were considered proof of this, and a new hero, a national hero in his time, would emerge and stimulate his *minjok* to become courageous again.[21] Even though Sin, along with other nationalist intellectuals such as Pak Ŭnsik and Chang Chiyŏn, promoted the image of national subjects who possessed disciplined bodies and minds, the image of heroes was fundamentally masculine; the physical and spiritual strength of the nation is embodied in Sin's heroes who survive in the competitive world.

THE CONSTRUCTION OF GOOD WIVES AND WISE MOTHERS (*HYŎNMO YANGCH'Ŏ*)

Having been caught up in the wind of progress, many nationalist intellectuals viewed women's ignorance and their unfair treatment by society as a sign of barbarism (*yaman*). The strict class divisions and neo-Confucian ethical codes of conduct for women came under vehement attack in print media: arranged marriage, concubinage, and women's confinement to inner chambers, for example, were viewed as barbaric customs to be uprooted. Reformist intellectuals' calls to eradicate the barbarity echoed strongly, though rarely did they consider class differences among women. Women were categorized as one group who deserved pity for their miserable living conditions. Social reformers seem to have been primarily concerned with educating women to be patriotic mothers, rather than promoting women's political rights or encouraging their participation in social activities.

One of the first Chosŏn bureaucrats of the patriotic nationalist movement period to advocate for women's education in this light was Yu Kilchun. Yu distributed his book, *The Impression of the West* (*Sŏyu kyŏnmun*), within bureaucratic circles as a report on his time in Europe and America. Yu could not be too assertive in his statements about women's education in that book due to the lingering conservative atmosphere in Korea.[22] He could only "introduce" Western ideas for the sake of national progress, referring to unidentified foreign authorities and inserting his opinion that

---

21. Sin, *Ŭlchi mundŏkjŏn*, 208, and *Yi Sunsinjŏn*, 320.
22. The report was dedicated to King Kojong and a few high-ranking officials in 1890, but it was only published in 1895 through the help of Fukuzawa Yukichi.

educating women is very important since "women's literacy will affect their children's intellectual development."[23] Yu's followers were more openly critical about the backwardness from the mid-1890s of government policies and cultural practices toward women; the most radical voices on the subject came from Christian groups who were particularly enthusiastic about promoting women's education as the foundation for liberal society.

One of the earliest newspapers that allocated significant space for gender issues was *The Independent News* (*Tongnip sinmun*). It frequently criticized the uncivilized state of Korea, which, in its view, was well reflected in women's lives: "The most pitiful women in the world are women in Korea ... Women have been treated so lowly for no logical reasons because men in Korea are not civilized and enlightened. What else can we call these men but barbarians who oppress their women by physical force while lacking reason and compassion?"[24] Besides advocating gender equality, the newspaper attacked men's ignorance, blaming them for making women blind and mute.[25] The condition that would allow men and women to develop reason and compassion, as promoted by most nationalist intellectuals, was education. Educating women in all classes was never considered necessary in Chosŏn, where women's ignorance was considered a virtue. This long-revered "virtue," however, was challenged at the end of the nineteenth century. "Reason" and "compassion," two of the most important teachings in Confucianism, were to be retaught with lexicons that came from different intellectual traditions.

Women's responses to male public figures' writings about women's education were scarce, and yet to women who could read *han'gŭl*, the availability of new information about contemporary world affairs was enlightening. As one elderly housewife wrote to *The Imperial News* (*Cheguk sinmun*), "The power of a newspaper rests on its delivery of knowledge" to a woman like herself who had been living as if "mute and blind." She hoped to overcome her "disability" through absorbing knowledge by reading newspapers.[26] Female readers' appreciation of *han'gŭl* papers

23. Yu Kilchun, *Sŏyu kyŏnmun* (The impression of the West), trans. Hŏ Kyŏngjin (Seoul: Sŏhaemunjip, [1895] 2004), 422–424.

24. *The Independent News*, 21 April 1896.

25. *The Independent News*, 31 March 1899.

26. *The Imperial News* (*Cheguk sinmun*), 3 April 1907; Yi Kyŏngha, "Taehan cheguk

could lead to considerable reader loyalty. When *The Imperial News* was facing bankruptcy due to financial problems, devoted female readers tried to raise funds to save the paper. They feared that they would lose their "eyes and ears" once the paper was gone.[27] As these responses demonstrate, newspapers were a source of learning for women, and women placed great importance on their ability to read them. Indeed, the fact that women now had the same access to information as men was a remarkable development that made them feel included in the society as equal members. Older generations of women were hopeful for the next generation—and that these younger women, like their male compatriots, "will let the world remember their names if they achieve social success through education."[28] The sense of inclusion led these women to see themselves as citizens who possessed not only the right to learn but also the responsibility to perform their roles as patriotic mothers for the nation.

Among those who actively promoted women's education, Chang Chiyŏn stands as a unique figure who produced a variety of writings on women—essays, fiction, and a compilation of exemplary women in Korean, Chinese, and Euro-American histories. In the compilation of exemplary women, Chang argued, "All young women will become mothers of national subjects. Children can grow to become good citizens only if their mothers properly educate them."[29] Chang did not recognize women themselves as "citizens," but considered them "mothers of citizens," a dominant view of women's role shared among nationalist intellectuals at the time, which was encapsulated in the term "wise mothers and good wives" (*hyŏnmo yangch'ŏ*). The idea of making women wise mothers and good wives in the service of nation-building had been widely spread through Japan since the late nineteenth century. It aimed to teach women to be solely responsible for domestic duties, child-rearing, and education, which

---

yŏin dŭl ŭi sinmun ilkki wa tokja t'ugo" (A study of female readership of newspapers and "women's opinion section"), *Yŏ/sŏng iron* 12 (2005): 282.

27. *The Imperial News,* 11 September 1907; Yi Kyŏngha, "Taehan cheguk," 293.

28. Hannam Yŏsa, "Kwŏn'go puin'gye" (Recommendations for my fellow women), *The Korea Daily News,* 20 March 1908; Hong Insuk, "Kŭndae kyemonggi kŭlssŭgi ŭi yangsang kwa yŏsŏng chuch'e hyŏngsŏng kwajŏng" (The writing patterns in the enlightenment period and the formation of female subjectivity), *Han'guk kojŏn yŏn'gu hakhoe* 14 (2006): 115–116.

29. Chang Chiyŏn, *Nyŏja tokbon,* April 1908, cited in Chŏng Hwan'guk, "1900 nyŏndae ŭi yŏsŏng" (Women in the 1900s), *Han'guk kojŏn yŏsŏng munhak yŏn'gu* 8 (2004): 268.

would constitute their patriotic contribution. This ideology gained currency in Korea at the turn of the twentieth century through the import of both Japanese and Chinese texts.[30]

Educating children, however, had not been married women's primary role in the previous era. Certainly, women were expected to educate their daughters on domestic matters. Yet, sons' education was largely left to their husbands and occasionally to their fathers-in-law. This division of labor on education in the domestic sphere would be revamped with the spread of the "wise mothers and good wives" ideology, which recognized men's labor as existing solely within the public sphere.[31] It was around this time that stories of mothers of men of great achievement in history began to be reconstructed through the lens of this ideology. Lady Sin, better known as Sin Saimdang (1504–1551) to modern-day Koreans, is a good example. The mother of an influential Confucian scholar, Yi Yulgok (1537–1584), Lady Sin was refashioned as one of the supreme examples of wise mothers even though in the previous era she had been better known for her artistic talent and intelligence.[32] On the other hand, a woman like Kollumba Kang Wansuk (1761–1802), a Catholic activist who not only contributed to the spread of Catholicism in Korea, but also led fellow Christian women to manifest their subjectivity through their religious practice, was to be ignored in the reframing of womanly virtues at the turn of the century.[33] Kang did not have a male heir and she had divorced her husband.

---

30. In Chosŏn, the term *hyŏnmo* (wise mothers) was widely used to emphasize mothers' role in their children's ethical development; by following Confucian principles, mothers would ensure that children became filial and loyal. *Yangch'ŏ*, on the other hand, referred to wives of *yang'in* (commoners). These two terms were combined around the turn of the twentieth century, referring to women whose motherly and wifely duties were redefined solely in the national context, making them responsible for educating children to become "good citizens." Chŏn Kyŏngok et al., *Han'guk yŏsŏng chŏngch'i sahoesa* (The political and social history of Korean women) (Seoul: Sukmyŏng Women's University Press, 2006), 57.

31. Hong Yanghi, "Singminji sigi 'hyŏnmo yangch'ŏron' kwa 'modŏnit'i ŭi munje" (The ideology of wise mothers and good wives in colonial Korea and the problem of modernity), *Sahak yŏn'gu* 99 (2010): 315.

32. Hong Yanghi, "'Hyŏnmo yangch'ŏ' ŭi sangjing, Sin Saimdang: Singminji sigi Sin Saimdang ŭi chaehyŏn kwa chendŏ chŏngch'ihak" (The symbol of wise mothers and good wives, Sin Saimdang: The representation of and the politics of gender of Lady Sin), *Sahak yŏn'gu* 122 (2016): 155–190.

33. Gari Ledyard, "Kollumba Kang Wansuk, an Early Catholic Activist and Martyr,"

Even though she was extraordinary woman she would not be commemorated in the "civilized" society simply because she lacked the condition of being a wise mother of sons.

But the most important womanly virtue was not associated with women's role as mothers; rather, it was their filial piety toward their parents-in-law who held enormous power over the daughter-in-law's life. As gender equality was emphasized as a sign of civilization, the relationship between women and their in-laws, especially mothers-in-law, was criticized as archaic and inhumane by reformers who sympathized with the powerless position of daughters-in-law while advocating equal relationships between wives and husbands.[34] The ideology had implications far beyond the patriotic; it was to become a gender hegemony for the next century that continuously compelled women to become good mothers, to gain respect from their husbands, and to claim membership as citizens in the society.

Although women's education was regarded as useless unless utilized for children and husbands, it would be a mistake to assume that women perceived this ideology as gender discriminative at the time. Reformers' encouragement of women's education was rather an opportunity for women to educate themselves with new knowledge. However, they did not place blind faith in education for civilizing their society, maintaining instead a critical view of the civilization discourses they were exposed to through newspapers. Female readers of newspapers did not refute nationalists' views on their role as wise mothers and good wives for national growth, although at times they were discontent with the blatant promotion of Western-inspired education and the generalization of feminine virtue. One young woman argued that those who publicly promoted Western education and new knowledge "tend(ed) to ignore the value of our own knowledge and education system with no logical explanations"; she was doubtful as to whether the dismissal of native culture and tradition was really a way to "civilize" society.[35] As well, women readers took

---

in *Christianity in Korea*, ed. Robert Buswell Jr. and Timothy Lee (Honolulu: University of Hawai'i Press, 2007), 38–71.

34. Hong Yanghi, "Singminji sigi 'hyŏnmo yangch'ŏron' kwa 'modŏnit'i ŭi munje" (The ideology of wise mothers and good wives in colonial Korea and the problem of modernity), *Sahak yŏn'gu* 99 (2010): 310–312.

35. Nongun nangja, "Kyoyuk i hyŏn'gŭm ŭi cheil kŭpmu" (Our first priority, education), *Taehan maeil sinbo*, 5 June 1908, cited in Yi Kyŏngha, "Taehan cheguk," 286.

issue with male social ideologues' tendency to problematize marriage practice from a moralist position, rather than as a social problem. One male writer, in a condemnation of concubinage (*ch'ŏp*), blamed the custom on the "promiscuity" of concubines and claimed that they harmed public morale by living with married men. Upon reading this column, a female reader who identified herself as a married woman living in a rural area wrote a letter attacking his dismissal of systemic problems surrounding the custom and his stereotyped view of female sexuality. She argued that since women's status does not automatically determine their moral character and vice versa, discussing the practice in a moral context was beside the point.[36] Nevertheless, once the female readers of newspapers had been exposed to information about the national crisis, they responded with nationalistic activities, such as fundraising to pay off the national debt (*kukch'e posang undong*, 1907)[37] and founding private academies for young girls.[38]

A CONFUCIAN JOAN OF ARC

Chang Chiyŏn understood fiction writing as the male intellectuals' duty to enlighten society and his translation was an extension of his intellectual labor that ultimately aimed to elevate the patriotic spirit of the masses. He was the chief editor of the *Capital Gazzette* (*Hwangsŏng sinmun*), where he serialized the translation of a biography of Joan of Arc entitled *The Story of a Patriotic Lady* (*Aeguk puinjŏn*, 1906) in pure *han'gŭl*. It is not known what intermediary text was used for Chang's translation of Joan of Arc. Some scholars suggest the Korean translation was likely based on either Liang or Lu Xun's text,[39] while others try to identify its origin among Japa-

---

36. "Ŏttŏn yujigak han sigol puin" (A wise woman from a rural village), *The Imperial News*, 10 November 1898.

37. Major nationalist papers initiated this campaign, which gained nationwide support. About thirty women's associations were formed, particularly aimed at raising funds among women who participated in the campaign by selling their jewelry and other personal items. Chŏng Chinsŏk, *Ŏllon kwa han'guk hyŏndaesa*, 102–103.

38. Between 1900 and 1910, about 128 academies were founded by women's organizations. Ch'oe Ch'angsu, "Sinsosŏl: yŏsŏng ŭi kŭndaehwa wa chagi chŏngch'esŏng" (Modernized women and their identity), *Ŏmun nonjip* 28 (2000): 262.

39. Hyun, *Writing Women in Korea*, 33.

nese sources.[40] Compared to the transliterary sphere in China at that time, where translators identified the original texts they translated,[41] Korean translators rarely identified the intermediary texts they used. And yet, like his Chinese compatriots, Chang often added commentary to connect the story's central historical event: the war between France and England, with Korea's confrontation with Japan.[42] Although he did not mention Japan in the text, possibly because of censorship, his repetitive use of England as France's "enemy" along with mention of "victorious moments in Korean history" are direct references to the domestic political situation.[43]

The Story of a Patriotic Lady narrates the life of Joan of Arc in chronological order, and it begins by emphasizing equality as an important condition for making women patriotic citizens. This work was also included in a two-volume textbook entitled *Readings for Women* that Chang published in 1908, a book that quite clearly conveyed Chang's position on equality for women through his selection of historical figures with various

40. Stories of two Western heroines, Joan of Arc and Madame Roland, were published in separate volumes in Korea in the early 1900s. While it is believed that the work on Madame Roland was based on Liang's work and chosen for its use of "maternal metaphor," portraying Madame Roland as the "mother of the nation," the intermediary text that was used for Chang's translation of *The Story of a Patriotic Lady* has not been clearly identified. No Yŏnsuk suggests that the original Japanese text, Iwasaki Sōdo and Mikami Kifu's *Sekai jūni joketsu* (Twelve world heroines) (Tokyo: Kōbundō shoten, 1902), shares many similarities with Chang's, yet I find that there are significant differences between the two in terms of their construction of the text, narrative techniques, and emphasis on feminine virtues. The story of Joan of Arc, in No's findings, was introduced in twelve different texts in Japan. See the discussions on Chinese translations of Joan of Arc and Madame Roland in Joan Judge, "A Translocal Technology of the Self: Biographies of World Heroines and the Chinese Woman Question," *Journal of Women's History* 21, no. 4 (November 2009): 59–83; Hu Ying, *Tales of Translation: Composing the New Woman in China, 1899–1918* (Stanford, CA: Stanford University Press, 2000). For discussions of Korean translations, see No Yŏnsuk, "20 segi ch'o tong asia chŏngch'i sŏsa e nat'anan 'aeguk' ŭi yangsang" (Expressions of "patriotism" reflected in political writings in the beginning of twentieth century East Asia), *Han'guk hyŏndae munhak yŏn'gu* 28 (2009): 7–34.

41. Judge, "A Translocal Technology of the Self," 63–65.

42. In certain places, he refers to France as Chosŏn by mistake. For example, in Joan of Arc's speech, she explains the crisis facing France to the crowds, yet in the same speech, she refers to France as "Chosŏn."

43. Lawrence Venuti defines a community who desires to share a common understanding with a foreign group through translation as an "imagined community." Inscriptions of domestic beliefs and values, he argues, are a manifestation of the desire of the readers who "imagine" the reconciliation of linguistic and cultural differences between the cultures. Venuti, ed., "Translation, Community, Utopia," 498–502.

social backgrounds. The first volume of *Readings* consists of stories of exemplary Korean women who were mostly widows and commoners. While the women in *Readings* devote their energy to educating their sons, *Patriotic Lady*'s heroine, Joan, is the daughter of peasants who educates herself through avid reading. Besides her drive to learn, Joan's religious belief makes her special from the beginning. She is chosen to be the savior of her nation because of her devotion to God. In the eyes of the villagers, however, it was her intelligence that stood out the most, leading them to say, "Had she been born as a man she would certainly make a great contribution to our country."[44] She reacts against this statement by showing her sense of equality in the service of the nation: "Men and women are equal before God, thus there is no reason why women cannot do for the nation as men do."[45]

The ambiguity of Chang's observations on Christianity is noteworthy in *Patriotic Lady*. He describes Joan's Christian beliefs as a spiritual foundation for equality, while the French are presented as people who have been lured into the trap of superstition. Their country was weakened, he suggests, due to the "unscientific" religious beliefs and practices of the time. Having been trained in the Confucian tradition, he may have had difficulty accepting the existence of the spirits that appeared before Joan, though he did not omit this part in *Patriotic Lady*.[46] He commented in the *Translator's Notes* that Joan's "inexplicable" (*pulgabul*) display of spiritual power was shown because she had to appeal to the French who were deluded by the world of gods at the time. It was Joan's political tactic to use religious belief in order to motivate and unite her people to regain their sovereignty, a view quite similar to that of Zhao Bizhan, a Chinese translator of Joan of Arc.[47] Chang tried to clarify his position by making Joan a heroine who "enlightened" the people through her intelligence and patri-

---

44. Chang Chiyŏn, *Aeguk puinjŏn*, in *Han'guk kaehwagi munhak ch'ongsŏ: yŏksa/chŏn'gi sosŏl* (A comprehensive series of literature produced during the Enlightenment period: Historical and biographical novels) (Seoul: Han'guk munhŏn yŏn'guso, 1979), 1.

45. Ibid., 2.

46. Zhao Bizhen, the translator of a Japanese text, *Twelve World Heroines* (*Sekai jūni joketsu*, by Iwasaki and Mikami), maintained a critical distance from the spirituality by inserting comments that the story of Joan of Arc was written at the time when "superstition had not yet been overcome by science." See the discussion of Chinese translations of Western heroines in Judge, "A Translocal Technology of the Self," 67.

47. Chang, *Aeguk puinjŏn*, 38. This line is almost identical to the translator's notes written by Zhao Bizhen. See Judge, "A Translocal Technology of the Self," 67.

otic attitude, commenting in the notes: "It cannot be said that a human being's action is determined by God."[48]

It was not uncommon to see Christian vocabulary used in political novels, even though their writers did not necessarily practice the religion; in particular, the Christian concept of equality was understood as a universal law, governed by an absolute power, which would eventually secure Korean independence. Well-known Christian writers such as An Kukson (1878–1926) and Kim P'ilsu (1872–1948) stood out for their use of specific biblical references and religious symbolism rather than relying on generalized notions of "the law of God." This is especially clear in An's translation of a Japanese political novel, *The Record of the Conference of Birds and Beasts* (*Kŭmsu hoeŭirok*, 1908), and Kim's translation of a Japanese novel, *The Bell of Enlightenment* (*Kyŏngsejong*, 1910), whose main objective was to criticize social injustice and overcome official corruption in order to modernize the country. Considering that social Darwinism was widely understood as determining a nation's survival, Korean writers' use of equality in a Christian context seems to have functioned as an ideology that could counter the Japanese colonial force.[49]

Countering the political hegemony of the West through a Western religion might have been peculiar had there been no attempt made to universalize religious doctrines through translation. An Kukson's specific Christian references, therefore, had to be translated in order to appeal to their intended audience. The Christian concept of God (*hananim*) was used interchangeably with the Confucian concept of "heaven" (*sangje*); for example, filial piety and chastity were emphasized as feminine virtues that were to be maintained according to the will of heaven. At times, Taoist and Christian ideas appeared side by side in the same text; the concept of women's equal rights was approached with both the Christian doctrine "God loves us all equally"[50] and the *yin-yang* theory, "the harmony between heaven (men) and earth (women)."[51]

---

48. Chang, *Aeguk puinjŏn*, 38.

49. Kwŏn Podŭre, "Sinsosŏl e nat'anan kidokkyo ŭi ŭimi: *Kŭmsu hoeŭirok* kwa *Kyŏngsejong* ŭl chungsim ŭro" (The meaning of Christianity in the New Novel: Focusing on *Kŭmsu hoeŭirok* and *Kyŏngsejong*), *Han'guk hyŏndae munhak ŭi yŏn'gu* 8 (1998): 7–30.

50. Ch'oe Pyŏngch'an, "Nyŏja kyoyuk p'iryo" (The necessity of women's education), *Nyŏjajinam* 1 (1908): 16–19.

51. Chŏng Haebaek, "Namnyŏ tongdŭng ron (On equality between men and women), *Nyŏjajinam* 1 (1908): 19–23.

Chang described Joan as a warrior who received great respect for her masculine appearance and militaristic skills: "In a golden armor, she held a long sword in her right hand ... her solemn and confident appearance inspired her people,"[52] and "her sword cut down innumerable British soldiers ... their heads piled up on the ground like fallen leaves."[53] He compared Joan to exemplary male military leaders in Korean history such as Yang Manch'un and Ŭlchi Mundŏk of Koguryŏ, as well as Kang Kamch'an of Koryŏ, thus erasing gender distinction in the service of one's nation. Chang also included an abridged rendition of *Joan of Arc* in the second volume of *Readings*, where he introduced stories of militant heroines, including Chinese women warriors such as Hua Mulan of Northern Wei (386–534), Xun Guan of the Western Qin dynasty (265–316), and Qin Liangyu of the Ming dynasty (1368–1644).[54] Chang's discussion of exemplary Korean women in history, however, is mostly limited to those who killed themselves to protect their chastity from the Japanese. Korean women's efforts to stay chaste, in other words, were understood as a nationalistic action in the *Readings*. This emphasis on chastity could be interpreted symbolically—a message to stay "pure" against the external forces, with the nation gendered as female—yet it also points to his notion that women's equality and freedom could be recognized only when their moral conduct met the Confucian standard.

Chang's appropriation, if not distortion, of the biography of Joan of Arc did not go unnoticed. Some criticized his *Story* for its historical inaccuracy. Florian Demange, a Catholic priest and an editor of the religious paper *Kyŏnghyang Daily*, warned his readers:

---

52. Chang, *Aeguk puinjŏn*, 19.

53. Ibid., 30.

54. The first volume of the *Readings* deals with women in Korean history, whereas the second volume introduces fifteen exemplary Chinese women, starting with Mencius's mother and ten Western heroines. The selection of ten Western heroines is a mixture of suffragists, educators, queens, and patriots, which seems to have been based on two Chinese texts, *Twelve World Heroines* (1903) and *Ten World Heroines* (1903). The second volume of the *Readings* features Charlotte Corday (1768–1793), Anita Garibaldi (1821–1849), Louise Michel (1830–1905), Joan of Arc (1412–1431), Madame Roland (1754–1793), Lucy Hutchinson (1620–1681), Harriet Beecher Stowe (1811–1896), Queen Louise of Prussia (1776–1810), Frances Willard (1839–1898), and Florence Nightingale (1820–1910). *Nyŏja tokbon*, reprinted in *Han'guk kaehawgi kyokwasŏ ch'ongsŏ* (A compilation of textbooks published during the enlightenment period), vol. 8 (Seoul: Asea munhwasa, [1908] 1977).

A history must be told based on factual events. But this New Fiction called *The Story of a Patriotic Lady* doesn't depict the story of Joan of Arc faithfully. Some historical dates are incorrect and the translator omitted some crucial points. Furthermore, it was wrong for the accompanying illustration to dress Joan of Arc as if she were a woman living in contemporary times ... can you, Korean readers, imagine King Sejong dressed in a Western suit?[55]

In fact, Demange made a list of the "mistakes" in Chang's works and corrected them, adding an admonishing critique of his translation practice. According to Ch'oe T'aewŏn, the distinction between translation and adaptation was not clear until the 1910s; before then, translators seem to have understood adaptation to be a translation technique,[56] which is illustrated in Chang Chiyŏn's "Translator's Notes" (*Pŏnyŏkhan ja*) in *Madame Roland.* The "looseness" of translation during this period conveys the historical moment in which the practice was conditioned. Translators strategized the "transfer" of unfamiliar culture by "indigenizing" it. When translation is strongly connected to cultural nationalism, this trend is more salient, something we can see in other societies as well.[57] Demange's cultural point of view saw "distortion" in Chang's "infidelity" to the original; however, from Chang's point of view, I believe, his text was a product of compromise, "a compromise between one's ideals and one's aims, and negotiation between the foreign and the self."[58] What might have appeared "anachronistic" in the eyes of an outsider was a practical choice for Chang; he tried to make sense of the history of others in his native language while viewing the material through his own cultural lens, a dual process that

---

55. "On books published these days," *Kyŏnghyang Daily*, 27 March 1908.

56. Ch'oe T'aewŏn, "Pŏnan iranŭn haeng'wi wa kŭ juch'e" (An act of adaptation and the adapting subjectivity), *Chōsen bunka kenkyūkai seminar*, Waseda University (24 November 2007), 1–2.

57. Maria Tymoczko discusses this relationship between translation and cultural nationalism in her investigation of modern Irish translation of early texts as a "mode of discovery and an assertion of the indigenous cultural heritage." *Translation in a Postcolonial Context: Early Irish Literature in English Translation* (Manchester, UK: St. Jerome Publishing, 1999), 177.

58. Hu Ying, in her discussion of the translation practice of Yan Fu at the turn of the twentieth century in China, argues that translators were clearly aware of their appropriation of original texts as a compromise in order to bridge the gap between "the foreign and the self, and between different facets of the self." *Tales of Translation*, 17.

bridged the gap between Korea and the foreign, and between the past and the present, through translation.

Chang's Joan argues that "every citizen has a duty to serve the nation as a soldier at a time of crisis"[59] because "one's fate is determined by the nation's fate, if citizens of the nation cannot defend the sovereignty, they will become nothing but slaves of invaders."[60] However, she also bears the obligation to serve her parents as a filial daughter. After winning a battle against the British army, she pleads with the king to let her visit her parents, saying, "I am an ordinary maiden from a small farming village where my parents live by themselves. I worry about my aging parents who have no one else to depend on."[61] This reference to Joan's filial piety exhibits the moral conflict a woman may face in serving the nation at a time of crisis, which requires not only the sacrifice of her life, but also her family's. As Chang states in *Patriotic Lady*, "It is difficult for one to be loyal to her country and filial to her parents at the same time," yet Joan's "truly loyal heart" chooses nation over family.[62] In the end, Joan's individuality is manifest only in her relationship to her family and the nation, never in relation to her religious spirituality.

Like Joan of Arc in *Patriotic Lady*, all of Chang's heroines in the *Readings* are historical figures. Their filial piety, chastity, and loyalty toward their husbands and families are shown to help their children's moral education and bring national security and prosperity. The texts' emphasis on women's child-rearing duties particularly appealed to female readers who were already familiar with the instruction, having read the compilation on virtuous women in China and Chosŏn. However, female readers were particularly inspired by the idea of women's education as the foundation for raising their children as patriotic citizens. In her letter to *The Korea Daily News*, a subscriber who identified herself as Chang Kyŏngju wrote, "Mencius's mother moved three times to find a right place for her son's education. Had she been ignorant it would not have been possible for her son to become a great scholar. This example shows us how important it is to educate women. When we see those heroines in novels such as *The Story of a Patriotic Lady* and *Madame Roland*, it becomes clear that even women can make great

---

59. Chang, *Aeguk puinjŏn*, 24.
60. Ibid., 22.
61. Ibid., 33.
62. Ibid., 34.

contribution to their country if they are properly educated."[63] Though women's education was the most fundamental condition for actualizing national wealth, in Chang's reconstruction of Joan of Arc as a filial daughter and a warrior, the concept of political rights and freedom for women does not surface. Similarly, his portrait of Frances Willard (1839–1898) in the *Readings* omits her work in the women's suffrage and temperance movement and instead focuses on her involvement in the abolitionist movement. This substitution was not a simple mistake; rather, it was undertaken to clearly deliver Chang's firm position on women as "mothers of citizens," not as "citizens" themselves. It is not a coincidence that the mother of Kim Yusin (595–673)[64] is introduced in the first volume of *Readings*, and the mother of Mencius in the second volume; both are mothers of eternal heroes of Korea and China. Chang's prioritization of these exemplary women represents the then-dominant imagination of women as dedicated mothers whose intelligence and wisdom encouraged their people.

The biography of Madame Roland was another novel that became highly popular in Japan, Korea, and China between 1880s and the early twentieth century, based on the biography that appeared in Grace Wharton's (1797–1862) *The Queens of Society* (1860). *The Queens* included biographies of eighteen women, and yet none of the other biographies received the interest that the biography of Madame Roland did from Japanese translators. Since the first translation in 1876, other renowned writers of the time also translated the story of Madame Roland. One of the giants in the field of translation in the Meiji period, Tsubouchi Shōyō, translated it twice, in 1886 and 1887, with Futabatei Shimei's foreword included in the latter version; and Tokutomi Roka published his translation in 1893. When Tokutomi published a compilation of biographies of women in the East and West in 1898, Madame Roland was introduced first in it.[65] The translators' devotion to Madame Roland perhaps reflected their own political

---

63. Chang Kyŏngju, "Nyŏja kyoyuk" (Women's education), *Taehan maeil sinbo*, 11 August 1908.

64. A military general of Silla (57–935) who played a crucial role in uniting the three kingdoms in the peninsula.

65. Son Sŏngjun, "Rolang puin chŏn'gi ŭi tongasia suyong yangsang kwa kŭ sŏngkkyŏk" (Adaptations of the biography of Madame Roland in East Asia and their characteristics), *Pigyo munhak* 53 (2011): 116–123.

views, since both Tsubouchi and Tokutomi advocated parliamentarism. Further, as the Freedom and People's Rights movement had waned by the 1880s and as the political radicalism associated with the movement had gone out of favor, Madame Roland might have been an ideal figure to represent a victim of radicalism.[66]

Chang Chiyŏn used Liang Qichao's text when translating the story of Madame Roland, which was introduced to Chinese readers in 1902. Although it is likely that Liang used Tokutomi Roka's version,[67] his emphasis shifted significantly. Unlike Tokutomi's description of Madame Roland's emotional conflict arising from her position as a mother, a wife, and a revolutionist, Liang lessened the domestic image of Madame Roland while underlining her bigger-than-life personality that enabled her political vision. In Tokutomi's text, consumed with sadness due to leaving her daughter, Madame Roland is described as "a good wife and loving mother … after all."[68] But in Liang's text, she is a revolutionary first, brushing aside the motherly feeling she expresses; instead, he views her sadness as a sign that shows "the great woman was also a loving person."[69] Liang rather presented her as "a metaphorical political and social mother," to borrow Joan Judge's expression. In the beginning of the text, Liang writes:

> [Madame Roland was] the mother of Napoleon, the mother of Metternich, the mother of Mazzini, the mother of Kossuth, the mother of Bismarck, and the mother of Cavour. In short, all great men of nineteenth-century Europe could not but regard her as mother; all civilizations of nineteenth-century Europe could not but regard her as mother. Why was this so? Because the French Revolution was the mother of nineteenth-century Europe, and Madame Roland was the mother of the French Revolution.[70]

The above lines were not in Tokutomi's text; they were created by Liang. In

---

66. Both translators were supportive of the revolution and the establishment of the parliamentary government; however, their attitude toward radical revolutionary figures such as Robespierre was negative. Ibid., 127.

67. It had long been believed that Liang used Tsubouchi Shōyō's text, *Rōran fujinden*, but it has been identified that he rather used Tokutomi Roka's, *Bukkoku kakumei no hana*, Ibid., 127–128.

68. Ibid., 128.

69. Ibid.

70. Translated by Judge, "A Translocal Technology of the Self," 71.

turn, they were translated in their entirety by Chang in the Korean translation, revealing that both translators maintained a distance from the human aspect of Madame Roland. In fact, there is another part of Madame Roland's life that was omitted by Liang and Chang, that is, her feelings toward François Nicolas-Léonard Buzot who was known to be her lover. Liang's appropriation of Tokutomi's text may indicate two objectives. First, his main target readers were men who were to be inspired by Madame Roland's political passion and morality. What may have been perceived as inappropriate feminine conduct associated with her relationship with a man outside of marriage thus had to be eliminated. Second, Liang maintained a conservative attitude toward a revolution that was, as reflected in the translation, not an ideal process for China.[71] Liang and his Japanese counterparts in fact shared views on the revolution, though the former stressed the manifestation of her masculine vision for political reform, making her "the mother of all men" while dramatizing the negative impact of radicalism, which sacrificed a great woman such as Madame Roland. The dramatization of the sacrifice was expressed in Liang's description of Madame Roland's final moment in the court. She is removed from domestic reality; instead, she appears as a spiritual mother whose purity and beauty, in a white dress with long hair, will soon be destroyed by tyranny.

Liang and the Japanese translators' skeptical view of radicalism, however, turned into something positive in the Korean translation. This is one noticeable instance where Chang distances himself from Liang's vision for Korea. In the translator's notes, Chang points out that France was able to make the revolution happen because of great people like Madame Roland even though its situation was less urgent and corrupt than Korea's. Thus, he continues, Korea can stand on equal footing with strong European nations if all Korean men and women follow in the footsteps of the exemplary mother and teacher, Madame Roland.[72] As Son Sŏngjun points out, the change may indicate that Chang, despite Korea's dire situation, wanted to remain hopeful for himself and his audience, dreaming of Korea's independence.[73]

---

71. Son Sŏngjun, "Rolang puin chŏn'gi ŭi tongasia," 130–131.

72. Chang Chiyŏn, *Raran puinjŏn*, 39–41.

73. Son Sŏngjun, "Rolang puin chŏn'gi ŭi tongasia," 136.

However, the implication of this change is wider than the imagination of national independence. The imagination of national community and its sovereignty embodied in the translation echoes Partha Chatterjee's argument about the formation of nationalism in non-Western/colonized societies, where the conventional story about modern nationalism as a consequence of "the contest for political power" overlooks anticolonial nationalism and its creation of an "inner domain of cultural identity."[74] The aesthetic construction of national culture with nationalizing/modernizing native language is one example; and the appropriation of the "new woman" who was expected to preserve national tradition is another in the Indian context, according to Chatterjee. To follow Chatterjee's highlighting of the spiritual dimension of the "inner domain" over the "material domain of the [colonial] state,"[75] Chang's translation can be seen as an example of Korean nationalism that formed first and foremost as an anticolonial movement, appropriating Western history and native tradition as a way to legitimize his imagination of national unity and independence. Madame Roland as the mother of the people, in this context, becomes a timeless symbol that produces and mediates a narrative of the nation. The story of Madame Roland in the Korean context, therefore, interrupts imperialism while recognizing Western political practices in building the fiction of a modern Korean nation in which the figure of mother operates as a never-changing spiritual ground for constructing cultural identity. Women's ability to nourish and reproduce men's nationalistic spirit manifests over and over again in stories of historical heroines in the field of culture and, in particular, literature in colonial Korea.

PUBLIC SPEECHES AND GENDERED PUBLIC SPACE

Authors and translators addressed their readers as members of a national community that emphasized the horizontal relationship among the masses. In Pak Ŭnsik's translation of *Wilhelm Tell*, for example, the people who came to hear the hero's speech are first referred to as "the masses" (*chungin*), then the term changes to "national subjects" (*kungmin*) who

74. Partha Chatterjee, *The Nation and Its Fragments: Colonial and Postcolonial Histories* (Princeton, NJ: Princeton University Press, 1993), 5–6.

75. Ibid., 9.

must be given equal political rights (*minkkwŏn p'yŏngdŭng*). In Sin Ch'aeho's biographical fiction about Yi Sunsin and Ŭlchi Mundŏk, the masses are deliberately called *minjok*, reflecting his attempt to define the nation-state as constitutive of one ethnic group. The Korean Joan of Arc's speech is highlighted in *Patriotic Lady* where the translator not only names the masses as "national subjects" of Korea but also creates an atmosphere of national unity by detailing the public space and the communication dynamics between the speaker and the audience. In a real-life setting of public speeches, however, those terms were likely censored by the Japanese, especially after the 1907 media and publication censorship law went into effect. As in the Korean translation of *Plum Blossoms in the Snow*, a heavily policed atmosphere likely led Korean speakers to use neutral terms such as "the masses" (*inmin*) and "society" (*sahoe*) instead of "national subjects" and "Korean nation," respectively.

Despite the conservative language needed, however, public speeches and debates are often seen in fiction produced in the early 1900s, reflecting the wide practice of these new forms of communication by various organizations that appeared one after another. Speeches and debates gained currency starting in the late nineteenth century through public activities organized mainly by three types of institutions: sermons delivered by Western missionaries at Protestant churches, celebratory statements delivered at government events, and debates established by political societies such as The Independence Club and Hyŏpsŏnghoe.[76] These religious and political institutions employed public speeches as a means of shaping people's political consciousness. In this political atmosphere, familiarity with and demonstration of behavior appropriate for public speeches and discussions were perceived as willingness to engage in the civilization discourse and nation-building following the example of Western countries.[77]

---

76. Shin Jiyoung, *Pu/jae ŭi sidae: kŭndae kyemonggi mit singminji sigi Chosŏn ŭi yŏnsŏl/chwadamhoe* (The age of absence/presence: public speeches and roundtable discussions in the enlightenment period and in colonial Korea) (Seoul: Somyŏng ch'ulp'an, 2012), 69–71.

77. This kind of promotion of public speeches and debates as practices of the West, as well as encouragement for people to learn such practices, continuously appeared in the advertisements and reports of these public events in *The Independent News* in 1897 and 1898. The Independence Club, for example, was introduced as a society where people study other nations' rules of assembly and discuss important social and political issues. "Tongnip hyophoe," *Tongnip sinmun* (*han'gŭlp'an*), 21 July 1898.

Social reformers played a significant role in popularizing public speeches and debates. Yun Ch'iho, for example, published *Accommodation of General Rules for the Assembly* (*Ŭihoe t'ongyong kyuch'ik*) in 1898, a translation of Henry M. Robert's (1837–1923) *Robert's Rules of Order* (1876), which introduces rules and regulations for a deliberative assembly. Yun's book was promoted in various newspapers until about 1910 as a guidebook for Koreans to obtain the knowledge necessary for participation in public debates. Around the time of *Accommodation*'s publication, Yun Ch'iho, together with Sŏ Chaep'il, had also established debating societies (*t'oronhoe*) in Hyŏpsŏnghoe and the Independence Club in 1896 and 1897, respectively.[78] An Kuksŏn published *Ways to Deliver Public Speeches* (*Yŏnsŏl pŏppang*, 1907), in which he instructs speakers on how to make effective public speeches. He published *The Record of the Conference of Birds and Beasts* a year later, a novel that consists entirely of public speeches. Regardless of the societies' political stances, public speeches and debates were an essential part of cultural and political organizations—and essential to their members who were expected to understand the rules involved in public meetings. *Accommodation* was advertised as a book to serve people's needs, and one was not "qualified to become a member of any society if he has no knowledge of the book."[79]

The dream of unifying the nationalistic spirit of Koreans is represented by the description of gathering places for speeches. The speech in *Story* happens in an open public space (*yŏnsŏltchang*) that is filled with hundreds of thousands of people—old and young men, women, and children. When Joan of Arc appears at the podium, the bustling and noisy space becomes orderly and silent at once; all eyes are fixed on her. However, a more realistic rendering of public space for political speeches in Korea at the time is seen in the Korean translation of *Plum Blossoms*, where the majority of the audience members are adult men. The speeches are held in the Independence Assembly Hall (*tongnip hoegwan*) in the novel. The Japanese police check the identities of the spectators meticulously at the entrance. The police have the power to examine speech drafts in advance

---

78. Ryu Chunghee, "Kaehawgi Chosŏn minhoe hwalttong kwa ŭihoet'ongyong kyuch'ik" (Activities of civil societies in the kaehwagi period and accommodation of general rules for the assembly), *Tongbang hakchi* 167 (2014): 11.

79. An advertisement for the "Accommodation of General Rules for the Assembly" in *Hwangsŏng sinmun*, 31 May 1906.

and stop anyone's speech if the speaker's political opinion is "too extreme" (*kwagyŏk*). Two policemen are seated by the podium, resting their hands on their swords. The policemen's menacing look and the measure of their policing are described as "revolting" (*anikkoptta*) in the eyes of the Korean spectators[80]—an aspect that does not appear in the original, whereas the general atmosphere and the state's intervention in the speech is translated quite faithfully. Despite the strict policing, the hall is packed with people who respond to each speaker with cheers and applause, showing their enthusiastic support for the speeches about the importance of political rights such as freedom of speech, freedom to act, and independence.

Other than the description of Yi Sunsin, which briefly mentions his physical strength, heroes and heroines in historical novels rarely display their physical strength. The young protagonist in *Plum Blossoms* delivers his speech in a passionate manner. He possesses youthful physical features with fair skin and red lips, and yet his eyes and voice are filled with vigor. Dignified facial expressions, intelligence, and youthful spirits are stressed. These fresh figures, like the protagonist in *Plum Blossoms* and Joan of Arc, are well-received by their audiences who are moved by the youths' passion and determination. In *Patriotic Lady*, Joan of Arc delivers her speech with a passionate voice and gestures; overwhelmed by emotion, she starts to weep toward the end of the speech, which in turn "warms their [the audiences'] blood."[81] Some men admit to one another that they are ashamed of their ignorance and lack of passion after seeing that "even a woman like Joan of Arc"[82] possesses such courage to fight for the nation. The speech, in other words, becomes a spectacle that causes the masses to identify themselves as national subjects, a spectacle that is dramatized by the feminine-looking young woman's manly spirit.

Despite the fact that nationalist writers represent public space as a national space and name the masses as national subjects, the discourse of publicness in a colonial society must come under scrutiny for its ambiguity. On the one hand, its assumption of egalitarian participation and public goodness is misleading; the colonial state did not intend to guarantee equal rights and public welfare for the colonized. Although the colonial

---

80. An Kuksŏn, *Sŏlchungmae*, in *Han'guk kaehawgi munhak ch'ongsŏ: sin sosŏl/ ponan(yŏk) sosŏl* 3, (Seoul: Asea munhwasa, 1978), 7–8.

81. Chang, *Aeguk puinjŏn*, 27.

82. Ibid.

state advocated democracy and public welfare by organizing public events such as sport competitions, hosting industrial expositions, and constructing public parks, the hierarchy between the metropole and the colony embodied in these events rather enforced the opposite. On the other hand, although the regulation of publicness was in the hands of the state, the idea of publicness for the colonized was a basis for their resistance against colonial control. In the latter case, the manifestation of publicness is not likely made in physical space or in actual activities; rather, it is revealed in nationalists' intellectual and cultural works where the publicness represents the Korean nation as a whole. Publicness was a metaphoric concept that embodied the political consciousness of the colonized.[83] In addition, publicness as a political metaphor does not refer only to the resistance. Between the opposite poles of collaboration and resistance there existed multiple manifestations of publicness. Yun Haedong thus coined the term "the gray zone" to refer to the publicness in colonial Korea, an area that requires careful observation in order to understand the ambiguity of colonial social space.[84]

The discourse of publicness also shows public space as masculine, a place women were barred from entering both in corporeal and symbolic senses. Feminist critics have challenged Habermas's conceptualization of the public sphere for this reason, and in fact Habermas dismisses the concern that his public sphere has excluded women since the late eighteenth century.[85] Nancy Fraser raises another important point: the disregard of gender and class differences resulted in the bourgeois class's "privatization of gender politics," in which women and the working-class were viewed as separate publics not included in "the public."[86]

In turn-of-the-century Korea, the public sphere was a male-dominated political arena where women were necessary to maintain the patriarchy. On a rhetorical level, women were indeed encouraged to participate in public debates so that they, too, would have an opportunity to study as

---

83. Yun Haedong, "Singminji kŭndae wa konggongsŏng" (Colonial modernity and publicness), *SAI* 8 (2010): 163–195.

84. Yun Haedong, *Singminji ŭi hoesaek chidae* (The gray zone in colonial Korea) (Seoul: Yŏksa pip'yŏngsa, 2003), 23–52.

85. Joan Landes, *Women and the Public Sphere in the Age of the French Revolution* (Ithaca, NY: Cornell University Press, 1988).

86. Nancy Fraser, "Rethinking the Public Sphere: A Contribution to the Critique of Actually Existing Democracy," *Social Text* 25/26 (1990): 56–80.

equal members of society, even though opportunities for them to do so in real life were extremely scarce. *The Independence News*, for example, reports that a public debate was held at the Chŏngdong Methodist Church in 1898 on the issue of gender equality. It is likely that the debate was offered at the church after a devotional service; these so-called Bible schools were set up by Western missionaries as a way to encourage all women, including illiterate women, to express their thoughts about social issues.[87] An interesting aspect of this rather lengthy report is a statement from Yun Ch'iho: it provides his justification for women not receiving the same opportunities to study and is intended to produce a counterargument. In response, women, based on the Christian notion of equality, argued for their right to learn and asserted that their knowledge will strengthen the nation and establish peace in households,[88] a narrative that commonly appeared in nationalist newspapers at the time.

In contrast to the scarcity of women's participation in real-life public space, women's presence in public space in novels was abundant. In most cases they possessed a demure, Confucian sense of femininity except for their passion for learning. For instance, the Korean Joan of Arc and Madame Roland are knowledgeable in many subjects since they read books avidly. The heroine in *Plum Blossoms* loves reading more than playing a Japanese string instrument (*koto*) as in the original. Thus in the translation the hero is attracted by the sound of her reading books aloud, not the sound of the *koto*. The image of a studying woman is not described as a sign of regression; rather it is portrayed as an image of a reform-minded woman who is diligent in educating herself with new knowledge.

The Korean heroine in *Plum Blossoms* has no prospects for herself except for her wish to find a fiancé, unlike the Japanese heroine in the original who maintains her profession as a teacher and her companionship with the hero based on their shared political vision. Just as a masculine passion for state organization came to define patriarchal public space in reality, it also reorganized the private sphere. Women who appeared in public space in novels stressed their domestic role through their assertion

---

87. Theodore Jun Yoo, *The Politics of Gender in Colonial Korea: Education, Labor, and Health, 1910–1945* (Oakland: University of California Press, 2008), 51.

88. "Editorial," *Tongnip sinmun (han'gŭlp'an)*, 4 January 1898. Although women's presence in physical public spaces was extremely limited, their writing appeared in newspapers from time to time in the early 1900s. See Yi Kyŏngha, "Taehan cheguk," 278–296.

of a motherly duty to encourage men to be active political agents. Although studying was assigned as a national duty for women, male writers
emphasized that traditional female virtues such as modesty and chastity
were the most important moral foundation for women. In their novels
even uneducated women who demonstrate filial piety and chastity are
more respectable than women who are educated but ignore these virtues.[89]

FROM VIRTUOUS MOTHERS TO ADVENTUROUS DAUGHTERS

Reformist writers and translators of biographical novels maintained a
conservative attitude toward women's roles, affiliating their femininity
with Confucian virtues while advocating women's education in the name
of the nation. The novels were intended to be read more like conduct man-
uals or instructions for both men and women, a top-down and didactic
approach to the novel that ultimately aimed to instill patriotism in the
readers. The kind of national masculinity in these novels was constructed
partially through the representation of exemplary women whose dedication to the nation in spirit and in action was to be modeled by men.

Since Korean writers and translators shared the goal of social reform
with some Chinese writers, and since their linguistic familiarity and intellectual training were based on Confucian traditions, many of their
ideas were influenced by Chinese texts. The paraphrasing of Japanese and
Euro-American texts by both Chinese and Korean translators indicates
that the social reformers were aware of the novelty of foreign texts in
terms of content, and yet they were also conscious of the necessity to negotiate with the imported knowledge and foreign power in order to embody domestic politics and cultural traditions. Their instrumental approach to fictional narratives is evident in their employment of public
speeches in fiction works. Korean translators' political ideas and thoughts
on the issue of nation-building are strongly reflected in public speeches
and speech-like narrative techniques, through which they talk directly to
their readers.

Public speeches and public spaces were a male-dominated arena
where women were included only rhetorically. Chang Chiyŏn's biograph-

---

89. An Kuksŏn, *The Record of the Conference of Birds and Beasts*, in *Han'guk kaehawgi
munhak ch'ongsŏ: sin sosŏl/ponan(yŏk) sosŏl*, vol. 2 (Seoul: Asea munhwasa, 1978), 10.

ical novels indeed featured exemplary women whose public appearances have historical importance. However, the content of their speeches and their emotional way of appealing to the masses rather affirms a gender boundary. The feminine appeal for patriotism dramatizes the heroines' acts while conveying where women belong: in the family and the home. This gender distinction is more visible in a number of novels such as *Plum Blossoms* and *The Record of the Conference of Birds and Beasts*, in which the female characters changed from active political agents in the originals to passive women whose fate is determined by patriarchal authority in the Korean translations. The imaginary public space as a national space thus remains patriarchal and masculine, and an arena to which women had no access in reality. Rather, the women in these novels and their emotional speeches are techniques of persuasion in order to turn the masses into national subjects.

Creative fiction writers had the freedom to compose their narratives without concern for biographical details or accuracy; they dealt with practical issues in the contemporary setting. While the writers examined in this chapter displayed an anti-imperial stance and a conservative attitude toward the role of women, writers in the following chapters focus more on young women and their mobility without an explicit anti-imperial expression. These differences do not entirely depend on the writer's political stance; they also depend on each writer's experiments with different modes of writing.

3

AS REAL AS FICTION

Gender, Mobility, and Domesticity in New Fiction (sin sosŏl)

IN POST-SECONDARY STUDIES OF LITERARY HISTORY in South Korea, Yi Injik and Yi Haejo are emphasized as the two most important fiction writers, their works distinguished by a drive to civilize and enlighten the nation. Thanks to the historicization of their position in modern Korean literature as pioneers of New Fiction, virtually every Korean citizen is familiar with their names, and probably can name a few works of "new fiction" (*sin sosŏl*). Despite this status, they are two of the most underrepresented writers in modern Korea—first because having been considered enlightenment texts rather than literary works, their works are hardly read outside academia. Second, harsh criticism of their pro-Japanese tendencies by scholars of literary history has obscured their contribution to the development of modern Korean literature until recently. During a time when most nationalist writers lost the space to write as print media faced serious censorship by the colonial state, the continuing publication of these writers' works in public media has often been pointed out as a sign of their collaboration with the colonizer.

However, the longevity of their writing careers was not solely based on the pro-Japanese tendencies in their works and in their personal intimacy with the colonizer. It also had to do with the mode of their writing, through which they presented their self-consciousness as fiction writers as well as public educators. While nationalist intellectuals chose biographic novels as a tool to civilize the nation, Yi Injik and Yi Haejo wrote creative novels in which protagonists with "all too ordinary" backgrounds become heroes and heroines. It is not a coincidence that the colonial newspaper, *The Daily*

News (*Maeil sinbo*, hereafter referred to as *The Daily*), enthusiastically supported the stories of ordinary, previously marginalized, and oppressed
people transforming into agents of civilization. The two writers' position-
ing of the feudal society in the global context and making characters socially mobile matched the colonial state's policy, especially its propagation
of the mission to civilize Korea. The writers' direct and indirect exposure
to transnational literary forces via Japan was also manifest in their works,
both original novels and translations, in which characters move freely
across geographical, gender, and class boundaries. The relationship between the two writers and *The Daily* was a cohabitation that happened by
chance, at least for a time.

Writers and translators at the turn of the twentieth century had different ideas about how "*sosŏl*" should be written and what purposes it must
serve, but they were linked by their conscious effort to detach themselves
from the traditions of fiction-writing in Chosŏn. Even though Sin Ch'aeho
and Chang Chiyŏn used materials from the past, their purpose was to
serve the general public in the present time by writing a selective reconstruction of the past, intended to offer an alternative vision that would
allow society to progress. Yi Injik and Yi Haejo, on the other hand, showed
a strong antipathy to the past, attempting to turn the world "upside down,"
so to speak. In their creative fiction, Yi Injik and Yi Haejo tried to enliven
the realistic elements of fiction by incorporating current social affairs that
were in stark contrast to the traditional world. Thus the mode of writing
they chose was based on their "revolutionary" vision but it also had to do
with their preoccupation with eradicating the past, which in their minds
was delaying Korean progress.

Yi Injik and Yi Haejo prioritized fictional stories as the most important
component of "the novel," conscious of their role in "rendering human affairs as they are ... in an interesting/fun way (*chaemi*)" so that their novels
would move readers to various emotions, such as "pleasantness, sadness,
danger, and humor."[1] Their anticipation of readers' emotional reactions
beyond patriotism indicates that how they saw their role in relation to
their readers was different from that of Sin Cha'eho or Chang Chiyŏn.
Rather than asserting their roles as visionary leaders of the national community, they felt a responsibility to entertain their readers. Their engage-

---

1. Yi Haejo, *Hwa ŭi hyŏl*, *Maeil sinbo*, 6 April 1911.

ment with other activities such as journalism and education was not as significant as that of the nationalist intellectual writers examined in the previous chapter. This is not intended to suggest that they had less desire to civilize the nation—this desire is well reflected in their novels—but to emphasize their recognition of fiction-writing as a career. In this regard, these two writers stand out among writers and translators in the first decade of the twentieth century for their professional attitude toward fiction writing.

Although Yi Injik and Yi Haejo attempted through novels to exorcise "barbaric" customs and manners existing in Korea, vestiges of the past were not something that could be easily erased. Most novels written by Yi Injik and Yi Haejo show residual influence of traditional fiction in their tendency to "reward the good and punish the evil" (*kwŏnsŏn chingak*)—a theme that resonates with the writers' cultural background that influenced their ideas about the relationship between literature and society and with the colonial state's emphasis on the civilizing process while annihilating Korea's past. Grand narratives about national heroes found no space to share their passion for the nation in these writers' novels. Instead, in their works men are antiheroes whose corrupt morality and lack of visionary thinking about their society are mercilessly rendered. The value of their novels is in the power of postulating the temporal and spatial gap between the old and the new realities, catapulting readers in the direction the characters are moving; the readers move along with the time and space of the characters. The "reward the good and punish the evil" theme, in other words, lies along the linear path of progress *The Daily* tried to convey in the early 1910s.

There is an arresting sense of the crisis of masculinity in the selected works by Yi Injik and Yi Haejo I analyze here. Their themes include the decline of patriarchal authority, the corrupted morality and intellectual weakness of *yangban* men, and feckless and selfish fathers, to name a few. Contrary to the negative images of men, female characters are highly mobile and independent, crossing geographical, class, and gender boundaries more freely than men do. The implication of this contrast goes beyond the writers' attempts to redefine gender roles and relations in the midst of political and social upheaval. Rather, it points to the ways that writers were self-critical of Korean men's moral and intellectual degradation. Paradoxically, this kind of self-criticism directed toward the Korean patriarchy functioned favorably for the colonial state since the criticism could legiti-mize the state's moral leadership. If nationalist writers and translators feminized the masses in order to create a sense of horizontal relationships among Koreans prior to the annexation, the colonial state feminized Ko-reans in order to affirm the hierarchy between the colonizer and the colo-nized.

NEW FICTION WRITERS AND NEWSPAPERS

Among the enlightenment writers of the early twentieth century, Yi Injik has probably received the most interest from scholars of Korean literature since the liberation; his first novel, *Tears of Blood*, is almost always brought up as the first work of new fiction. The term "New Fiction" (*sin sosŏl*) ap-peared in Japan in 1889 and in China in 1902, in both cases as the title of a literary magazine. It is only in Korea that the term was continually used for approximately three hundred individual works of fiction produced be-tween 1906 and the early 1910s.[2] Partly due to the larger volume of fiction and the longevity of the term, scholars in Korean literary scholarship tend to view New Fiction as a "Korea-specific literary form that embodies the social and intellectual discourses [that] arose in the midst of the modern-izing process."[3] Although no unifying effort was made to define New Fic-tion among writers and translators at the time, the idea of enlightenment and civilization was the thematic thread through their works.

Most scholars approach New Fiction as an established literary form, although Kim Yŏngmin points out that newspapers frequently used the word "new" in order to appeal to readers by emphasizing the "newness" of information and knowledge. New Fiction, in his view, can be regarded as a rhetorical device (*susa*) used to promote newspapers through serialized novels that could appeal to a larger audience.[4] In fact, soon after the publi-cation of *Tears of Blood* in *The Independence News* (*Mansebo*, 1906), the term New Fiction began to be used frequently in other newspapers such as

---

2. Kim Yunsik and Kim Hyŏn, *Han'guk munhaksa* (The history of modern Korean literature) (Seoul: Minŭmsa, 1973), 158.

3. Ibid., 16.

4. Kim Yŏngmin, *Han'guk ŭi kŭndae sinmun kwa kŭndae sosŏl I* (A study of modern Korean newspapers and modern novels, vol. I) (Seoul: Somyŏng, 2006), 46–47.

The Korea Daily when referring to their serial novels, be it a translation or original. Sin Ch'aeho and Chang Chiyŏn's writings and translations of biographical novels were also introduced as New Fiction, for example. This lexical inconsistency reveals that no unifying effort was made to define the genre at the time. It was only in the late 1930s that the first systematic attempt to define the genre was made by Im Hwa.[5]

Nonetheless, Kim Yŏngmin's critical reevaluation of the historical significance of New Fiction, especially in its relationship with modern newspapers, is important since the concept of the novel was being reconstructed by the advance of modern print media. Most New Fiction works were authored by newspaper journalists and editors whose interest in the novel did not rest solely on literary curiosity. Although these authors were concerned with the political function of the novel, we cannot assume they had a clear concept of "the novel," and New Fiction specifically. Making sense of the novel itself took time, thus it is important to understand the status of New Fiction as it was perceived by writers at the time. In their newspapers, works like critical essays (*nonsŏl*) and explanatory articles (*sŏlmyŏngmun*), for example, were also classified under the term "the novel" (*sosŏl*) at this time.[6] At times, *nonsŏl* and *sŏlmyŏngmun* elements were incorporated in fiction, as seen in Sin Ch'aeho and Chang Chiyŏn's historical and biographical novels. Furthermore, there was no specific standard in terms of its length; short stories, novellas, and novels were all called novels. All these factors indicate that novel writers used the term *new* loosely when referring to their works; their self-awareness of the "newness" of their time was a catalyst for the use of the term. In other words, journalists and editors situated their writings in the purview of the political function of the newspaper, which was the very site where the concept of fiction was being reconfigured.

Since 1910 the governor-general of Korea (hereafter GGK) tightened the political control over the colony, including the publishing industry,

---

5. Im defined New Fiction as a body of fictional narratives that was written in traditional narrative form but with Western thoughts and ideas. In his essay, however, Im does not seem to be consistent when referring to New Fiction despite his argument that Yi Injik was the first New Fiction writer. Im Hwa, "Kaesŏl sinmunhaksa" (Establishing a history of new literature), *Chosŏn ilbo*, 2 September 1939–31 October 1939.

6. Kim Yŏngmin, *Han'guk kŭndae sosŏlsa* (A history of modern Korean fiction) (Seoul: Sol, 1997), 56.

forcing all the vernacular newspapers to close down, thus leaving only *The Daily News* available to Korean readers. *The Daily* was a mouthpiece for the GGK to deliver Japan's colonial policies. In this period of cultural drought, however, *The Daily* also provided a window of opportunity for fiction writers to further experiment with the novel genre and express their ideas of civilization in novels. Yi Haejo in particular dominated the paper's novel section in the early 1910s. His novels were introduced as New Fiction in *The Daily*, indicating that the colonial newspaper attempted to promote the novel by employing the term that had become a cultural currency at the time. It was a strategic choice for *The Daily* to promote New Fiction as a way to spread the GGK's assimilation policies throughout the colony.

Yi Injik and Yi Haejo are unique figures among writers and translators in the early twentieth century prior to 1910 in terms of the consistent length of their novels, the absence of an anti-imperial stance, and the strong antipathy to the Sino-centered cultural sphere, all of which can be explained by their social and cultural backgrounds. In the case of Yi Injik, his firsthand experience of Japanese journalism and culture industry may have affected his ideas of civilization and the novel genre. Yi Injik went to Japan in 1908,[7] and studied political science and journalism there, while most writers and translators at the time had not stepped outside the national boundaries. Nonetheless, he seems to have been more interested in journalism and cultural sectors rather than in politics. In these sectors he could enlighten Koreans in the areas of ethics, self-discipline, hygiene, public morality, literature, industry, agriculture, and so on. He hardly mentioned his view on politics or the cultural figures and movements in Japan that influenced his career. But his experience as a trainee reporter at *Miyako Newspaper* (*Miyako shimbun*) between 1901 and 1903 may have shaped his ideas about newspaper journalism as well as cultural works such as literature and theater, which would later become his career focus. In fact, *Miyako Newspaper*, from its establishment

---

7. It is said that he went to Japan as an asylum seeker because of his involvement in pro-Japan activities. Ko Chaesŏk, "Yi Injik ŭi chugŭm, kŭ poiji annŭn yusan" (The death of Yi Injik and his invisible legacy), *Han'guk ŏmunhak yŏn'gu* 42 (2004): 221–252; Ham T'aeyŏng, "Yi Injik ŭi hyŏnsil ŭishik kwa mosun" (The contradiction in Yi Injik's understanding of the reality), in *Kŭndae kyemonggi munhak ŭi chaeinsik*, ed. Munhak kwa sasang yŏn'guhoe (Seoul: Somyŏng ch'ulp'an, 2007), 222–223.

year, actively promoted the novel and theater in Japan. Yi Injik's observation of the cultural scene in Japan probably led him to write an opera piece, *The Silver World* (*Ŭnsegye*), in 1908—the first modern theater piece, we are told, that was inspired by the new kabuki movement that he witnessed in Japan.[8]

Yi Injik took the chief editor's position at *The Independence News* (*Mansebo*) shortly after he returned to Korea in 1906.[9] Despite the fact that the paper was established by the Religion of the Heavenly Way (*Ch'ŏndogyo*), most editorials were dedicated to domestic and international political affairs, society, education, and the economy.[10] Its attempt to reach the lower strata of the populace was evident in its low price—it was about two-thirds cheaper than *The Korea Daily* —and its *han'gŭl*-only policy.[11] In addition, it encouraged its readers to send their opinions on various issues of interest by publishing an opinion section. The opinions that were put forth in the newspaper can be characterized by their lightness; they were humorous, satirical, and at times speculative presentations of social affairs, politics, and cultural works such as novels and theater.[12] Shortly after the newspaper closed down due to financial difficulties, Yi moved to the *Korea Newspaper* (*Taehan sinmun*), which was established by Yi Wanyong, then to the colonial newspaper *The Daily* at the time of the annexation. The trajectory of his career resonates with his belief that Korea must model itself after Japan for social development. However, it is questionable whether he considered his pro-Japanese activities to be a betrayal of his own country. He differentiated reformists from traitors, arguing

---

8. Pak T'aegyu, "Yi Injik ŭi yŏn'gŭk kaeryang ŭiji wa *Ŭnsegye* e mich'in ilbon yŏn'guk ŭi yŏnghyang e kwanhan yŏn'gu" (A study of the influence of Japanese theater on Yi Injik's *Ŭnsegye* and his involvement in the reforming of Korean theater), *Han'guk ilbon hakhoe* 47 (2001): 287–303.

9. Son Pyŏnghŭi established the newspaper in order to receive popular appeal from Koreans. Ibid., 206–208.

10. Only a handful of editorials in *The Independence News* were written about the religion, less than 3 percent of all editorials published over one full year from 1906 to 1907: Chŏn Ŭn'gyŏng, "*Mansebo* ŭi tokja t'ugoran kwa kŭndae taejung munhak ŭi hyŏngsŏng" (Readers' responses in *Mansebo* and the formation of modern popular literature), *Ŏmunhak* 111 (2011): 364.

11. Unlike other newspapers that used a mixture of *han'gŭl* and Chinese script, *Mansebo* used a unique writing style, placing small annotated glossaries in *han'gŭl* to the right side of Chinese characters, so-called *rubi* character style.

12. Chŏn Ŭn'gyŏng, "*Mansebo* ŭi tokja t'ugoran," 365–370.

that the former wholeheartedly took on the duty of national development while the latter prioritized their individual interests over national matters.[13]

Since he passed away in 1916, and since there was a lapse in his writing career between 1913 and 1916, we have very little knowledge as to how Yi Injik reflected on the effects of his own cultural productions. What we can detect, however, is the mirroring of his own experience of crossing spatial and temporal boundaries and his imagination of a positive future in the *bildungsroman* genre, such as in *Tears of Blood* where a sense of selfhood "linked the individual to the nation and projected their entangled fate into the future as destiny."[14] In addition, some of the characteristics of the *bildungsroman*, such as the free movement of Yi's young protagonists from one city/country/continent to another through the aid of modern transportation for the sake of the character's spiritual growth, are also significant for the development of the novel as a modern literary genre.[15] Yi perhaps held faith in the future that he had yet to see.

Archival materials on Yi Haejo's personal history are scarcer than those on Yi Injik, mainly because he minimized his public exposure. He came from a royal family whose ill fate resulted in their lineage being deprived of social privileges, starting with Yi Haejo's grandfather's generation.[16] Except for a short period working as a low-ranking government official from 1901 to 1903 at Yangmuamun, an institute that was responsible for land surveying, Yi Haejo was involved in the education reform movement, working at various schools such as Nagyŏn School (Nagyŏn ŭisuk), Kiho School (Kiho hakkyo), and Sinya School (Sinya ŭisuk). All these schools focused on modern education, offering courses such as Japanese-language education, math, geography, and so on. However, Yi Haejo seems to have experienced conflict with some groups of neo-Confucian literati who were displeased with his modern curriculum and

13. This is based on Tajiri Hiroyuki's research, which examined Yi Injik's writings that appeared in *Miyako Newspaper*. Cited in Pak Sŏnyŏng, "Yi Injik ŭi sahoe ch'ŏrhak kwa ch'inil ŭi hamŭi" (Yi Injik's social philosophy and the implication of his collaboration)," *Sahoe wa Yŏksa* 89 (2011): 194.

14. Janet Poole, *When the Future Disappears: The Modernist Imagination in Late Colonial Korea* (New York: Columbia University Press, 2014), 13.

15. Moretti, *Atlas of the European Novel*, 64–69.

16. For a detailed explanation about Yi's family background, see Song Minho, "Yŏlchae Yi Haejo ŭi saengae wa sasangjŏk paegyŏng" (The life and the philosophical background of Yi Haejo), *Kŭgŏ kungmunhak* 156 (2010): 245–246.

his handling of resources while running Nagyŏn School.[17] His conflict with these literati, who were defensive of their Confucian academies, may have also been rooted in his discontent with the social privileges attached to these elites. The anachronistic and morally corrupt image of *yangban* in his works thus reflects Yi's attitude toward socially privileged people who bring tragedies to underprivileged people such as women and slaves.

Unlike Pak Ŭnsik, Sin Ch'aeho, and Chang Chiyŏn, who relied on Chinese intermediary texts and valued Confucian tradition, Yi Injik and Yi Haejo stayed away from Sinosphere culture and the Sino-centered civilization discourse altogether. The cultural distance the writers created partly derived from their critical view of Chinese culture, but it can also be interpreted as an artistic endeavor, experimenting with creative novels that directly deal with contemporary Korean society. Yi Haejo was especially productive and industrious, experimenting with different literary genres that were either motivated by Western science fiction—such as Jules Verne's (1828–1905) *Les Cinq Cents Millions de la Bégum*, which he translated and entitled *The Iron World* (*Ch'ŏlsegye*)—or reinterpreting and restyling traditional novels such as *The Tale of Ch'unhyang* and *The Tale of Sim Ch'ŏng*. The longevity of these writers' careers even after the annexation, especially in the case of Yi Haejo, is explained by their criticism of social practices embedded in their novels, which overlapped with the colonial newspaper's civilizing mission. At the same time, it also had to do with Yi Haejo's continuing effort to learn about literature of the West and experiment with traditional novels in order to appeal to his readers.

It is noteworthy that, although Yi Injik and Yi Haejo were producing creative novels, they did not refer to themselves as novelists or authors (*chakka*) but as "journalists" (*kija*), revealing that fiction writing was not commonly understood as an independent profession at the time. Further, its meaning was formed with writers' and readers' associations with newspapers on a cognitive level. However, Yi Haejo left a number of writings about his attitude toward the novel, discussing the concept of the novel and the purposes it serves, illuminating his self-assumed position as an author who was burdened with enlightening and entertaining his readers.

---

17. Song Minho's biographical details on Yi Haejo are based on the diary that was written by Cho Ch'angyŏng (1875–1948) in 1914. According to the diary, Cho and Yi maintained a close relationship, especially regarding the education reform movement.

He often added his ideas on the novel in the foreword or epilogue of his serialized novels. He states:

> Generally speaking, there are numerous materials that can be used for the novel [*sosŏl*] such as politics, detective work, social criticism, domestic affairs, ethics, science, etc. All these are based in events in our lives that are re-created by writers [*kija*]. Some are pleasant and humorous while some are sad and inspiring. However, half of novels that are available today are about the contemporary life events while the rest portray meaningless stories about the past ... I now start serializing a novel, *Blood of Flower* [*Hwa ŭi hyŏl*], from today, and I will not write a word about meaningless or fictitious things but truthfully depict a life of a real person. My style of writing is not elegant or great but I intend to write a story that can delineate the good and the evil as clearly as a mirror. Readers will feel as if seeing and listening to the story with their eyes and ears.[18]

One characteristic of Yi Haejo's conceptualization of the novel is that he refuses to intervene in the novel as a commentator. Other writers such as Sin Ch'aeho also used the foreword section to explain what moral values their novels embody, but they would play the role of a commentator in the novel as well by inserting their opinions about historical figures and events. Yi Haejo, on the other hand, stays away from this position. He refers to himself as "author" only in the foreword or epilogue. The narrator always remains in the third person and omniscient in the novel. This kind of distancing differentiates writers such as Yi Haejo and Yi Injik from the nationalist writers.

UPROOTED FAMILY AND THE ABSENCE OF THE FATHER

As the sound of roaring gunfire, which entirely devoured Pyongyang during the war, finally stops, there is no trace of human beings on the street. Mountains and fields are covered by dust and dusk is slowly enveloping Peony Hill. As if she wishes to hold the faint sunlight a little longer, a bewildered woman is rushing about the street madly. She appears to be thirty-something and her face is as white as if it were covered with white

---

18. Yi Haejo, *Hwa ŭi hyŏl*, *Maeil sinbo*, 6 April 1911.

powder. Her breasts are fully exposed as her top has been rolled down while her skirt drags on the ground. Even though she tries to walk fast she can only advance a few steps.[19]

This is the opening scene of *Tears of Blood*, which was serialized in *The Independence News* in 1906. It describes the main character's mother, Ch'oe Ch'unae, searching for her lost child right after the First Sino-Japanese War. She was also separated during the war from her husband, Kim Kwanil, a low-ranking but wealthy government official in Pyongyang. The Kim family is uprooted by the war, a metaphor for the destruction of the Korean nation by the clash between the old and the new imperial hegemonies. The image of the national disaster is represented by the physical and mental state of a *yangban* woman who is not only displaced from her home but also unaware of the shameful state of her physical appearance, that is, a full exposure of her breasts in a public space. Adding to the already devastating situation, she has no male family member to protect her. The war also deprives her husband of his status and wealth and makes him rely on his wife's family.

While the parents lose their power to find their daughter or reclaim their wealth and status, the life of the protagonist, the then-seven-year-old Ongnyŏn, will be transformed by the war, pushing her to make the journey to "civilized worlds" such as Japan and America where she obtains modern knowledge so that she can become a leader in women's education back home. The war becomes a catalyst that makes the daughter's transformation possible. As Ongnyŏn's Japanese foster mother states, the war brought fortune to Ongnyŏn since she has the opportunity to go to a school: "If you were to stay in Chosŏn, you would not have been able to even dream about studying,"[20] she says. In Yi Injik's political imagination, the clash that Ongnyŏn survives represents Korea's situation at the time. The disempowered position of the father represents the decline of the old social order and the diminished patriarchal power that can no longer govern domesticity. Blaming China for initiating the war,[21] the novel describes "violent" Chinese soldiers who "loot" properties and "rape" Korean

---

19. Yi Injik, "Hyŏl ŭi nu," in *Han'guk kaehwagi ch'ongsŏ I: sin sosŏl pŏnan(yŏk) sosŏl*, vol. 1 (Seoul: Asea munhwasa, 1978), 3.

20. Ibid., 49.

21. Ibid., 27.

women, thus becoming "enemies" of Korea. The only Chinese people who are portrayed positively are Kang Youwei and his students in America with whom Ongnyŏn studies.[22] Yi Injik's imagined Korean nation is reconstructed through gendering the national community and its social space; the national territory is "looted and raped" by the declining power, while the young child's survival and the reunion of her family is guaranteed only through obtaining modern knowledge.

A dominant number of New Fiction works center on the domestic sphere, supporting Yoon Sun Yang's claim that the idea of home or domesticity (*kajŏng*) and its prominence in New Fiction is in fact significant, for "it was for the advocates of nation-building to transform Korean domestic norms in line with the global standard at the turn of the century."[23] Yoon observes that the traditional use of the term "*ka*" (home or domesticity) was being replaced with "*kajŏng*"—a translation of the Japanese "*katei*"— at the turn of the century. Women remain only within the domestic boundary in *ka* whereas they serve the nation by performing their child-rearing and domestic duty in *kajŏng*. However, Yoon notes that the idealization of the traditional notion of *ka* to rebuild the family-state structure is also evident: the old patriarchal order and modern notion of gender equality coexist in Yi Injik's New Fiction, reflecting the nationalists' "dilemma" that was "deeply seated in the modern nation-building project of early twentieth-century Korea. If nationalists had to make a radical break from the past to create the 'modern' nation, they also ought to keep recalling an 'invented' past to unite a class-divided populace into one imagined community."[24]

The father in *Tears of Blood* indeed transforms. He studies in America and plans to come home, where his chaste and submissive wife awaits him. Ongnyŏn's future husband, Ku Wansŏ, accompanies Ongnyŏn to America and studies there as well. However, the focus is given to Ongnyŏn, which adds another dimension to the "dilemma" felt by writers such as Yi Injik and Yi Haejo; namely, the imposition of a sense of shame and humiliation on men as a social criticism of the traditional social elites' moral corruption, ignorance, and anachronism. The pitiful state of Ongnyŏn's mother

---

22. Ibid., 70.

23. Yoon Sun Yang, "Nation in the Backyard: Yi Injik and the Rise of Korean New Fiction, 1906–1913," PhD diss., University of Chicago, 2009, 6.

24. Ibid., 59.

in the above passage is symbolic of the deprivation of social status and self-control that pushes her near death; she attempts to kill herself out of despair. The implication of her attempted suicide, in other words, goes beyond the representation of the old world where women lacked agency; it also shows the powerless state of men who failed to protect the family, which, by extension, represents the nation.

The politics of shame and humiliation are more prominent in Yi Haejo's novels than Yi Injik's. The "man of disgrace" in Yi Haejo's *Snow on the Temple Hair* (*Pinsangsŏl*, 1907),[25] for example, is Mr. Sŏ, a wealthy man with *yangban* lineage who evicts his legal wife from his home and lives with a fiercely jealous and manipulative concubine instead. He appears to be an enlightened man on the surface, wearing a Western suit (*yangbok*) and spectacles that were imported from France. And yet his mind is blinded by lust, causing him to lose his sense of morality and responsibility as the head of a family. He does not support his wife and is often tricked by the manipulative concubine, and is eventually driven to attempt to murder his legitimate wife. Through the effort of the wife's twin brother, the crime is revealed to the public and Sŏ runs away from home. Contrary to Sŏ's negative image, his wife maintains unbending faith in traditional feminine virtue by maintaining her respect toward her husband while enduring the humiliation with silence.

It is useful to visit Yi Haejo's discussion of the novel as "a mirror" of social affairs and his emphasis on the novel's capability to evoke various emotions.[26] The emotion of shame in particular is worth paying attention to in terms of its association with social bonds. Drawing on Émile Durkheim and Erving Goffman's social theory of shame, Thomas J. Scheff sees it as a social emotion that is "generated by a threat to the [social] bond, *no matter how slight*, then a wide range of cognates and variants follows … since most ideals are social, rather than individual."[27] The source of shame, Scheff argues, is the fear of losing the social bond, which can be applied to Yi Haejo's attempt to provoke shame in order to strengthen social cohe-

25. Yi Haejo, "Pinsangsŏl," in *Sinsosŏl, pŏnan(yŏk) sosŏl*, vol. 4 of *Han'guk kaehwagi munhak ch'ongsŏ*, compiled by Han'gukhak munhŏn yŏn'guso, 3–44. Seoul: Asea munhwasa, 1978. Originally published in Seoul: Kwanghak sŏp'o, 1908.

26. Yi Haejo, "Hwa ŭi hyŏl," *Maeil sinbo*, 6 April 1911.

27. Thomas J. Scheff. "Shame and the Social Bond: A Sociological Theory," *Sociological Theory* 18, no. 1 (2000): 97 (emphasis in original).

sion. Based on Yi Haejo's dedication to modern education, he seems to be attempting to move the national community in a positive direction by using the novel to generate this sense of shame. The final purpose of shame, as shown in *Freedom Bell*, is to change all people to be equipped with morality and intelligence, making them all *yangban* as he noted in *Freedom Bell*. This assertion should not be considered bizarre, despite the fact that criticism of *yangban*'s immoral and ignorant behavior is the main theme in Yi's novels. What we can infer is the point already raised by Yoon, that the nationalists' objective was to reinvent the past to create the social unity of the national community.

Nonetheless, unlike Ongnyŏn who actively seeks ways to advance her life, Sŏ's wife has no other way to escape her impending death but to depend on others, such as her brother. However, what these two characters share is their role in making their men look inferior by comparison—in terms of knowledge in the case of Ongnyŏn and morality in the case of Sŏ's wife. The emphasis on women's intellectual and moral superiority is intended to criticize the weakened patriarchy that cannot be maintained by traditional male virtues alone; instead, it must be regained through new knowledge. Yi Haejo's *Freedom Bell*[28] consists of speeches made exclusively by women who argue, "The reason for the corrupted government and the people in our nation is the absence of knowledge ... our nation's independence and people's freedom all depend on knowledge."[29] While Yi Haejo's women argue for new knowledge it is his men who must act on it. The desire to restore the reduced masculinity of Korean men is expressed in Yi Haejo's works by humiliating the male characters, destroying their patriarchal authority, a necessary process for eventually restoring them at home as enlightened fathers and sons. This supports the idea in these works that the retrieval of traditional femininity is necessary. Women in Yi Haejo's works are clearly divided into two groups, the "wicked" and the "obedient," like the concubine and the wife. Unlike Ongnyŏn in *Tears of Blood*, women in Yi Injik's later novels lack political agency. These female characters are either sacrificed by the practice of

---

28. Yi Haejo, "Chayujong," in *Han'guk kaehwagi ch'ongsŏ I: sin sosŏl pŏnan(yŏk) sosŏl*, vol. 4 (Seoul: Asea munhwasa, 1978), 4.

29. Ibid., 4.

concubinage or rewarded for keeping traditional virtues as shown in *Voice of Ghost* (*Kwi ǔi sǒng*, 1907–1908).

The image of traditional women in these works is of the "eternal feminine ... as the repository of a lost truth that man had to regain."[30] This view is based on the observation of the artistic trend in industrialized Western Europe during the nineteenth century where nostalgia for the past resulted in an image of the ideal woman who retained archaic virtues. While Korea had yet to experience the process of industrialization at the time, the writers' reconstruction of traditional women embodies their ambivalent attitude toward the present and the future. Both writers emphasized a clear severance from the past for the sake of national development, but their anxiety over the unknown future is manifested in the re-creation of traditional feminine virtues that had to be protected. The head of the family remains powerless, but he is always given a chance to redeem himself at the end, like the father of the sacrificed concubine in *Voice of Ghost* who "honors" his daughter by murdering the killer and Sǒ in *Snow on the Temple Hair* who runs away to Shanghai and enters a school to obtain a modern education.

The redeemed father, then, exercises moral judgments both in and beyond the domestic sphere. The male head of a family in Yi Injik's works usually reacts to the injustice done to his family members through violent acts of revenge. Yi Haejo, on the other hand, relies on law enforcement as a means to protect the home. Rarely are Yi Haejo's wicked or evil characters punished by means of death but rather by imprisonment, like the concubine in *Snow on the Temple Hair*. Even in works such as *Demon-Expelling Sword*, which is meant to criticize women's practice of superstition, Yi makes them pay for their wrongdoings through legal measures. This element becomes even more prominent in novels produced shortly after Japan's annexation of Korea that criminalized old social practices such as trafficking children and the imprisonment of shamans. Yi Haejo's employment of modern legal force implies more than his vision for renewing the nation. It was also aimed at reinforcing the patriarchal order in the national context. Like the father in *Tears of Blood* and the stepson in *Demon-Expelling Sword*, the once-reduced masculinity is restored

---

30. Rita Felski, *The Gender of Modernity* (Cambridge, MA: Harvard University Press, 1995), 50.

through education, which enables these men to contribute to the nation-building process as educators and judges.

WOMEN'S MOBILITY AND THE MALE ANXIETY OVER REPRODUCTION

The heroine in *Tears of Blood*, Ongnyŏn, constantly moves from one geographical location to another. She travels from Korea to Japan by boat, leaves for Tokyo from Osaka by train, and eventually arrives in America by boat again. While traveling, she encounters various individuals: a kind Japanese doctor, Inoue, who sends her to his home in Osaka; a wounded soldier who is returning home from Korea after the Sino-Japanese War; a Chinese laborer, who introduces her to Kang Youwei on her way to Korea, and so on. These travel sketches signify the heroine's progress in moving closer to the source of civilization. The new modes of transport thus represent modern technologies that enable Ongnyŏn's relocation; but more important, they epitomize the speed of modernization with which Ongnyŏn must keep up.

The heroine's time flows differently from her mother's, who exists in a fixed state while waiting for her daughter and husband to return home. While the mother remains the "eternal feminine," she is also symbolic of the present Korea that cannot move forward without venturing into the world like her daughter. The importance of "catching up" is also demonstrated by the contrasting images of the Japanese soldier and the Chinese laborer whom Ongnyŏn encounters on her way to Japan and the United States respectively. One is returning home as a "victor" of the Russo-Japanese War while the other is leaving home to seek a means to survive. In this scene the weakened state of China is juxtaposed with Japan, which rose to become a global power after winning the war. In between these two different realities is the image of Korea: young, immature, and yet needing to sail with the wind of civilization.

The mobility of female characters in *Tears of Blood* is quite unusual compared to the social reality at that time, whereas the heroine's mother's retreat into domesticity is more realistic. At a time when crossing the domestic boundary was a rarity for a *yangban* woman, crossing national boundaries was even more radical. But the fantasy of self-advancement through going abroad seems to have appealed to readers. A reader's message that was published in *The Independence News* read: "I hear that a former courtesan [*kisaeng*] in Pyongyang, Ransa, returns home after spending ten years of studying in Japan. What a pioneering woman we witness in this land. The civilization of our nation starts from educating women."[31] Some made a direct reference to Ongnyŏn in *Tears of Blood*, stating, "I wish I could go to Japan or America and study there but my husband stops me from pursuing my dream."[32]

Yi Haejo's *Freedom Bell* stands out among his works because its narrative is told in a fixed location—a woman's chamber—and because of its limited number of characters and their class backgrounds. The deconstruction of class for national unity and the importance of mobilizing women are expressed more directly in this than any of his other novels. Although it is introduced as a "debate novel" (*t'oron sosŏl*), *Freedom Bell* reads more like a collection of individual speeches. Four female characters are gathered on one character's birthday and they agree to spend their time productively; that is, seeking ways to improve the nation's fate. The opening speech is made by Lady Sin who introduces herself as "a wife of a high government official in the past but now is just another person who belongs to the pitiful masses" (*minjung*). By social convention, she must be older and her social position must be higher than the other three women, since she initiates the discussion. However, by downplaying her own status, she encourages her fellow women to present their thoughts in a liberal atmosphere. Women, she says, are as intelligent as men, thus they shall make the gathering productive by leading the discussion in a "scientific manner" (*hangni*).[33] Although women in the gathering agree that they possess intelligence, they lament their lack of knowledge, criticizing the lack of education for half of the Korean population as the main cause for the national crisis.

On the issue of education, women blame Korea's past close ties with China, viewing this as the main cause for the absence of national culture. Some women argue that Koreans must use *han'gŭl* only in order to de-

---

31. Ilŏnsaeng, "Tokja t'ugoran," *Mansebo*, 8 August 1906, cited in Chŏn Ŭn'gyŏng, "*Mansebo* ŭi tokja t'ugoran," 373.

32. P'albuin, "Tokja t'ugoran," *Mansebo*, 17 November 1906, cited in ibid., 375.

33. Yi Haejo, *Jayujong*, in *Han'guk kaehwagi munhak ch'ongsŏ I: sin sosŏl, pŏnan(yŏk) sosŏl*, vol. 4 (Seoul: Asea munhwasa, [1910] 1978), 2.

velop national culture away from China, though some point out the challenge of abandoning the use of Chinese characters immediately. Lady Kungnan, for example, gives a realistic assessment of the *han'gŭl*-only policy, which cannot accommodate the immediate need to educate the populace since knowledge has been accumulated in Chinese script for many centuries. It will only be possible to "discard" after major texts are translated into *han'gŭl*.[34] While the women emphasize their active participation in national affairs, it is often justified by men's incompetence, especially the social elites and patriarchs, whom the women can no longer expect to provide solutions to Korea's predicament. In this regard, the absence of men—and *yangban* men in particular—in *Freedom Bell* is noteworthy for its deliberate description of them as the immobile fathers and husbands, which also appears frequently in Yi Haejo's other novels.

Most *yangban* men in Yi Haejo's works do not have male heirs. In *Snow on the Temple Hair*, Sŏ and his wife have no children, and Sŏ shows no interest in having children with the concubine either. In other words, he is described as a man who is not ready to father a son—an immature man who needs to be enlightened first. In *Demon-Expelling Sword*, the male protagonist Ham Chinhae also does not deserve to have a male heir. He tries and fails to save his only son who eventually dies of illness because Ham's wife is encumbered by superstition. There is also no mention of children of the elderly man, Pak, in *Mountains and Streams* (*Sanch'ŏn ch'omok*, 1910). The absence of male heirs in Yi's novels adds another layer to the symbolic meaning of women's mobility. It is an expression of male anxiety over the uncertainty about "the origin of reproduction" under the force of modernity; unlike women's capability to reproduce, men's contribution to the next generation can be affirmed only by their claim of patrimony.[35] Viewed in this light the deprivation of fatherhood in these novels, either due to natural cause or ignorance, likely stems from the writers' preoccupation with revamping the traditional world and their fear of the unknown future. The displacement of women from the home and the death/absence of male heirs is a harsh self-criticism by the authors at a time when the disruption of family genealogy was considered a sin.

---

34. Ibid., 13.

35. Luce Irigaray, *Speculum of the Other Woman* (Ithaca, NY: Cornell University Press, [1975] 1985), 22–24.

Perhaps this is why traveling women were not always depicted positively in Yi Haejo's novel. When women are displaced from home against their will they are brought back to a newly constructed home at the end of the novel. However, when they decide to leave on their own accord they are no longer members of the family when they return. This aspect of women's willful mobility is another dimension of the male anxiety over women's desire to control their home. In this regard, Yi Haejo's *Mountains and Streams* (*Sanch'ŏn ch'omok*)[36] is significant for its representation of traditional morality and the corruption of youth, both of which show a sense of anxiety about the present and the future. In this work, an elderly former government official, Pak, lives with his young and beautiful concubine and supports her parents. The concubine, however, falls in love with a young playboy called Yi Sijong whose interest in her is based solely on erotic desire. Driven by the flame of love, the concubine runs away from home and secretly lives with Yi. At the end Yi abandons her, and despite his anger and feelings of betrayal, Pak lets her stay at his house out of pity. Although the concubine returns to the house, the possibility of her reuniting with Pak is slim, and Pak in turn dwells in a home devoid of love and harmony.

The description of the concubine's expression of her desire to "live with someone she loves even if it lasts one day"[37] is quite radical for its straightforwardness about romantic desire, which is rarely seen in Yi Haejo's novels. The initially reserved woman is "awakened" by the feeling of love, a powerful emotion that emasculates her elderly male partner. Further, her act is unfilial, as she risks an economic downfall that will directly affect her parents' livelihood since they receive financial support from Pak. Pak realizes that her love (*chŏng*) is directed at the young man, but he cannot alter his feelings for her.[38] This work may have intended to criticize the problem of the male-centered sexual practice of concubinage, but it also demonstrates how controlling female sexuality was becoming a grave concern for colonized men. As Anne McClintock rightly observes, the colonized land was often represented by figures of women; relegated to a position outside history and knowledge, women in the colony and at home

36. Yi Haejo, "Sanch'ŏn ch'omok," in *Han'guk sinsosŏl chŏnjip* (Seoul: Ŭlyu munhwasa, [1910] 2011).

37. Ibid., 69.

38. Ibid., 57.

symbolically became a "natural" object of male contest.[39] In Yi Haejo's novels, the force of modernity is described as both threatening and necessary, yet as far as female sexuality is concerned, there is the danger that the newly organized social sphere will make women "uncontrollable."

It is noteworthy that the concubine in *Mountains and Streams* "encounters" love in a new public space, a theater, which may "corrupt" women. The concubine was brave enough to show her face in the public space where men and women are gathered for the purposes of entertainment, and yet as soon as she is exposed to the theater's "liberal atmosphere" she discovers her private desire that endangers her and her parents' safety. The idea of romance is not only the expression of new selfhood that is formed in the midst of social change; it is also an expression of male anxiety over losing control of reproduction to the colonial force. The handling of romance from the early 1910s thus is rested on the colonial discourse in which female sexuality becomes an object of domestication for colonialists and Korean nationalists. This partly explains why Ongnyŏn, in the sequel to *Tears of Blood* entitled *Peony Hill* (*Moranbong*, 1913), returns home, and why Yi Haejo's attitude toward female sexuality became more conservative in the early 1910s. Domesticity, through which social relations and racial hierarchies were formed and mediated, became a great concern for the colonial state. The function of the novel was ambivalent, for it served conflicting and variable purposes for the colonial state and the colonized.

SCRIPTING "REALITY" IN THE 1910S

There was a significant change in the publication industry right after Japan fully annexed Korea. The GGK forced the closure of nearly all Korean newspapers, leaving only three newspapers that came under their direct control: the English paper *The Seoul Press*, the Korean-language paper *The Daily*,[40] and the Japanese-language newspaper *Keijō shinpō* (*Seoul News*). As censorship became stricter the publication industry concentrated on

---

39. McClintock, *Imperial Leather*, 35.

40. The Japanese Inspector General (*T'onggambu*) tried to purchase *Taehan maeil sinbo* from its owner, Ernest Thomas Bethel (1872–1909), for some time. The purchase attempt was instigated by the paper's anti-Japanese stance and by its high subscription

the relatively innocuous genre of writing: fiction.[41] While most of the formerly prominent publishing houses were having financial and management crises, some prospered by shifting their editorial focus. Tongyang sŏwŏn and Sinmun'gwan are good examples; the former successfully monopolized the publication of New Fiction while the latter concentrated on translating European and American literature. Although there had been a serious decline in the publishing industry,[42] there was still a niche market for fiction, and New Fiction in particular. Korean publishing houses and *The Daily* competed for this market until the end of 1912, when *The Daily*'s serialization of Japanese domestic fiction became hugely popular.

Tokutomi Sohō (1863–1957) oversaw the management of *Seoul News* and *The Daily* between 1910 and 1918. Sohō was an experienced journalist as well as a fervent supporter of Japan's military expansionism and colonialism.[43] The key decision-making figures at *The Daily* were the Japanese, while its general editors and journalists were Koreans.[44] The police were responsible for censorship, however, and there were only six policemen assigned to censor all printed media until 1919.[45] The GGK's censorship practice became more systemized after the March First Movement, when it allowed Koreans to publish vernacular newspapers and magazines, and the number of censors, including Koreans, also increased after that.[46] Although *The Daily* was a state newspaper, it would be too simplistic to conclude that the state exercised all-encompassing power over the content of

rate. Chŏng Chinsŏk, *Han'guk ŏllonsa yŏn'gu* (A study of Korean journalism) (Seoul: Il-tchogak, 1988), 246–249.

41. Pak Chinyŏng, *Pŏnyŏk kwa pŏnan ŭi sidae* (The age of translation and adaptation) (Seoul: Somyŏng ch'ulp'an, 2011), 202.

42. The increased number of fictional works did not necessarily elevate the quality of fiction, which became a cause for the serious decline of the industry in the mid-1910s. The publishers Sinmun'gwan and Tongyang sŏwŏn failed to maintain an innovative edge in terms of their translation techniques and the diversification of fiction genres, thus they had lost a substantial portion of their readership by the 1910s. Ibid., 226.

43. See his view on Japanese imperialism and military expansion in East Asia in John D. Pierson, *Tokutomi Sohō 1863–1957* (Princeton, NJ: Princeton University Press, 1980), 234–247.

44. Ham T'aeyŏng, "1910 nyŏndae *Maeil sinbo* sosŏl yŏn'gu," PhD diss., Yonsei University, 2009, 18–19.

45. Chŏng Chinsŏk, "Ilche ha kŏmnyŏl kigu wa kŏmnyŏl kwan ŭi pyŏndong" (The censorship bureau and censors in colonial Korea), in *Singminji kŏmnyŏl* (Seoul: Somyŏng, 2011), 21.

46. Ibid., 50.

the newspaper. While it played its role as an agent to carry out the colonial state's policies, it was also necessary for the paper to consider the native condition by offering Koreans the ability to participate in the public space. It constantly negotiated with native organizations, as well as with individuals whose interests were not limited to civilizing projects only but in the preservation of traditions.[47] This kind of negotiation is reflected in the overall organization of the newspaper shortly after the annexation.

The GGK's assimilation strategies were most clearly laid out on the first page of *The Daily*. Accompanied by visual materials such as photographs that delineated Korea's subordinate position in the Japanese empire, the political hierarchy between the metropole and the colony was visualized. A portrait of the Meiji emperor appeared first,[48] and photos of Japanese officials soon followed. The visualization of the political hierarchy between Koreans and the Japanese was also made clear by the introduction of photographic images of former Chosŏn palaces that appeared in the paper during the first few years of the colonial rule. The transformation of the Ch'angdŏk Palace's Rear Garden (*Huwŏn*) to the Secret Garden (*Piwŏn*), for example, denoted the end of the Chosŏn monarchy's history, bringing what was once the private property of the royal family to the public. The image of the royal garden lost its secretive aura by being fully exposed to common folks; the changed name of the garden ironically accentuated the absence of secretiveness.

While the public exposure of these places projected the dissolution of Korea's monarchy, the colonial administration also tried to create the sense of equality. The inclusion of all classes and the celebration of leisure time culminated in the nationwide Chosŏn Industrial Exposition (*Chosŏn mulsan kongjinhoe*) in 1915, which was advertised in *The Daily* for nearly three months. As Hong Kal argues, the exposition visualized the improved economic and social status of Korea under the tutelage of Japan while simultaneously constructing the hierarchy between Korea and Japan using exhibition techniques.[49] Kal's analysis of the reception of the

---

47. Kim Hyŏnju, "Singminji esŏ 'sahoe' wa 'sahoe jŏk' kongongssŏng ŭi kwejŏk" (The stance of "society" and "social publicity" in colonial Korea), *Han'guk munhwa yŏn'gu* 38 (2016): 224.

48. *Maeil sinbo*, 3 November 1910.

49. Hong Kal, *Aesthetic Constructions of Korean Nationalism: Spectacle, Politics, and History* (New York: Routledge, 2011), 13–31.

exposition also shows how the time and space stimulated Koreans' "desire for progress." The creation of the progress-desiring subject was a crucial element in the nation-building process, which is reflected in *The Daily's* serial novels.

Placed on the first or last page, the novel section stood out visually due to its use of pure vernacular, whereas editorials and essays predominantly used Chinese script. But more important, a greater use of photography is also seen in the construction of reality in the novel:

> Sitting alone, Sujŏng is resting her chin on her hand in a seated position. She is facing the mountain across from her with tears streaming down on her cheeks. This view of her, if it had been taken as a photograph and hung on a wall, would evoke sympathy from all women (with vulnerable hearts) who probably can't help weeping by looking at it.[50]

Sujŏng is the heroine of Yi Haejo's novel *The Flower World (Hwasegye)*,[51] and in this scene she is waiting to hear from her long-lost lover. What draws attention is the author's visualization of the supposedly sad atmosphere through the use of a photograph. Yi Haejo used a photograph to speak for the scene, making the scene "realistic" to convey the mood. The photograph would not produce the effect the author intended had there been no contextualization provided by the description to begin with. But this photographic mode of expression of the image points to a transformation in fiction writing, which was beginning to embody a new kind of visuality in constructing narrative in order to represent the scene "as realistically as possible."

A photographic image also appeared in the Korean translation of Suehiro Tetchō's *Plum Blossoms in the Snow*: the female protagonist keeps a portrait photo of her fiancé. The function of this portrait is to serve as a reminder or an objective proof of the existence of the fiancé that somehow guarantees the truthfulness of his identity. The scene in *The Flower World*, however, does not do "justice" to the physical likeness of the heroine. Instead it tries to convince the readers of the heroine's emotional state through the photographic mode of description. I contend that this is a new turn within literature, an attempt to deliver the inner landscape of the

---

50. Yi Haejo, *Hwasegye, Maeil sinbo*, 7 December 1910.
51. Yi Haejo, *Hwasegye, Maeil sinbo*, 12 October 1910–16 January 1911.

character through the aid of modern science. Yi Haejo did not continue experimenting with photography in other novels; instead he incorporated other signs of modern knowledge into his works (which often appear in *The Daily*), such as trains, motorboats, legal trials, and so on, all of which are important props to make people perceive the changing social reality.

Around this time, real events reported in newspapers were often compared with fiction to stress their dramatic elements. For example, we see a reversal of what Yi Haejo intended: various news of "fictionlike reality" appeared almost daily in the newspaper in the society and crime section, such as "A Fictionlike (*sosŏl kat'ŭn*) Encounter"[52] and "A Fictionlike True Story."[53] Family disputes, the kidnapping of young girls, murder of spouses and family members, and female suicides were daily events, and they were often reported in the paper. The distinction between fiction and reality becomes unstable; from time to time, *The Daily* carried nonsensical news reports such as mermaids being captured[54] or stories demonizing the Righteous Army (*ŭibyŏng*) as mere bandits (*chŏkdo*).[55]

Despite the fact that *The Daily* considered the novel an important apparatus to domesticate the colony, its editorial team's attitude toward the novel was not coherent. One published editorial shows a deep concern for the publishing industry in Korea, arguing that the industry is obsessed with generating profit only while ignoring the quality of "books" (*sŏjŏk*): "There is a flood of vernacular novels in Seoul, proving the low standard of the publishing industry these days ... Refined [*kosanghan*] books refine people."[56] *The Daily* does not clarify what kind of vernacular novels are harmful for people, but criticizes that they are not useful for elevating the society's level of civilization. It recommends that people read "books from Japan first in order to overcome the current state of barbarity and ignorance."[57] This contrasts with the paper's active promotion of New Fiction, as it had serialized the works of the most popular writer of the time,

---

52. *Maeil sinbo*, 9 April 1912.

53. *Maeil sinbo*, 15 August 1912.

54. "Inŏ p'ohoek" (A mermaid captured), *Maeil sinbo*, 12 July 1912.

55. From a detailed story of a "bandit" who participated in the military campaign against the Japanese in 1906. Reports of the capturing of bandits appeared frequently in 1910 and 1911, during which time the Righteous Army was still providing resistance against the Japanese. "Chŏkdo ŭi pulbok" (A bandit's denial), *Maeil sinbo*, 12 July 1912.

56. "Sŏjŏkkye e taehaya" (On the publishing industry), *Maeil sinbo*, 16 April 1911.

57. "Sŏjŏk ŭi chŏngdo" (The standard of books), *Maeil sinbo*, 21 September 1911.

Yi Haejo, from its inception. In an advertisement for Yi Haejo's *Touch-Me-Not* (*Pongsŏnhwa*, 1912), *The Daily* emphasizes the entertaining value of the novel, stating, "You will lose sense of time when reading this New Fiction, *Touch-Me-Not*. It is not an exaggeration to say that you will miss out on some of the greatest fun in your life should you miss reading this novel … Subscribe to *The Daily* so that you can kill two birds with one stone, that is, reading the novel and the newspaper every day."[58]

The Daily's frequent discussion of vernacular novels in its own editorials shows that it did recognize the impact of the novel on readers.[59] Another reason for the ambivalent attitude toward the novel, presumably, is the editorial team's conscious effort to compete with the native publishing industry as a way of controlling the culture industry in the colony. An alternative to native novels, which the paper devalued in comparison with "refined books from Japan," would be made a few years later. But for the time being, Yi Injik's and Yi Haejo's New Fiction came in handy toward achieving the newspaper's double agenda: to gain a wide readership[60] and promote the new social order at the expense of annihilating the past.

DOMESTICITY AND LAW ENFORCEMENT

Yi Injik continually published his work in *The Daily*, although his period of absence was long: only one novel, a sequel to *Tears of Blood* titled *Peony Hill* (*Moranbong*), was serialized in *The Daily* in 1913.[61] In this regard, Yi Haejo deserves greater attention since his novels enjoyed continuous pop-

---

58. "Sinsosŏl yego" (Notice on a new novel), *Maeil sinbo*, 5 July 1912.

59. Ham T'aeyŏng, "1910 nyŏndae *Maeil sinbo* sosŏl yŏn'gu," 55.

60. Kim Yŏngmin, "1910 nyŏndae sinmun ŭi yŏkhal kwa kŭndae sosŏl ŭi chŏngch'ak kwajŏng" (The role of newspapers in the 1910s and development of the novel), in *A Study on the Relationship Between Modern Korean Narratives and Media*, ed. Kim Yŏngmin (Seoul: Somyŏng ch'ulp'an, 2005), 152–153. The subscription rate subsequently rose, reaching almost 10,000 at its peak in the 1910s. Ham T'aeyŏng, "1910 nyŏndae *Maeil sinbo* sosŏl yŏn'gu," 33.

61. Yi Injik worked for pro-Japanese newspapers, *Mansebo* and *Taehan sinmun*, prior to 1910, and the pro-Japan and anti-Qing tendencies embedded in *Tears of Blood* may have worked favorably for his writing career. However, it is not clear why there was a relatively long absence of his work in print media, including *Maeil sinbo*. Even his *Peony Hill* ended incomplete in 1913. His absence may have to do with his illness, neuralgia, which was the cause of his death in 1916.

ularity throughout the early 1910s. Praising him as "the best novelist in contemporary Korea,"[62] *The Daily* stressed the "entertaining quality" (*chaemi*) of Yi Haejo's novels. No other writers were given such a privileged opportunity from *The Daily* between 1910 and 1912; during these years, fifteen of Yi's novels were serialized consecutively.

Yi Haejo's concentration on crimes and troubled family relations forces us to investigate the value of his works within the purview of newspapers, since *The Daily* provided a heuristic space for readers to recognize their shared time and space. The protagonist in Yi Haejo's *The Flower World*, for example, displays her vulnerability, which was formed by old customs and traditional moral values. Born into a poor family, this young woman, Sujŏng, is about to be sold by her parents to become a concubine of a high-ranking military officer. Sujŏng runs away from home to avoid this terrible fate, but then faces a series of hardships on the road until she is "saved" by her future husband. Her savior, Ku, is a former soldier of the Chosŏn army who now travels around the peninsula aimlessly; he has transformed from a greedy and corrupted official to "a man of integrity and virtue" by the time he meets Sujŏng. In the climax of this story, the accusation that Ku is a bandit is revealed as false by a public prosecutor (*kŏmsa*) at a trial, a crucial condition that secures the couple's bright future, allowing them to form a happy family. Frequent appearances of police (*sunsa*) and *kŏmsa* in Yi Haejo's stories are an important apparatus for making happy endings, signifying the institutional change that is constitutive of civilization. This is not merely a means to inform the readers about the colonial government's effort to civilize Korean society by modern legal standards; it represents the moral authority of the colonial administration to establish social order by correcting the morality of Koreans.

In another of Yi's stories, *Youth in Spring* (*Ch'unoech'un*, 1912),[63] a young, talented woman, Yŏngjin, is about to be sold to a brothel by her stepmother. She decides to kill herself rather than become a prostitute, but regains her will to live after conversing with a kind woman who provides her with shelter. At the end, her former teacher helps Yŏngjin to go to Japan to study, where Yŏngjin meets her future husband. Yŏngjin's trans-

---

62. "Pon sinbo ŭi tae swaesin" (A great innovation of *Maeil sinbo*), *Maeil sinbo*, 14 June 1911.
63. Yi Haejo, *Ch'unoech'un*, *Maeil sinbo*, 1 January 1912–14 March 1912.

Figure 3-1. A cross-examination in a police station in Yi Haejo's *Youth in Spring, Maeil sinbo,* 10 March 1912 (Photo credit: Korea Press Foundation).

gression against the "old time and space" is made through her travel from Korea to Japan, leading her to enter a civilized world. While this innocent and vulnerable woman becomes empowered by relocating to Japan and encountering her soulmate, those who made her suffer receive punishment according to the law. What is noteworthy about this novel is the insertion of illustrations in the novel, visualizing the central scene in each

installment, where the hierarchy is made clear in the juxtaposition between the "uncivilized" Koreans and the "civilized" Japanese.

An illustration that was inserted in *Youth in Spring*, for example, depicts a cross-examination in a police station (Fig. 3-1).[64] A man in uniform
in the illustration is the chief of police and a man in a traditional Korean
jacket is Yŏngjin's father who is being interrogated for his wife's involvement in the kidnapping of Yŏngjin. In the image, the chief, with his sword
by his side and a stern expression, is positioned above everyone in the
room. The chief talks down to Yŏngjin's father who in turn answers in
formal speech. It goes without saying that the uniform and the sword
symbolize the law and its enforcement. The way the chief of police addresses Yŏngjin's father is overtly condescending, criticizing his inability
to manage domestic affairs. The moral lesson for the father, who is ashamed
of having neglected his daughter, was not expressed in fiction only. Head-
lines during this time from reports on domestic violence, robbery, and
gambling, for example, were also judgmental, describing the immoral
character of those who were involved in these crimes.

It is not an unusual practice for modern empires to attempt to charac-
terize the ruled as ignorant and immoral,[65] yet it would be too simplistic to
judge the moral lesson embedded in Yi Haejo's novels as part of the colonial administration's effort to circulate the image of Koreans as ignorant.
Yi's handling of moral concerns over society through domestic settings in
his fiction, in fact, is consistent from the early stage of his writing career,
and he openly expressed that the most important value of the novel is "to
correct wrong customs and habits and awaken the society."[66] Yi Haejo's
attitude toward the novel is no different from that he expressed in the
body of New Fiction he had produced prior to the annexation in terms of
its imagination of the Korean community as morally renewed. Thus it is
questionable whether we can accept Yi's emphasis on the moral reconstruction of society as his "moral defeat" by the colonial power.[67]

---

64. *Maeil sinbo*, 10 March 1912.

65. Ann Stoler, *Along the Archival Grain: Epistemic Anxieties and Colonial Common
Sense* (Princeton, NJ: Princeton University Press, 2010), 248.

66. This line is inserted at the end of his fiction entitled *Haw ŭi hyŏl*, *Maeil sinbo*, 21
June 1911.

67. Ham T'aeyŏng argues that Yi's fiction aimed to lead his readers to succumb to the
colonial power, "1910 nyŏndae *Maeil sinbo* sosŏl yŏn'gu," 99.

The civilization discourse was not formed with the colonization of Korea; rather, it emerged when the necessity of enlightening society was first presented by New Fiction writers like Yi Haejo and Yi Injik. This is where the dilemma of civilization reveals itself in colonial Korea: inasmuch as reform-minded Korean intellectuals tried to convey their will to civilize the society, the colonial authority tried to display the same message. Although the difference between the two is the problem of agency, it is not clear whether a writer like Yi Haejo can be regarded as an accomplice of the colonialists. It is possible that writers like Yi Haejo faced the dilemma of producing novels to enlighten their fellow Koreans while continuing to write for the colonial power. In this regard, inculcating shame cannot be solely interpreted as the colonial administration's intervention into the daily life of the ruled in order to establish moral order based on racial hierarchy. These concerns reveal the writers' criticism of their own society through invoking shame among Koreans. Yi Haejo's concentration on domestic life in particular shows how home became both a metaphorical and physical place where personal and political interests overlapped and clashed. Yi Haejo's novels in *The Daily* demonstrate that the novel possessed the possibility of claiming something beyond the private realm; he presented domesticity as a facet of colonial society, where private life was a barometer of civilization.

It took some time for Yi Injik to come back to novel writing with *Peony Hill (Moranbong*, 1913), his serialization of the sequel to *Tears of Blood* entitled.[68] The novel begins with Ongnyŏn, her father, and her fiancé Ku Wansŏ in San Francisco, enjoying a stroll around a park. The novel takes place at the outbreak of the Russo-Japanese War, reminding Ongnyŏn and her father of the tragic event that displaced their family. Worried about her mother left alone in Pyongyang, Ongnyŏn decides to delay her studies and return to Korea with her father while her fiancé, Ku Wansŏ, remains in America to further his studies. Upon their return to Korea, however, the visionary Ongnyŏn, who desires to devote her life to enlightening the nation, vanishes. From there, the story revolves around her keeping faith in her fiancé despite unfortunate circumstances that force her to marry a person she does not love. Although the feeling of love and the term "love" itself are not explicitly invoked, the strong emotional attachment between

---

68. Yi Injik, *Moranbong, Maeil sinbo*, 5 February 1913–3 June 1913.

Ongnyŏn and Ku is evident. In other words, a sense of romantic love and the anticipation of happiness is implied in their relationship, which will, they believe, manifest in their marriage in the future.

As Yoon Sun Yang observes, Ongnyŏn's relationship with Ku was intended to stress new domestic practices where "marriage is depicted as the main site where traditional Korean customs encounter West-influenced new domestic practice."[69] The reason for the shift of thematic focus from nation-building to domesticity, as Yang rightly points out, stems from colonial suppression of nationalistic content in cultural productions. But the more important point she raises is Ongnyŏn's placement back in the old domesticity, thus creating conflicts between the "uncivilized" and the "civilized" worlds. This immobile position perhaps points to nationalists' frustration over the impasse of the nation-building project,[70] which is symbolized by the delay of the wedding of Ongnyŏn and her fiancé.

The serialization of *Peony Hill* stopped suddenly, leaving the story incomplete. While this novel does highlight the waning spirit of patriotism and the ambiguity of the civilization process in the colonial situation by placing Ongnyŏn between two worlds with no way for her to overcome the impasse, Yi Injik's novels, including *Peony Hill*, do not leave his heroines in the shadow of civilization. The endings of his novels almost always cohere with the "reward the good and punish the evil" theme, bringing the heroines from their predicament to the light of civilization.

What links Yi Injik and Yi Haejo is their preoccupation with free choice marriage. Similar to *Peony Hill*, Yi Haejo shows a deep interest in the idea of individuality that culminates in free marriage. In *The Flower World*, the hero Sujŏng's fiancé stresses the importance of a peaceful conjugal relationship as a condition to make a happy family, arguing, "We are living in a different world now. If husband and wife face irreconcilable differences they can take a separate way through divorce."[71] Similar rhetoric about the idea of free marriage appears in other novels,

---

69. Yoon Sun Yang, "Nation in the Backyard," 144.
70. Ibid., 174–175.
71. Yi Haejo, *Hwasegye*, *Maeil sinbo*, 10 December 1910.

such as *Blood of Flower*, where the heroine encounters her future fiancé while studying in Tokyo.

Even though the descriptions of heroines' romantic encounters are implicit and brief, what is noteworthy about the marriage theme in Yi Haejo's novels is twofold. First, the encounter with the marriage partner takes place when the heroine is displaced from home. Before her departure, regardless of her will, her home is dysfunctional and full of chaos, which is usually created by an evil stepmother or mother-in-law who overpowers the head of the family. Marriage is suggested as a new beginning for the colonial community, and the heroine, like Ongnyŏn in *Tears of Blood*, must go through a series of challenges outside the home. Marriage, in this sense, is a symbolic representation of the reworking of domesticity through the help of modern law and the interaction with the "civilized Japanese" like the heroine in *Blood of Flower*.

Second, even though it is implicit, the sense of individuality manifests in the marriage theme. Free choice marriage in particular becomes a sign of young Koreans entering into modern civilization, a channel through which they express their inner feelings. As Yi Haejo's novels in the early 1910s demonstrate, class divisions no longer acted as a barrier for young people's marriages, and this sense of class equality, together with the young characters' self-advancement through education, presents a positive picture for colonial subjects. The anticipation of modern civilization, in other words, is not only aligned with modern knowledge; it is also conjoined with the aspiration for upward social mobility through education as well as the expression of private desire in the form of romantic encounters.

The marriage saga delineates something beyond that positivity associated with the new colonial social order. In the next chapter, young people's conflicts in their pursuit of love are emphasized in novels wherein heroines are portrayed as "uncontrollable." Placing women at home, in other words, becomes more challenging than ever before, and the role of parents is significantly reduced. Free marriage and heterosexual romantic desire become central in novels where the traditional order emphasized by Yi Haejo's and Yi Injik's works no longer functions. The fear that women will become uncontrollable can be a projection of the writers' fear of the external realities that seduce women, such as the desire for elevated social status, consumerism, and—most notably—romance. It will take much emotional work to bring women back to the domestic realm, a struggle that embodies the tension that arose from both the opportunities and closures created by colonial modernity.

4

THE EMOTIONAL LANDSCAPE OF THE COLONIZED IN KOREAN TRANSLATIONS OF DOMESTIC FICTION

Romantic Vision of Social Mobility

"SO! YOU MEAN TO MARRY HIM AFTER ALL! You wicked woman," Kan'ichi cried, kicking Miya in the knee. Miya fell to the ground. Lacking the strength to voice her pain, she lay sprawled on the sand. Like a beast about to attack its prey, Kan'ichi's eyes were fixed on Miya who was in prostrate form, showing no sign of any movement. Looking at her with hateful eyes, he spoke in fury.

"Miya ... you ... you are a wicked woman! By simply changing your mind, you have killed my hopes and made a madman of me. You have just ruined one life. I shall give up my studies. My hatred will turn me into a demon and I will devour the flesh of animals like you. Mrs. ... Mrs. Tomiyama, raise your head and look at me, because this will be the last time you will see me as an honest man."

(…)

Miya tried to rise suddenly. But the bruises on her thigh prevented her from doing so. She dragged herself along the ground and clung to his knees while sobbing.

"Kan'ichi! Kan'ichi w-w-w … wait please. Where are you going?"

Kan'ichi turned. Seeing the bloodstains on her dress, he said with more tenderness than he perhaps really felt.

"Are you hurt, Miya?"

"It doesn't matter, but where are you going? I have something important to tell you. Come with me and talk. I beg you."

material and physical hardships they faced.[10] Throughout the serialization of the column, these talented people were most frequently described as "diligent," "excelling at their studies," "good-natured," and "virtuous," qualities that were deemed essential for success. The introduction of these young, upwardly mobile people cannot be separated from the colonial government's goal of encouraging Koreans to make diligent efforts to elevate their level of civilization to match the Japanese. *The Daily* aimed to educate Koreans about the importance of Japan's assimilation policy,[11] arguing that Koreans needed to make a genuine effort to reform their society. As these exemplary young men and women demonstrate, *The Daily* instructed Koreans to take the initiative to reform Korean society and economy through education and hard work. In describing the Viscount Yi Hayŏng, for example, the paper emphasized how he advanced to his current position "through his resilient spirit and diligence" despite his "lowly family background" (*mich'ŏnhan sinbun*).[12]

The fact that the columns were printed in the newspaper's society section is noteworthy, since it meant that the "greatness" of these young men and women stood out in contrast to the reports of various crimes and family tragedies deriving from Korea's old customs and manners. The contrast of "good" and "bad" people, customs, and manners was meant to emphasize the level of civilization Koreans would need to achieve to distancing themselves from their disorderly and "backward" past. The introduction of successful Koreans was just one segment of the *The Daily* that delineated the gap between the educated and the uneducated, and by extension, the productive and harmful members of society.

The potential for advancement through education, however, was presented in a contradictory manner in the newspaper. An editorial published in *The Daily* warned young Koreans and their parents to be "realistic"

---

and graduates such as Na Hyesŏk and her younger sister, Na Chisŏk, who demonstrated excellent intellectual ability.

10. Among others, a story of a young blind woman is noteworthy: it discusses her successful completion of the high school curriculum and her plan to study in Tokyo, a rare event that was "happen[ing] for the first time in Chosŏn." *Maeil sinbo*, 12 July 1913.

11. Mark Caprio, "Marketing Assimilation: The Press and the Formation of the Japanese-Korea Colonial Relationship," *The Journal of Korean Studies* 16, no. 1 (2011): 12.

12. *Maeil sinbo*, 28 January 1913.

about their expectations of education. The goal of education is not to make children into lawyers and politicians, it says. Rather, Koreans must concentrate on "practical" (*sirhaengjŏk*) studies that are urgently needed to increase the "wealth of Korea" (*chosŏn ŭi puryŏk chŭngjin*).[13] Even with the paper's emphasis on women's education, the editorial argued that the goal of women's education is to produce women who can perform their child-rearing duties well, thus educating their children to become "*kungmin*" (national subjects).[14] The gap between the potential for advancement as reflected in the *Chosŏn inmulgwan* column and the editorial's guidelines for Koreans to find a place "appropriate" to their social position in the Japanese empire demonstrates an inconsistency in the colonial administration's message concerning the civilization of Korea. The inconsistency, however, was to be expected based on the colonial state's position on education; it had no serious intention to educate Koreans and only began to do so in the late 1930s, when the state began recruiting young Korean men to the army.[15]

Framed in a rectangular box with their immovable expressions in the portrait photographs, these talented agents of civilization are brought to life by *The Daily*'s serial novels. By overcoming challenges faced by villains and the ignorant, characters that resemble the "agents" demonstrate their resilient spirit by participating in the civilizing mission. The stories that entangled romantic and family relationships in particular are narrated with emotionally charged descriptions of their struggle, a persuasive technique to make readers feel the necessity of civilization.

Ann Stoler argues that colonial states intervened in the emotional life of the everyday, both among their agents and among the people they ruled, in order to establish moral order in their colonies.[16] Thus, she continues, the use of sentiment was intended to construct colonial relations accord-

---

13. *Maeil sinbo*, 27 November 1912.

14. It even uses Mencius's mother as a good example for young female students to model themselves after by dedicating their lives to their children. "Yŏja kyoyuk" (Women's education), *Maeil sinbo*, 3 March 1912.

15. Mark Caprio, *Japanese Assimilation Policies in Colonial Korea 1910–1945* (Seattle: University of Washington Press, 2009), 100.

16. Ann Stoler, *Along the Archival Grain*, 69.

ing to emotional affiliation and response in accordance with social rank.[17] The Japanese colonial state's investment in the establishment of moral order among Koreans in *The Daily*'s serial novels rationalized the idea of social reform, yet it also embodied the racial hierarchy between the Japanese and Koreans. *The Daily*'s serial novels published in the early 1910s are especially noteworthy to understand how the power shift had affected social imaginations of civilization in literature, and how these imaginations were contested.

At the time of the publication of the selected fiction of my investigation that follows, the shame-based narratives of Yi Injik and Yi Haejo were no longer being published. Instead, the serialized novels in *The Daily* focus on young professionals and students, just like those introduced in the *Chosŏn inmulgwan* column, who promote the narrative of civilization by traveling from one place to another. This spatial condition is crucial because the source of their emotional struggle is their feudal past and their struggle is resolved with the help of modern, foreign education. *The Daily*'s fiction not only presented the possibility of upward social mobility, but was also a screen to project personal desires and emotions against the backdrop of the nation-building process.

JAPANESE DOMESTIC FICTION AND NEWSPAPERS IN JAPAN AND KOREA

The emergence of Japanese domestic fiction (hereafter, domestic fiction) took place at a time when a vast quantity of Western fiction, and particularly fiction about romance and marriage, flooded into Japan.[18] The subjects of these works primarily consisted of troubled romantic relationships, familial conflicts, and marriage; and their target readers are believed to have been middle-class women, urban workers, and students, though recent studies suggest that there is insufficient evidence for this assumption. Newspaper sales figures often do not match their readership, since it was common for a group of people to share a single newspaper by circulat-

---

17. Ibid., 22.

18. Kathryn Ragsdale, "Marriage, the Newspaper Business, and the Nation-State Ideology in the Late Meiji Serialized Katei Shōsetsu," *The Journal of Japanese Studies* 24, no. 2 (1998): 233.

ing it among themselves, and it is difficult to precisely assess the diversity of readership for this same reason.[19]

Besides the expansion of the publishing industry during this period, which is attributed to the burgeoning popularity of domestic fiction,[20] another important factor for the phenomenal popularity of domestic fiction was the partnership between Meiji writers and new school drama (*shimpa* or *shimpa geki; sinp'a* in Korean) producers in late Meiji. Though it began in Japan in the late 1880s as a reaction to traditional theater genres such as *kabuki* and *bunraku* by a coterie of amateurs, *shimpa* had become one of the major forms of theater at the dawn of the twentieth century. Its popularity soared around the Russo-Japanese War, during which the genre of war plays was particularly well-received.[21] *Shimpa*'s popularity traveled far beyond Japan as well, influencing theater reform in China[22] and Korea in the early twentieth century.

Japanese, European, and American novels were also adapted for *shimpa*. Thus, some of the most influential literary figures such as Izumi Kyōka (1873–1909), Ozaki Kōyō (1868–1903), Tokutomi Roka (1868–1927), and Kikuchi Yūhō (1870–1947) were not unfamiliar to *shimpa* audiences since their novels had been adapted to the form. Writers first serialized their novels in newspapers and magazines, and based on their popularity, theater producers adapted these novels for *shimpa*. If the *shimpa* became popular, then the serial novels would be published in book form, bringing more attention to their authors. *Shimpa*, in other words, benefited both writers and newspapers since its popularity brought an increase in the sale of books as well as newspapers.[23]

---

19. Ibid., 234.

20. Between 1897 and 1911, 236 papers were published. Carol Gluck, *Japan's Modern Myth: Ideology in the Late Meiji Period* (Princeton, NJ: Princeton University Press, 1987), 171.

21. By this time, even *kabuki* actors, who were reluctant to join the new school drama, participated in *shimpa*; and female actresses were brought into *shimpa* as well. Benito Ortolani, *The Japanese Theatre: From Shamanistic Ritual to Contemporary Pluralism* (Princeton, NJ: Princeton University Press, 1995), revised edition, 233–240.

22. It is said that *shimpa* influenced the early formation of *huaju* (spoken drama), also known as *xinju* (new drama). Siyuan Liu, "The Impact of *Shimpa* on Early Chinese *Huaju*," *Asian Theatre Journal* 23, no. 2 (Fall 2006): 342–355.

23. Cody Poulton, "Drama and Fiction in the Meiji Era: The Case of Izumi Kyoka," *Asian Theatre Journal* 12, no. 2 (Autumn 1995): 283.

The rise of an urban middle class was another factor that boosted sales of newspapers in Japan,[24] thus increasing the consumption of domestic fiction. In fact, most heroes and heroines in domestic fiction come from middle-class backgrounds—a class whose social role was being redefined in an urbanized and industrialized environment. The rapid circulation of popular fiction among the urban middle class, however, was a concern for the Meiji government, which labeled the stories "nauseatingly vulgar" and socially dangerous, especially for young women.[25] Schoolgirls were also severely criticized by commentators for their use of the "male form" of language, as they mimicked the language spoken by female characters in such novels.[26] As school curriculums for young girls were tailored to produce "good wives and wise mothers," their use of such language was perceived as a transgression of gender boundaries and a challenge against patriarchal authority.[27] However, the government's censorship of morally harmful materials that challenged the patriarchal order does not seem to have been very strict. Nor were the commentators' scornful remarks very effective in stopping women from reading domestic fiction.

In a number of domestic fiction works, heroines seek marriage without receiving approval from the male head of their household. As Ken Ito points out, heroines in a number of popular domestic fiction works contradict the state ideology of home and family through their desire to satisfy self-interest.[28] The schoolgirls' modeling of language spoken by fe-

24. The commercial and industrial bourgeoisie and the middle class, groups which emerged between the Sino-Japanese War and the end of Meiji period, played a significant role in producing cultural capital and knowledge. Their participation in education within the perimeter of state structure, in particular, is noteworthy in terms of their direct and indirect influence on policy decisions. See David R. Ambaras, "Social Knowledge, Cultural Capital, and the New Middle Class in Japan 1895–1912," *The Journal of Japanese Studies* 24, no. 1 (1998): 1–33.

25. Carol Gluck, *Japan's Modern Myth*, 170.

26. Young girls in domestic fiction used language such as *kango* (Chinese words) and English words, which were both perceived as the language of elite males. Miyako Inoue, *Vicarious Language: Gender and Linguistic Modernity in Japan* (Berkeley: University of California Press, 2006), 63–66.

27. The New Civil Code of 1898 emphasized patriarchal authority within the family, legalizing the head of the household's control over female members. For example, marriage decisions for any woman under age 25 and any man under 30, and the subsequent distribution of inheritance, were in the hands of the male head of the household. Kathryn Ragsdale, "Marriage, the Newspaper Business, and the Nation-State Ideology," 23.

28. Ken Ito argues that the ideological contradiction of "home," in fact, is one of the

male characters in fiction points to women's discontent with rigid gender boundaries, thus encouraging them to "speak out" against the patriarchal imagination of modernity.

By the time *The Daily* began serializing Korean translations of Japanese domestic fiction, Yi Haejo, who had almost singlehandedly provided the content of the novel section in the paper, had ceased to appear there. In addition, two of the most representative private publishing houses, *Sinmun'gwan* and *Tongyang sŏwŏn*, failed to diversify their fiction genres and develop translation techniques around this time, thus losing significant portions of their readership by late 1912. In this context, Cho Chunghwan emerged as a unique figure for his decision to publish his first translation of Japanese fiction, *Puryŏgwi* (*The Cuckoo*, 1912),[29] through a prominent private publisher in Japan.[30] The editorial directions of the native publishing houses did not fit with his goal of publishing such a work as none were willing to venture into the new form of literature. The fact that the work was unusually long also made publishing houses doubt its marketability.

Cho Chunghwan's strategy to publicize *The Cuckoo* was to adapt it into *shimpa* in 1912. Japanese *shimpa* traveled to Korea in the early 1900s, staged mainly for Japanese residents, especially in Seoul, Yongsan, and Inch'ŏn, where *The Cuckoo* was one of the most popular productions in their repertoires.[31] Furthermore, Korean-produced *shimpa* gained a significant level of popularity among Korean audiences from 1911. *The Daily's* reports on these *shimpa*, including Cho's work, reveal that theater was becoming a new cultural site, drawing a significant number of spectators in Seoul. *The Daily* frequently reported about *shimpa* theaters in Seoul that

---

most salient characteristics reflected in *katei shōsetsu*. Ken Ito, "Class and Gender in Meiji Family Romance: Kikuchi Yūhō's *Chikyodai*," in *An Age of Melodrama: Family, Gender, and Social Hierarchy in the Turn of the Century Japanese Novel* (Stanford, CA: Stanford University Press, 2008).

29. A translation of Tokutomi Roka's *Hototogisu* (The cuckoo, 1898–1899), which was serialized between November 1898 and May 1899 in *Kokumin shimbun* in Japan.

30. It was published by a Japanese publisher in Yokohama, Keiseisha shoten, and printed by Fukuin gōshi insatsu kaisha (Fukuin Printing Ltd. Partnership), also in Yokohama. Pak Chinyŏng, *Pŏnyŏk kwa pŏnan ŭi sidae*, 93–98.

31. Hong Sŏnyŏng, "T'ongsok e kwanhan isŏl" (Another theory of popular narratives), *Ilbon munhwa yŏn'gu* 29 (2009): 235.

were "flooded with people every night."[32] *Shimpa* was perceived as a site where Koreans could experience modern culture in terms of the new acting style and narratives in addition to their spatial experience of the indoor theater.

The success of the *shimpa* version of *The Cuckoo* was followed by other novels by Cho Chunghwan serialized in *The Daily*, which actively promoted these Korean versions of *shimpa*. Reports on *shimpa* often appear, accompanied by photographic images of plays and the theater itself packed with spectators. It is not an exaggeration to say that Cho was one of the major figures in the colonial culture industry who popularized domestic fiction and *shimpa* simultaneously. As soon as he was employed by *The Daily* in 1912, Cho began to serialize other Korean translations of Japanese domestic fiction, dominating the novel section for the next two years. *The Daily*'s new choice of writer not only appealed to readers for his choice of sensational subject matter, such as premarital pregnancy and marriage fraud, but also for the expression of individuality that was implied in his fiction. As Pak Chinyŏng notes, Cho's presence in *The Daily* was a turning point in the literary scene in Korea at the time. His skillful translation techniques, together with provocative subject matter, revitalized readers' interest in fiction.[33] Partly due to the popularity of Cho's fiction, *The Daily*'s sales increased from approximately 2,500 subscribers in 1910 to more than 10,000 by the mid-1910s.[34]

Urbanization, the nuclear family, consumerism, and communication technologies are crucial elements in domestic fiction, all of which Korea had yet to experience. However, the unfamiliar became familiar in Cho's innovative translation. Except for his first translation of *The Cuckoo*, where he familiarized only a few cultural terms in the Korean context such as *shinto* shrine and *koto*,[35] Cho changed the geographical back-

---

32. "Yŏnyegye chŏnghwang" (The entertainment news), *Maeil sinbo*, 5 March 1913.

33. Pak notes that *Maeil sinbo*'s concentration on serializing Yi Haejo's works resulted in the author's growing insensitivity to readers' demands for newness, along with readers' waning interest in his conventional plotlines. *Pŏnyŏk kwa pŏnan ŭi sidae*, 120–121.

34. *Maeil sinbo* announced that its sales had reached almost 100,000 subscribers at one point, which seemed exaggerated to an extreme. According to Ham T'aeyŏng's research, it likely maintained about 10,000 subscribers during the 1910s. Ham T'aeyŏng, "1910 nyŏndae *Maeil sinbo* yŏn'gu" (A study of *Maeil sinbo* serial novels), PhD diss., Yonsei University, 2008, 32–34.

35. Shinto shrine is replaced with *sŏnghwangdang*, *koto* with *kŏmun'go*, and some

grounds and characters of original texts into Korean versions, and experimented with syntax that naturalized dialogues.

Besides Cho's translation technique, I believe that the following three factors were behind the popularity of the domestic fiction in *The Daily*. First, main characters in domestic fiction are young men and women who have received Western-inspired education. Their exposure to newly emergent ideas such as free love and marriage by choice appealed to readers not because there was the possibility to attain them, but because they gave moral justification to young people's desire to pursue them. Second, as an extension of the first point, the pleasure of conjugal love portrayed in domestic fiction was a step toward the construction of domestic space, home, as a harmonious unit in society that was in contrast to a space maintained by duty and obligation. Third, the urban setting and the stories of professionals in these works, which included themes of consumerism, might have motivated young people to achieve upward social mobility. One term that encapsulates these factors is individuality; it manifests itself in romance and marriage by choice. Individuality, however, is contested and contrasted in domestic fiction wherein characters struggle hard to succeed against the traditional social order and practices. Home, in this context, is represented as a central location of generational and gender conflicts, which simultaneously sharpens the meaning of individuality in the national/Japanese and colonial/Korean context.

HOME IN MEIJI JAPAN: FOCUSING ON *THE CUCKOO*

In Meiji Japan, home (*katei*) was understood as a living environment for a family rather than a physical building, where a new set of practices—mainly Western-based—on family life was recommended and advertised as a process of reforming society.[36] Although the state was not directly involved in the construction of the new concept of *katei* in Japan,[37] the

---

proverbs are replaced with Korean proverbs that retain the same meanings.

36. See how the concept of home was constructed during the Meiji period through the reformation of the architectural space of the house, family etiquette, and the role of housewives in Jordan Sand, *House and Home in Modern Japan: Architecture, Domestic Space, and Bourgeois Culture, 1880–1930* (Cambridge, MA: Harvard University Asia Center, 2005).

37. Sand argues that the idea of home was rather cobbled together by experts of West-

project of reforming "home" (*kajŏng* in Korean) in Korea became a great concern for the colonial state. *The Daily* promoted the importance of the conjugal relationship (*pubu ŭi kwan'gye*), publishing a series of editorials that emphasized the "respect and love" (*kyŏngae*) between husband and wife. By using a Confucian precept, it argued that the nation could not be regulated if families were not regulated.[38] According to these articles, the "beautiful custom" of respect and love, which had been passed down to Koreans for many generations, was being "deteriorated" by those "morally corrupt" men and women who were not fulfilling their duty of regulating their families. The editor was doubtful about allowing women to divorce and remarry, since he felt that this system was being exploited by the corrupted, thus producing dysfunctional families.[39]

Pointing to women as the cause for the destruction of domestic peace was not uncommon in fiction and the newspaper, making women solely responsible for harmonious homes. A noteworthy point is the restoration of "beautiful traditions" for making a new home. Reforming the home implied the reaffirmation of the traditional division of physical and emotional labor in an elite household. An ideal home—which the newspaper describes by using an example of home in Japan—is one in which husbands, on returning from their full day of work, can find comfort, drinking sake warmed up by their wives while carrying on a friendly conversation together. This image of a middle-class home in Japan was far from realistic for most people in the colonial context.[40] And yet, the new image of home in domestic fiction functioned in two ways in the colony: first as a location of generational and gender conflicts, and second, as a space where gendered roles are performed in the service of the Japanese empire. Home, in this sense, is a symbolic and material site where Japan intervenes to modernize Korean society and transform Koreans into proper imperial subjects.

---

ern domestic practice who disseminated it through popular magazines and other commercial vehicles. Ibid., 54.

38. "Kajok chedo ŭi kaesŏn" (Reforming family system), *Maeil sinbo*, 14 January 1911.

39. "Pubu ŭi kwan'gye" (On conjugal relationship), *Maeil sinbo*, 11 April 1911.

40. *Maeil sinbo* published a series, called *Ilbonin kwa kajŏng* (The Japanese and their home), between 10 and 14 September in 1913, wherein Japanese women are portrayed as diligent, clean, and educated women who serve their husbands well and keep their households in order.

Tokutomi Roka's *The Cuckoo* is an exemplary work where the making of a new home was closely related to the nation-building process in Japan, interweaving Japan's military expansionist endeavor into the story of a newly married couple who remain faithful to each other and to their nation against all odds. The hero, Takeo, is a young naval officer of the Japanese empire, and the heroine, Namiko, is a daughter of a prominent family with a military background. This couple lacks nothing to make an ideal home; both received high levels of education in a modern school system, and yet they are modest, diligent, selfless, and filial, retaining their respect for traditions. Most of all, they are not as shy as their parents' generation in expressing their affection for each other and treating each other with respect. If this happy couple represents what *katei* should be like, Takeo's family stands as *ie*, the traditional notion of home, where duty and obligation are prioritized over love and respect.[41] Takeo's mother, whose dislike of things from the West is represented as a regression, represents a closed state of home that makes no contribution to the nation. The mother demands filial piety and obligation from Takeo and Namiko only to maintain the family line; she is selfish and lacks compassion and understanding both for her children and the nation. Namiko, as a consequence, has a difficult time living with her mother-in-law on account of their differing views on family values and relations.

Takeo's mother stresses his duty to carry on the family line, encouraging her son to divorce Namiko since the disease she carries might be passed on to their children. Upset with his mother's heartless attitude toward Namiko, Takeo challenges his mother, who justifies her position based on the "common custom" that is devoid of "compassion" (*ninjō*) and "loyalty" (*giri*).[42] A more radical expression against the "custom" is Takeo's declaration that he will leave the house. Partially out of anger, and mainly because of the call of duty, Takeo leaves home, participating in the first Sino-Japanese War and in Japan's colonization of Taiwan. During his absence, Namiko passes away. The last part of the novel shows Takeo shedding tears before the grave of Namiko, where he meets his father-in-law, with whom he shared a life-threatening experience during the war. The

---

41. Ken Ito, *An Age of Melodrama*, 71.

42. Section 3 in chapter 6 in the first volume. Tokutomi Roka serialized the novel in *Kokumin shimbun* from 1898–1899. I use an online version based on the book-volume published by Iwanami bunko in 1938.

father-in-law then states that he will always consider Takeo as his son (*yappari anta no oyajija*), showing that even though Takeo has lost his wife, he has found an alternative family and a father who is eager to hear about his recent experience in Japan's newly acquired colony that is Taiwan.[43]

The formation of the father-son relationship between Takeo and Namiko's father indicates that the young man has emerged out of the familial obligation of his *ie* and forms a new familial bond. His bold decision to leave the *ie* behind is based on his love for Namiko, but this passionate act is also infused with his patriotic spirit and comradeship. Both domestic boundary and familial relationship are newly formed as the national territory is expanded. The young man's discovery of an alternative home and family thus implies a deconstruction process of the old world upon which they build a new home constitutive of the Japanese empire.

Of all his translated works, *The Cuckoo* is the only one Cho Chunghwan translated with what modern readers of foreign literature would call fidelity: he transliterated names of characters and geographical locations and did not appropriate the narrative. The work proved its marketability thanks to the appeal of its new expression of conjugal love, which gave Cho an opportunity to pen other works for *The Daily*. But when he began serializing other translations in the newspaper, he appropriated original texts, at times extensively. Though Japanese domestic fiction does not lack moral lessons exhorting young women to be frugal, chaste, and diligent, the Korean versions valorized the moral dimension of the fiction. Almost always, male characters' unbending faith in love "corrects" women's deviant behavior, eventually leading them to return home to assume their role as dedicated mothers and subordinated wives. Descriptions of sexual relations in original texts are either erased or subdued extensively and women's desire for social mobility is denounced.

These appropriated moral attributes are a symbolic gauge that delineates the paradoxical nature of colonial patriarchy. On the one hand, they were aimed at disciplining the colonial society by defining gender boundaries, transforming uncontrollable women to controllable. On the other hand, they display colonized men's desire to have complete control of the domestic realm where their masculinity will not be challenged and where

---

43. Tokutomi Roka, *Hototogisu* (Tokyo: Sinchōsha, 1930), 267.

the domestic boundary also functioned as a symbolic space of cultural identity against the imperial force. In this way, "home" served complex purposes in the colony, wherein the colonialist desire of controlling and the colonized men's nationalistic vision collided. Home in the colony was a contentious field where the politics of love were played hard, something *The Gold Demon* shows best.

CHASTE WOMEN AT HOME IN THE COLONY: FOCUSING ON THE KOREAN TRANSLATION OF *THE GOLD DEMON*

The Gold Demon is based on a work by a popular writer of dime novels in England, Charlotte M. Brame's (1836–1884) *Weaker Than a Woman*. Introduced as "Bertha Clay" in America without her knowledge, Brame's works were wildly popular in America in the last quarter of the nineteenth century.[44] Brame probably could not have imagined what remarkable popularity she would gain in America, Japan, and Korea during and after her lifetime; and yet the global trajectory of her novels indicates that the Victorian romance genre traveled along with capitalist development and imperialist expansion. This does not mean that Victorian romance and its moral attributes were fully accepted and appreciated outside England. The ambitious, bold, and remorseless female protagonist in Brame's *Weaker Than a Woman*[45] was transformed by Ozaki Kōyō, who gave her a deep sense of guilt about her immoral conduct. In the Korean version, her body and morality were disciplined and corrected by young male characters in the name of true love.

Young men's struggles to establish themselves as new patriarchal authorities at home in the new era are more prominent in Ozaki Kōyō's *The Gold Demon*[46] than in *The Cuckoo*. In Japan, the popularity of *The Gold Demon* during and after its serialization in *Yomiuri Newspaper* (*Yomiuri shimbun*) was so remarkable that it went through 189 printings during the Taisho period alone; five stage versions were also launched by 1903, fol-

---

44. Graham Law, "Out of Her Hands: On the Charlotte M. Brame Manuscripts in the O'Neill Collection (MSS 0141)," *Waseda Global Forum* 8 (2011): 110.

45. Ida Yūko, *Karera no monogatari* (Men's stories), Nagoya daigaku shuppankai (Nagoya: Japan, 1998), 35–42.

46. Ozaki Kōyō, *Konjiki yasha* (Tokyo: Kadowaka Shoten, 1971).

lowed by twenty film adaptations produced up until 1954.[47] The Korean version of *The Gold Demon*, entitled *A Dream of Long Suffering* (*Chang-hanmong*, 1913), was also phenomenally popular. First published as a newspaper serialization, it was then published in a volume that went through numerous printings until at least 1956.[48] In 1913 it was staged as a theater production and adapted into films in 1925 and 1965.

In its Japanese original *The Gold Demon* portrays a tragic love story between Kan'ichi, a promising high school student and an orphan, and Miya, the only daughter of a middle-class family. Their romantic relationship develops to the point of each promising to marry the other. However, Miya betrays the promise and marries a wealthy banker instead. The scene introduced at the beginning of this chapter depicts Kan'ichi's response to Miya's betrayal; readers were captivated by Kan'ichi's frank and emotional expression of despair and anger. Kan'ichi is deeply wounded and completely demoralized; as a result, he abandons his education and becomes a moneylender. Interpreting Kan'ichi's career choice as a self-destructive act based on her choice to abandon his love in order to satisfy her material desire, Miya suffers from guilt. She is consumed by remorse and longing for Kan'ichi and seeks his forgiveness. Without Kan'ichi's forgiveness to redeem her conscience and her love, Miya becomes physically and mentally debilitated, eventually reaching a suicidal state. The conflict remains unresolved, and the novel ends with a long letter from Miya to Kan'ichi, expressing her longing for him and her unfulfilled dream of their reconciliation.

Unlike *The Cuckoo*, the hero in *The Gold Demon* has no father figure; the task of building his new home rests solely on his shoulders. The Korean Kan'ichi, Suil, also lacks a father figure, but unlike the original, his dream of reconciliation is fulfilled, thus completing the task of building a harmonious home at the end. There are a number of such changes in the Korean translation. Some significant changes are the happy ending for the couple and the emphasis on female chastity. Whereas Miya has a child

---

47. Ken Ito, *An Age of Melodrama*, 20.

48. The book was published in three volumes. The second volume was printed at least six times and the third volume seven times until the 1930s. Pak Chinyŏng, "'Yi Suil kwa Sim Sunae iyagi' ŭi taejungmunyejŏk sŏngkkyŏk kwa kyebo: *Changhanmong* yŏn'gu" (Characteristics of "Yi Suil and Sim Sunae" and its popularization: A study of *Changhanmong*), *Hyŏndae munhak ŭi yŏn'gu* 23 (May 2004): 234–241.

with her wealthy husband in *The Gold Demon*, the Korean Miya, Sunae, resists having sexual relations with her husband for almost four years after marriage. Sunae is eventually raped by her husband; traumatized by the event, she tries to kill herself, but she does not attempt to challenge her husband's wrongful conduct. Instead, her shame and guilt drive her to madness. This emphasis on female chastity was a distinctive feature of many Korean novels and translations produced in the early 1900s and 1910s, in which female protagonists tried to remain chaste at all costs, signifying loyalty and dedication to their lovers and husbands. With the chaste female body representing the colony and the male aggressor symbolizing Japan's economic exploitation of the colony, Sunae's adamant resistance against her capitalist husband can be read as an allegory for Koreans who refused to succumb to the colonial power, as Karen Thornber points out.[49]

However, the reading of female chastity solely as a national allegory runs the risk of masking the gender hierarchy that was legitimized by male writers in colonial Korea. Colonized men may have become more possessive and controlling of their women due to their reduced authority under the colonial force, and this reduced masculinity becomes the central element in a rape fantasy where men's awareness of their marginalized position and their desire to regain power is released. The loss or reduction of masculinity, however, is never personal but social and ideological.[50] It rationalizes men's desire to bar external powers from penetrating their territory. The rape fantasy is thus a location where the social distinction of gender and sex is embedded, making women an "object of exchange or catalyst for rivalry within male conversation and male power struggles."[51]

---

49. Thornber, *Empire of Texts in Motion*, 171.

50. In her discussion of the theme of rape in twentieth-century European literature, Sharon Stockton argues that the representation of rape is primarily social and masculine, reflecting the self-organizing form of capitalism that "functions without recourse to human agency"—thus making the raped female body a symbol of subordinated and marginalized masculinity. In short, the representation of rape, particularly by male writers, is an indication of men's "lack" or "loss" derived from the capitalist social order. Sharon Stockton, *The Economics of Fantasies: Rape in Twentieth-Century Literature* (Columbus: Ohio State University Press, 2006), 1–25.

51. In her analysis of E.M. Forster's novel, *A Passage to India*, Brenda R. Silver argues that the theme of rape in literature is an "enactment of power" for men. Brenda R. Silver, "Periphrasis, Power, and Rape in *A Passage to India*," in *Rape and Representation*, ed. Lynn A. Higgins and Brenda R. Silver (New York: Columbia University Press, 1991), 124.

The ways in which national culture and identity are expressed articulate the categories of women and men, thus gendering the space of struggle as feminine/domestic and the struggling act as masculine/public.

In the Japanese version, Miya and Kan'ichi never reconcile and the novel ends with Miya's letter to Kan'ichi, in which she recognizes that it is impossible to reverse the situation and seeks Kan'ichi's forgiveness. The ending of the Korean translation, on the other hand, describes Suil's and Sunae's determination to dedicate their lives to socially marginalized people, the poor, and the uneducated, expanding their harmonious relationship from the domestic to the public sphere. Home embodies a psychological dimension of colonized men who seek emotional compensation for their repressed masculinity by displaying their moral superiority and compassion toward women and their community. Sunae's transformation from uncontrollable to controllable is thus imperative for making "a harmonious household" (*tallanhan kajŏng*).

This kind of family–nation association can also be understood as the colonial newspaper's ideological representation of home, wherein private interests and individual happiness are ensured as long as home is at the service of the Japanese empire. However, we cannot rule out the possibility that Korean readers may have perceived the family–nation association differently because the translator Cho himself had intended for the text to be read in the Korean context. In the mid-1930s, he recalled his motive for translating *The Gold Demon*: "I had a hope that I would encourage young men and women in Korea to be spiritually uplifted through *A Dream of Long Suffering*. In order to achieve this, I felt compelled to make the Japanese domestic fiction entirely Korean."[52] He indeed possessed the literary ability to domesticate the original texts so that their contents could appeal to his readers by using cultural familiarities. In light of the depressing colonial environment, he may have tried to create cultural space for the manifestation of collective fantasy and the desire for cultural unity for Korean readers through this story of home and a happy family.

---

52. Cho Chunghwan, "Pŏnyŏk hoego: *Changhanmong* kwa *Ssangongnu*" (Recalling the translation of *The Gold Demon* and *My Crime*), *Samch'ŏlli* 6, no. 9 (1934): 234–236.

Figure 4-1. Yi Suil and Kim Tosik, *Changhanmong*. *Maeil sinbo*, 9 August 1913 (Photo credit: Korea Press Foundation).

THE IMAGE OF YOUNG MALE ELITES IN
A DREAM OF LONG SUFFERING

The fact that the story's central character was a student may have attracted the newly emerging social elites in Korea, where public expectations of the educated were often linked to national progress.[53] In fact, it was hard for public intellectuals, especially learned men, to avoid criticism if they were seen—in the public's eyes, at least—to be engrossed in "personal" interests. Therefore, while obtaining higher learning in Japan was a desirable goal for many young Korean men and women,[54] Suil's determination to become a moneylender symbolizes the moral collapse of a youth who not only abandons his obligation to serve society, but also abandons the educational opportunity that would have ensured his personal growth. The

---

53. Yunsik Kim and Hyŏn Kim, 115.

54. *Tonggyŏng yuhak* (studying in Tokyo) was one of the most frequently used themes in novels written in the early 1900s and 1910s. In those novels, "studying in Japan" often functions as a source of self-advancement and serves as a solution to predicaments faced by the characters.

image of young men obtaining higher education in modern education systems, therefore, is an important condition to establish them as patriarchal authorities at home and in the national community.

Another notable change made in the Korean translation is some characters' occupations, for example, replacing Kan'ichi's employer's educator son, Tadamichi, with a religious figure, Kim Tosik. While Tadamichi is described as a teacher and a scholar in the Japanese version, the Korean version is vague except for one illustration where Kim Tosik appears to be a Catholic priest (Fig 4-1).[55] Although the original Tadamichi represents the spirit of a Confucian samurai, whose indifference to materialism was meant to inspire Japan's social elites to perform benevolent acts for their community, a suitable and native Korean counterpart was not available. The *yangban* were frequently accused of being "uncivilized" and "corrupt" by the government and media; thus the insertion of Christian ethics and Christian figures may have been intended as a critique of the *yangban*. The family head of the home in colonial Korea, in other words, found an alternative ideology to maintain traditional order in the domestic space while acquiring social mobility through modern education.

Christian rhetoric often buttresses the status of young men as new authority figures in *A Dream of Long Suffering*. The Japanese original does not have this Christian element. Suil's schoolfriend Paek in particular exemplifies this point. A man of letters, indifferent to self-advancement, morally superior, and of staunch Christian beliefs, Paek becomes the central voice of paternalism in *A Dream*. When Suil decides to quit the moneylending business, Paek says, "So, you are baptized today. You are renewed" (*puhwal han saram*).[56] Paek continues to deliver this Christian message by persuading Suil to forgive Sunae in the name of Jesus Christ. Indeed, terms such as "baptism" (*serye*), "repentance" (*hoegae*), and "resurrection/renewal" (*puhwal*) appeared frequently in literature from the turn of the century onward.[57]

When Sunae's father seeks Paek's help in persuading Suil to visit his sick daughter, Paek replies with harsh criticism, blaming the father's in-

---

55. *Maeil sinbo*, 9 October 1913.

56. Cho Chunghwan, *Changhanmong*, ed. Pak Chinyŏng (Seoul: Hyŏnsil munhwasa, 2007), 493.

57. Yi Mihyang, *Kŭndae aejŏng sosŏl ŭi yŏn'gu* (A study of modern romance novels) (Seoul: P'urŭn sasang, 2001).

ability to supervise his daughter properly in the first place. Despite the fact that the age difference between Sunae's father and Paek was greater than twenty years, Paek doesn't lower his position in his speech as expected by social norms. Paek's moral superiority and the tolerance of his condescending attitude by his elder signifies the respect given to Korean youths for their higher education; this implies that there is a heavy responsibility assigned to them to contribute their knowledge to the national community rather than pursuing their individualistic desires. That said, although at first sight Paek's stern attitude toward his elder seems to suggest a moral failure of the traditional order, his stress on the importance of women submitting to male members of their family echoes the Confucian notion of women's place in society. This is an example of how the Christian critique of gender equality was reconfigured in a Confucian context through the "evocation of another modern metanarrative: nationalism."[58] In this contradictory fashion, the process of reconfiguring gender equality in Christian rhetoric would continuously be used as a literary device to support the political mandates of Korean nationalists.

Although the colonial government promoted class equality as a part of their assimilation policy, the opportunity to achieve economic success was limited for most young Koreans since their access to educational and economic resources was scarce. Reports of events in the education sector and advertisements that attempted to recruit students for technical schools appeared frequently in *The Daily*, yet these enticing images of the future were less reality and more constructions of colonial control that aimed to mask the predicament faced by the colonized.

Cho likely felt ambivalent about the changing social landscape. As indicated by his statement on his translation policy to "Korean-ize" Japanese fiction, he tried to appeal to his readers by applying domestic cultural sentiments, to *The Gold Demon*, the perception of grief in particular. Besides its historical connection with the love story of the Tang emperor and Yang Gui-fei that was widespread in East Asia through the song *A Song of Long Suffering (Changhan'ga)*,[59] the title of the translation, *Changhanmong*, res-

---

58. Choi Hyaeweol, *Gender and Mission Encounters in Korea: New Women, Old Ways* (Oakland: University of California Press, 2009), 14–15.

59. The literal meaning of *Changhanmong* is "a dream of long suffering," which originated from the famous love story between the Tang emperor Hsüan Tsung (685–762) and his consort Yang Gui-fei (719–756). The tragic conclusion of their love affair and the em-

onates with a sensibility that represents Koreans' collective consciousness. In the original, Kan'ichi expresses his feeling of betrayal and bitterness as *urami*. Although the same Chinese character is used in the Japanese and Korean versions, the meaning of the term is considerably different. The word used for Kan'ichi's feelings toward Miya in the original, *urami*, can be translated as "hatred." However, the term used in the Korean text, *han*, might be better associated with mute grief and suffering. *Han* is deeply embedded in one's personal psychology, and the possibility to resolve it during one's life is slight. Thus Korean ghost stories and traditional fiction, which draw upon the concept of *han*, commonly feature dead souls who creep back into the real world or protagonists who wander the realm of dreams in order to fulfill their desires. Some scholars associate the concept with Korean shamanistic rituals, which seek to pacify the traumatized soul of a deceased person by resolving the deceased's *han* and liberating the soul. Since shamanistic rituals are community-based activities, the religious language of *han* can be conceptualized in terms of the "collective consciousness" or "representations of collectives."[60]

In other words, while grief over death is said to be private and individualistic in Western societies, shamanistic ritual in Korea reflects a collective society in which death is associated with a communal belief system.[61] The inability of the dead to speak in real life carries significance here; their voices are audible to the community through such rituals. *Han*, in other words, was a strategically chosen term that reflected the popular view of suffering. The rewriting of the plot, namely to include the happy

---

peror's longing for his departed lover are portrayed in a long poem, *Changhan'ga* (A song of long suffering), composed by Bai Juyi (772–846). The overall feeling of the poem is thought to be very romantic, and Bai's poetry—*Changhan'ga* in particular—significantly influenced Japanese literature from the Heian period onward. Kondō Haruo, *Chōgonka/ Biwakō no Kenkyū* (A study of *chogōnka* and *biwakō*) (Tokyo: Meiji shōin, 1981), 64–90.

60. According to Jae Hoon Lee, the concept of *han* developed in two streams— *chŏnghan* and *wŏnhan*—in the Korean literary tradition, from premodern folktales to modern literature. While *chŏnghan* signifies a permanent state of depression caused by the loss of the love object, *wŏnhan* calls for revenge. In short, *wŏnhan* and *chŏnghan* can be identified as feelings of love and hate. Lee supports his observation with a limited selection of historical and literary accounts. Because his focus is the popular imagination of *han* in the democratic movement in the 1970s and onward, his analysis lacks historical consistency and continuity. Lee, *The Exploration of the Inner Wounds—Han* (Atlanta, GA: The American Academy of Religion, 1994), 4.

61. John Archer, *The Nature of Grief* (London and New York: Routledge, 1999), 33.

reunion of the lovers, mirrors the dialectic of *han* that was concluded by going through a pathos that would be recognized by Cho's readers, pacifying their repressed psychology under the various social restrictions they faced at the collective level.

Both Sunae and Suil show their grief through shedding tears throughout the story. The source of Sunae's grief is her guilt for betraying her lover, but Suil's grief extends beyond the romantic relationship; his tears express his ultimate hope to regain his patriarchal authority at home, which will extend to his community. In this regard, what appears to be a love story, in fact, narrates multiple social issues that derived from the colonial situation. Inasmuch as home had to be redefined, the meaning of love also had to be translated for the male head of the family.

THE POLITICS OF LOVE IN *A DREAM OF LONG SUFFERING* AND *TEARS OF TWIN JADE*

In *The Gold Demon*, it is self-centered, materialistic desire that initially destroys the lives of the young couple. Miya decides to betray her lover when she sees an opportunity to elevate her status by marrying a rich man. Kan'ichi inflicts pain on himself by entering the moneylending business where he experiences the dark side of human nature. While materialistic pursuits are disdained in *The Gold Demon*, the portrayal of the middle-class lifestyle is not something young Korean readers would have viewed with disdain. In the Korean story, the lifestyles of Kan'ichi/Suil's circle of friends is alluring; by obtaining their education in Japan, they become government officials and lawyers, professions Suil could have achieved had he continued his studies. The signs of material wealth appear in the illustrations in the Korean translation of the fiction as well. Sporting a trendy chignon hairstyle (*hisashigami*) of the period and carrying a parasol, a symbol of wealth, Sunae appears to be a woman following the most current fashions.

The advertisement section of *The Daily* is filled with ads for consumer goods such as Western-style shoes, hats, and parasols that targeted the wealthy former *yangban* and up-and-coming elite classes. While materialistic desire is denounced in Japanese domestic fiction, the availability of luxury consumer goods invites readers to the pleasure of material affluence. In *The Daily*, the moral lesson for Koreans to be frugal and diligent

for national progress appears side by side with the encouragement of consumerism, conveying the ambivalence of the colonial state's policies on
establishing moral order. Furthermore, native writers' participation in
The Daily and their appropriation of Japanese original texts challenge the
notion of the Japanese empire as a fixed totality. The challenge that *The
Daily* faced, in other words, was to "translate" the socioeconomic contexts
of the middle-class home in the Japanese original into Korean contexts in
order to make sense of the moral struggle that young men and women
manifested in their romance.

Yi Haejo dealt with romance in his works, yet the happy pairing of
young couples almost always came as a "reward" for suffering heroines in
his fiction. On the other hand, romance becomes the cause of suffering for
young characters in domestic fiction; it is their encounters with love that
bring them a series of hardships they must overcome. In this regard, love
is a synonym for civilization in these works, since it is a reality that young
people desired to achieve, a condition that guaranteed a happy conjugal
relationship, and by extension, a happy family life. This domestic order
and social reality was manifested in the name of love in *The Daily*'s serial
novels, demonstrating that love was a communicative device that delineated overlapping and contradictory expectations of the modern imagined by the colonial authority and the native writers.

Love (*renai* in Japanese) was a very popular term that captured the
liberal mood of the late Meiji period, and writers emphasized its spiritual
dimension based on their observations of a "civilized West," where men
and women, in their understanding, maintained partnerships based on
equality, freedom, and respect rather than erotic attraction.[62] In Edo literature, the nature of love was expressed with different words such as *iro*
(eros), *koi* (attraction/passion), and *jō* (sentiment/emotion), and yet when
sexual relationships were described, *iro* was most commonly used. In the
late Meiji period the words *ai* and *renai* began to replace *iro* in literature
when referring to a romance between lovers that included, but also went
beyond, the sexual. When the purely spiritual aspect of the relationship

---

62. This clear hierarchy between the physical and the spiritual characterized *katei
shōsetsu*. Saeki Junko, *Renai no kigen* (The origin of love) (Tokyo: Nihon keizai shimbunsha, 2000), 13–17.

was emphasized, originating from the English word "love" (*raabu*), was written in *katakana*.

Why had Japanese culture changed to the extent that a foreign language had to be adopted in order to explain heterosexual love? Noguchi Takehiko explains how the Protestant concept of love influenced Meiji writers in their exploration of heterosexual relations.[63] In Meiji literature, sexual intercourse for the sake of pleasure tended to be downgraded, and the spiritual bond between lovers was emphasized. Some Meiji writers went so far as to denounce *iro* as barbaric or a "lower form of love."[64] Saeki Junko points out that the perception of *iro* in the Edo period was not limited to erotic desire only; it also embodied the feeling of longing. However, during the Meiji period the meaning of *iro* was primarily understood within the context of eroticism. This clear split between physical and spiritual, and the hierarchy given to the two, derived from Meiji intellectuals' observation of a "civilized world"—the West—where men and women, in their understanding, maintained partnerships based on equality, freedom, and respect rather than erotic attraction. Tsubouchi Shōyō's (1859–1935) categorization of love, for example, epitomizes this cultural milieu; he defines the highest form of love as based on the spiritual bond with the partner, while the lowest is based on pure eroticism.[65] While the West became a source of inspiration for Meiji writers in reconceptualizing love, their emphasis on the spiritual dimension of love also reveals a strong sense of fear and despair over the loss of traditional culture. In a number of Meiji romance novels, the confrontation between different generations and individuals is depicted through the polarization of moral sentiments, positing faithfulness and compassion as the antithesis of material desire. In *The Gold Demon*, the male protagonist, Kan'ichi, exemplifies this point when he vilifies the materialism that undermines human feelings.

The equivalent of the Japanese *iro* in Korean, *saek*, generally belongs to the sensual realm, which was seen as "vulgar" in the Chosŏn period. On the other hand, the word *sarang*—which originally meant having someone special in mind over a long period of time—was used to express deep affection for friends, family, and lovers. In Christian circles, it was also used

---

63. Noguchi Takehiko, *Kindai nihon no renai shōsetsu* (Modern Japanese romance novels) (Osaka: Osaka shoseki, 1987), 9–44.

64. Saeki Junko, *Renai no kigen*, 13–17.

65. Ibid., 13–14.

to express divine benevolence—the "love of God"—from the late Chosŏn period on. *Renai* (*yŏnae* in Korean), a neologism of love, would be translated for use in Korea, beginning to appear in the public media and literature from the early 1910s and used interchangeably with the Korean word for love—*sarang*. Since it also connotes courtship that will lead to marriage, before long the term was used in a spiritual context and understood as the fundamental condition for entering into an "ideal marriage."[66]

The imagination of *yŏnae*, however, was highly gendered in Japanese domestic fiction. Women are often represented as ignorant and emotionally vulnerable, prone to losing control over their bodies and minds. They almost always need paternal guidance from their future husbands who will correct their ideas about *yŏnae*. The representation of women's emotional vulnerability is well described in Cho's translation of Kikuchi Yuhŏ's *My Crime*, which Cho titled *Tears of Twin Jade* (*Ssangongnu*, 1912–1913). This is a novel in which the concept of love is quite extensively laid out. *Tears of Twin Jade* deals with a series of tragedies faced by a young woman, Kyŏngja. Kyŏngja's dark fate begins with her desire to pursue free love (*jayu yŏnae*), yet her innocent dream is shattered when her lover deserts her after she becomes pregnant. Realizing that her imagination of *yŏnae* is naive, she laments:

> "When young men and women encounter each other, they experience the wonderful feeling of excitement and deep inspiration. There is nothing unnatural about this kind of emotional reaction because it is such a special thing that does not happen in everyday life." This was what the imaginative Kyŏngja thought about *yŏnae*. Deep in her mind, she truly believes in the sacredness of *yŏnae*. She has never desired to fulfill her sexual desire through a romantic relationship: she just wanted to be a person who can devote her whole being to the sacred *yŏnae*. Although her attitude toward *yŏnae* is pure, her mind is feeble like a wall on sand.[67]

Kyŏngja's sexual encounter is not described at all in the work; it is only suggested by the pregnancy. Her reaction toward the sexual relationship rather describes the act as a mistake. The cost of the mistake is immense.

---

66. Kwŏn Podŭre, *Yŏnae ŭi sidae* (The age of love) (Seoul: Hyŏnsil munhwa yŏn'gu, 2004), 11–18.

67. Cho Chunghwan, *Ssangongnu*, reprint, ed. Pak Chinyŏng (Seoul: Hyŏnsil munhwa, 2007), 27.

She loses her children; her second husband abandons her because of her tainted past; her father kills himself out of shame; and she loses her social connections. Like Sunae in *A Dream of Long Suffering*, Kyŏngja also attempts to kill herself twice, though she fails in both attempts. The guilt and remorse drive her to the abyss of sadness and she can only pull herself out of this hapless state by serving the sick at a hospital as an act of repentance.

The link between women's emotional and mental vulnerability is commonly made in domestic fiction, which culminates in the medical term "hysteria." After Kyŏngja is abandoned by her lover, she is diagnosed with hysteria. In *Tears of Twin Jade*, hysteria is described as an advanced form of depression (*uultchŭng*), which can eventually develop into a mental disease (*chŏngsinppyŏng*). Kyŏngja's physical and mental condition is very similar to that of Sunae in *A Dream of Long Suffering*. In the Japanese original, *The Gold Demon*, Miya suffers from "hysteria" (*hisŭt'eria*[68]), whereas Sunae's condition in *A Dream of Long Suffering* is diagnosed as "acute melancholia" (*kŭpsŏng mellangkollia*).[69] The female protagonists in these works are susceptible to mental illnesses such as hysteria while male protagonists are overtly determined in terms of their belief in moral and ethical principles. Women's suffering is often caused by their greed or misjudgment of men's characters while men's suffering derives from their moral conflict over the failure to protect their women. In both novels, women's crises are resolved through men's acts of forgiveness, though the forgiveness comes only after women demonstrate their repentance in a violent form: attempted suicide. In this regard, women's mental illness such as hysteria was a literary device to inflate the power of forgiveness that brings her back to reality, the patriarchal power that manifests at the expense of female subjectivity.

THE FATE OF BAD WOMEN IN THE COLONY

Ambitious women, regardless of whether they are driven to pursue material wealth or romance, are heavily criticized in domestic fiction, especially when their ambition lacks motherly love, chastity, and a na-

---

68. Ozaki Kōyō, *Konjiki yasha*, reprint (Tokyo: Kadowaka shoten, 1971), 467.
69. Ibid., 472.

tionalistic mindset. They had to be "tamed" by their lovers and husbands, and the Korean version of *The Gold Demon* demonstrates the taming process by putting the female character in danger of death and madness. In the Japanese original, the female protagonist Mitsue, who is Man'gyŏng in the Korean version, is a pursuer of Kan'ichi as well as the mistress of a wealthy moneylender who is forty-something years her senior. Both Japanese and Korean versions describe Mitsue as a wicked woman who has succumbed to the power of gold. She is beautiful, and she knows how to use her beauty for profit. Unlike the main female protagonist Miya who benefits from her middle-class background in addition to her beauty physical charm is Mitsue's only asset, one that possesses a high exchange value in capitalist society.

Mitsue's ambition is quite different from Miya's. She actively participates in her partner's business and becomes economically independent. Unlike Miya, she does not seem to be interested in pursuing a powerful man; instead, she goes after Kan'ichi, who lacks money and power. She tries to seduce Kan'ichi through her physical charms and wealth. Yet Kan'ichi is rather turned off by Mitsue's excessive display of wealth. Looking at her "gold tooth, gold watch, gold ring, gold bracelet, even her gold-colored cigarette papers"—Kan'ichi thinks to himself, "Gold, gold, and more gold."[70] Although he is attracted to Mitsue's beauty, he is reluctant to associate with her precisely because of her obsession with gold, the cause of his pain and suffering. He cannot separate Mitsue's beauty from materialism; her beauty is as dangerous as gold, with its potential to destroy human passion.

Sensing her desire for him, Kan'ichi says,

> First, I am determined that I won't marry for the rest of my life. Perhaps you know this already, but I was a student. I quit school not because I was leading a dissipated life or I failed to pursue it further (...) The profession I am engaged in is the most dishonest business of all. An extremely disappointing event motivated me to enter this business. The feeling was so intense I wanted to kill the enemy and kill myself. I trusted people before that point, but they discarded their morality and broke their promise. In other words, I was completely deceived. (...) In fact, it is money that makes people throw their morality and compassion away, and deceives

---

70. Ozaki Kōyō, *Konjiki yasha*, 131.

an innocent person like myself. I will never forget the feeling of betrayal as long as I live.[71]

On hearing Kan'ichi's emotionally charged confession about his past, Mitsue concludes that his obsession with "morality/moral obligation" (*giri*) and "compassion/sympathy/kindness" (*ninjō*) is a sign of his "narrow-mindedness." Kan'ichi does not know the pleasures of love yet, she thinks, and she is determined to teach him how to enjoy life. Mitsue is well aware of Kan'ichi's distrust of women, but her obsession with him continues to grow regardless. It is not based, however, on her intention to marry him, as he suspects. Rather, she identifies with his pain over engaging in "the most dishonest business." It is his honesty, contrary to his presentation of himself as dishonest, that attracts Mitsue. After all, *giri* and *ninjō* are what Mitsue lacks; pursuing Kan'ichi is, in a way, her attempt to compensate for what she has been missing in her life.

While Mitsue is originally the mistress of a Japanese man, the Korean Mitsue, Ch'oe Man'gyŏng, is coupled with Tchireman, a male foreigner whose nationality is not identifiable. The description of Tchireman focuses on his carnal nature, especially in the way he "tricks" Ch'oe's parents in order to possess the then-sixteen-year-old girl as his mistress. A sense of hostility and fear toward Westerners is expressed in the translator's description of Tchireman as "*sŏyangnom*" (a Western bastard),[72] and the fact that Ch'oe habitually appears in Western dress (*yangbok*). Contrary to Sunae in *A Dream of Long Suffering*, who always wears the traditional Korean *hanbok*, Ch'oe's revealing dress emphasizes her sexual appeal.

In the following illustration from *The Daily* (Fig. 4-3), Ch'oe's directness, which seems associated with the general conception of Western things, is expressed in visual form. For example, her frank expression of erotic desire is enhanced by her clothing and hairstyle. The illustration of Miya and Mitsue from the *Yomiuri shimbun* focuses on the physical struggle of the two women (Fig. 4-2) while the one from *The Daily* differentiates their personality through gestures and attire (Fig. 4-3). Both figures represent the women struggling over a knife with which Ch'oe tries to get Suil to kill Sunae, and after Suil hesitates, Ch'oe tries to kill Sunae herself.

---

71. Ibid., 139.
72. Cho Chunghwan, *Changhanmong*, 113.

Figure 4-2. Mitsue and Miya, *Konjiki yasha, Yomiuri shimbun*, 12 January 1901 (Note: This image was photocopied from the printed version of *Yomiurin shimbun*. Attempts to reach the copyright holder of the image were unsuccessful.)

Figure 4-3. Ch'oe and Sunae, *Changhanmong, Maeil sinbo (The Daily)*, 26 August 1913 (Photo credit: Korea Press Foundation).

Sunae wrestles for the knife and finally thrusts it into her own throat. The dying Sunae then seeks forgiveness from Suil. This incident takes place in Suil's dream, a fact revealed at the end of the chapter. The connection of eroticism to violence conveys Suil's obsession with eternal love, which he has been trying to deny all along.

Cho drew from the Japanese sequel *Konjiki yasha*, written by Kōyō's pupil Oguri Fūyō, especially toward the end of his translation.[73] Whereas Mitsue appears throughout Kōyō's version, in Cho Chunghwan's version there is no further mention of her after Suil's dream scene. There is, however, a description of her corpse. The fate of a woman who lives according to her own will is ultimately tragic. Her frank expression of romantic desire was seen as an act that endangered the moral order of the society.

THE POLITICS OF TEARS OF COLONIZED MEN

Tears were used as an important device that conveyed the humanness of characters. Both Sunae and Suil in *A Dream of Long Suffering* show their grief and suffering by shedding tears throughout the novel. In fact, tears are a key motif that frequently appeared in the domestic fiction genre in early and mid-1910s Korea. Another popular serial novel in *The Daily* was even entitled *Tears* (*Nunmul*, 1913),[74] wherein the excessive feelings of sadness are often displayed by weeping men, women, and even children. However, a clear pattern can be detected in the act of crying men and women: the gendered process in which both men and women are reborn as members of a new family.

The source of female protagonists' grief and tears is their betrayal of lovers or misjudgement of their own feelings, whereas the source of male protagonists' grief and tears derive from their frustration over the inability to protect their women and their struggle to maintain their moral principles. What moves the female characters' minds so that they are "renewed" as good wives is their husbands' unbending faith in love, which is

---

73. Nakagawa Akio, "*Changhanmong* ŭi pŏn'an hyŏngt'ae e taehan chaegŏmt'o" (A reevaluation of the translation of *Konjiki yasha*), *Kugŏ kyoyukhak yŏn'gu* 12 (2001): 454–489.

74. It was written by Yi Sanghyŏp (1893–1957) and serialized in *Maeil sinbo* from 16 July to 25 October in 1913.

expressed in their paternalistic gestures of protection, guidance, and admonition delivered with a display of excessive emotion crystalized in men's tears. The hierarchy at home thus is established through the reconfiguration of men's emotions that become the basis of the patriarchal order.

Like their female counterparts, male protagonists in *A Dream* and *Tears of Twin Jade* are often featured as high school students or professionals who are prepared to achieve upward social mobility. In both cases, women's education allows women to be lured by materiality while men's status will be measured not only by their professions but also by their moral strength. In domestic fiction discussed, female protagonists work as nurses or volunteers at the Salvation Army at a time when the opportunity for women to engage in these modern professions was extremely scarce. Yet their pursuit of a career is not based on ambition, but on guilt; they aim to undo their mistakes by helping others. Furthermore, their final destination and ultimate source of happiness is home, where they faithfully serve their husbands.

Inasmuch as the allure of modernity appealed to the colonized through the emphasis on education, the fear of losing traditional values is communicated in the endings of these novels, in which tears become the sign of moral resistance against the new material reality brought to the colony that suppresses and exploit the colonized. As Haiyan Lee argues in her discussion of the theme of romance in literature during the first half of the twentieth century in China, "Discourses of sentiment are not merely representations or expressions of inner emotions, but articulatory practices that participate in (re)defining the social order and (re)producing forms of self and sociality."[75] This observation can also be applied to the overflow of emotions over romance in domestic fiction in colonial Korea, in which the expression of sentiments is deeply related to the frustrating and unstable social conditions for young colonized men.

The expression of sadness derived from separation, betrayal, and the transience of life in particular has been criticized as a tool for disguising the powerless mental state of the colonized, and thus diluting their nation-

---

75. Haiyan Lee, *Revolution of the Heart: A Genealogy of Love in China, 1900–1930* (Stanford, CA: Stanford University Press, 2007), 8.

alistic sentiments.[76] However, the politics of emotion framed in these translations were products of the translator's negotiation with colonial authority and ideology. He subverted the hegemonic power through the protagonists' moral victory over the "temptation" of material wealth, which would lead to the solidification of the unity between the characters. The expression of sadness, in other words, was a literary device that was to amplify the meaning of unity. Cho Chunghwan's emphasis on unity grows out of Confucian virtues that appear in the garb of Christian and patriarchal rhetoric, which form a moral basis for young Korean men to assume moral authority and leadership in restructuring society. Since the concept of home had to be redefined for colonized men, the meaning of romance also had to be translated in the colonial context, thus Cho's depiction of romance deserves our attention.

Although female protagonists in Cho Chunghwan's translations are punished by moral judgment instead of juridical discipline, it is apparent that women's challenges to the patriarchy are criminalized and women must pay for their crimes with various misfortunes such as suicide, mental illness, and loss of their children. In the selected novels I analyze in the next chapter, crime becomes the main impetus of narratives in which the rationality of law and policing and the emotional justification of patriarchy become questionable. Law cannot protect victims as it does in Yi Injik's and Yi Haejo's works, and men's tears do not hold the power to make women return home as they do in Korean translations of Japanese domestic fiction. Bringing justice to innocent victims is left to men who are either betrayed or highly suspicious of the judicial system in the Korean translations of European crime novels serialized in *The Daily* in the mid 1910s; the discourse of criminality and justice embedded in the novels reveals the ambiguity of colonial modernity.

---

76. Kwŏn Podŭre, *Yŏnae ŭi sidae*.

5

Vengeance Is Mine

Romantic Vision of Mobile Masculinity in Crime Fiction

Writers from the West such as Shakespeare or Tolstoy may have been influential figures in the circle of literary elites in colonial Korea, but writers like Alexandre Dumas and Arthur Conan Doyle were far more popular among readers. Certainly, *A Dream of Long Suffering*, with the changed title *Yi Suil and Sim Sunae*, enjoyed a long period of popularity, but its authorship was not revealed to the public until about two decades ago, whereas Dumas and Conan Doyle have been widely identified as the writers of *The Count of Monte Cristo* and the *Sherlock Homes* series. The delayed identification of *A Dream of Long Suffering*'s author may have to do with the overall tendency to discredit the influence of Japanese literature on the development of Korean literature, despite the fact that readers' knowledge of modern novels was mainly formed through Japanese novels and Japanese translations of Western novels.

The wide recognition of Dumas and Conan Doyle, however, was possible partly due to the colonial government's relaxation of censorship shortly after the March First Movement in 1919, at which time newly established native publishers and translators actively sought ways to reach audiences by introducing works that were deemed to be commercially viable. This period marked the first wave of popularity for crime fiction in colonial Korea. Before the arrival of the bigger wave in the 1930s, Dumas maintained his status as one of the most popular foreign writers since the late 1910s. A translation of Dumas's *Man in the Iron Mask* (*Musoet'al*, 1922), the third part of *Le Vicomte de Bragelonne ou Dix Ans Plus Tard* (1847–1850), for example, was a steady bestseller for a number of years.

153

At the same time native Korean writers such as Yi Kwangsu and Kim Tongin, having returned from their studies in Japan, were publishing their works in vernacular newspapers and magazines. *The Daily* continued to popularize itself by introducing new literary materials to readers, including Western mystery/crime fiction in the mid-1910s that had previously gained significant popularity in Japan between the 1890s and the 1900s. An obvious source for *The Daily*'s selection of literary genres was material that had already been successful in Japan, a safer way to ensure the popularity of an entirely new genre. Considering how stories of crime and vengeance possessed the possibility to challenge the social order, *The Daily*'s new literary endeavor was a bold step. There are, in fact, places in the novels that present the limit of social and political governing, but these are skillfully disguised with a sense of "otherness" that contains little to no traces of colonial Korea at first glance.

However, in the process of *The Daily*'s negotiation of the transnational literary force, alongside the negotiation between the translator and *The Daily* through "Western novels," gender boundaries became more rigid than before. Committing crimes and exercising the power to take vengeance on the enemy were actions solely of male characters, while female characters remained passive and obedient. Women's passivity is highlighted by men's rational thinking process and righteous actions in these novels. Reinforced by their knowledge of science, men could exert their power with their rationality. This enhanced gender boundary surely has to do with the characteristics of the genre, in which "rational, brave and virtuous men" solve crimes.

The Daily's decision to replace Japanese domestic fiction with crime fiction also had to do with readers' diminished enthusiasm for Cho Chunghwan's translations due to the repetitive narrative structure and rhetoric of civilization in his works. *The Daily* halted the serialization of Cho's translation of Watanabe Katei's novel *Maelstrom* (*Uzumaki* in Japanese) at the end of 1915, before it was even completed, due to its rapidly waning popularity.[1] It was around this time that the translator Yi Sanghyŏp (1893–1957) emerged, with his translations of new serial novels in *The Daily*.

---

1. Pak Chinyŏng, *Pŏnyŏk kwa pŏnan ŭi sidae,* 332.

Crime became a dominant theme in novels in the mid-1910s. While translations of works by Dumas and Mary Elizabeth Braddon are significant for their departure from localized contexts—changing foreign backgrounds and customs into Korean versions, for example—they are also marked for their shift in focus from women's to men's stories in which descriptions of home and the domestic order are largely absent. Female characters no longer desire money, careers, or fame in these stories but are passive victims. Romance is relegated to the margin of the narratives in which female characters elicit sympathy for their unbending faith in their male partners. These virtuous women's fidelity and powerlessness are contrasted with male villains' corrupted minds and merciless acts, heightening the need for the sympathetic women to be saved by righteous heroes.

Korean translations of crime fiction in the mid-1910s are about men's rivalries over wealth and fame. Here, men's tears do not function as an important apparatus to establish moral order in the domestic sphere as they did in Cho Chunghwan's translations of Japanese domestic fiction. Men, both villains and heroes, chase and are chased, and their rationality, intelligence, and cold-heartedness over emotion become important conditions for them to achieve their goals. Villains in these works are as mobile as protagonists and their respectable professions (such as medical doctors or public prosecutors) enhance their evil power. Burdened with the task of bringing justice solely on their own without the help of the law and law enforcement, the socially marginalized and wrongfully accused heroes, like the Count of Monte Cristo, maneuver to bring justice for themselves and others through their extraordinary intelligence and resilience.

Unlike the strong presence of Korea in the novels analyzed in previous chapters, Korea remains invisible in these works of crime fiction. The geographical backgrounds and characters are foreign and the only Korean element is the Korean names that are given to the characters. The invisibility of the Korean component in these novels is noteworthy because it projected a colonized man's imagination of mobility beyond the colonized territory; it affirms the otherwise invisible people whose immobility is conditioned by the colonial power. The interplay of the visible and invisible in the Korean translations challenges the inconsistency and contradictions of colonial discourses propagated by the Japanese empire. This is accomplished first by criticizing the hypocrisy of the scientific rationality of modern law imposed on the colonized by Japan in both works; second, by hierarchizing the West and Japan in order to authenticate the cultural superiority of the former; and finally, by reflecting the reduced freedom of the colonized man in *The Count of Monte Cristo.*

The Korean translations of Mary Elizabeth Braddon's (1837–1915) *Diavola*[2] (1866–1867) entitled *A Virtuous Woman's Resentment* (*Chŏngbuwŏn*, 1914–1915), and *The Count of Monte Cristo* (1845–1846) by Alexandre Dumas (1802–1870), entitled *Neptune* (*Haewangsŏng*, 1916–1917), were commonly called detective fiction in colonial Korea, but the role of detectives is insignificant and the translator did not make a genre distinction at the time.[3] Therefore, I generally refer to these works as crime fiction since in them crime takes center stage. These works are based on Kuroiwa Ruikō's intermediary texts,[4] although the Korean translator Yi Sangyŏp did not publicly identify the sources of his intermediary texts. Yi rather emphasized the Western origin of the works, authenticating himself as a translator of Western novels, a strategy that erases the colonial reality to invalidate the colonial rule. With the portrayal of the West in *A Virtuous Woman's Resentment* and the vengeful man and his mobility in China in *Neptune*, Yi demonstrated translation's ability to manifest colonial subjectivity at the expense of female subjectivity.

EUROPEAN CRIME FICTION IN THE COLONIAL CONTEXT

There had been a native literary genre dealing extensively with crime in Korea prior to the 1910s; *songsa sosŏl*, or courtroom narratives, was a genre

---

2. *Diavola,* or *The Woman's Battle,* was serialized in *The London Journal* in 1867 and was retitled *Run to Earth* when published in the United States in 1868. Ian McArthur and Mio Bryce, "Names and Perspectives in *Sute-Obune*: A Meiji-Era Adaptive Translation of the Mary Braddon's Mystery Novel, *Diavola,*" *The International Journal of Humanities* 4, no. 3 (2007): 144.

3. No significant body of Korean translations of detective fiction appeared until the early 1920s, during which time the term began to be popularized.

4. Kuroiwa Ruikō's translation of *Diavola,* entitled *An Abandoned Little Boat* (*Sute obune*), was serialized from 25 October 1894 to 4 July 1895 in *Yorozu chōhō.* His translation of *The Count of Monte Cristo* was published from 18 March 1902 to 14 June 1902 in *Yorozu chōhō* and was entitled *The King of the Cave* (*Gankutsuō*).

that flourished from the late Chosŏn period. Based on folktales and real-life events, that genre is characterized by the role of law and policing interwoven with supernatural events.[5] However, moral precepts and social criticism were more important than the actual process of trials and punishment. Some good examples are beloved Korean folktales such as *A Tale of Two Sisters* (*Changhwa hongnyŏnjŏn*) and *The Tale of Yangban* (*Yangbanjŏn*); the former is a horror/mystery while the latter is a satire, though the role of law enforcers is important in both. Some detective undertakings are made in these novels but they are carried out through the help of supernatural phenomena.

Courtroom narratives hardly influenced the formation of modern crime fiction in Korea, though. It was a series of crime fiction from the West via Japan that formed the first wave of crime fiction in Korea in the mid-1910s. Yi Sanghyŏp began to publish a serial titled, *A Virtuous Woman's Resentment,* starting in October 1914, and readers responded enthusiastically. Yi's works are devoid of didactic rhetoric about civilization, and they minimize the importance of education, frugality, or women's roles in the domestic realm. This largely had to do with the content of the originals, but the works also reveal Yi's attempt to appeal to the readers with newness; that is, the novel of the West where stories are set outside the familiar territory that is Korea.

The translator Yi Sanghyŏp was well informed of the literary scene in Japan, since he had studied at Keio University in Japan from 1909 to 1911. He also had knowledge of French since he was trained in a national French-language institute for five years prior to Japan's annexation of Korea.[6] It is not known whether Yi consulted the French original of *The Count of Monte Cristo* for his translation, but it is apparent that he relied on intermediary texts translated by Kuroiwa Ruikō, who enjoyed phenomenal popularity in 1890s Japan. Yi Sanghyŏp worked exclusively with Ruikō's translations beyond *The Count,* though he altered Ruikō's texts.

---

5. Sin Yŏngju, *Chosŏn sidae songsa sosŏl yŏn'gu* (A study of *songsa sosŏl* in Chosŏn) (Seoul: Sin'gu munhwasa, 2002).

6. The French curriculum in the national French-language institute Hansŏng pŏbŏ hakkyo ran for five years. Yi Sŭnga and No Sangnae, "Pŏnan sosŏl ŭi t'eksŭt'ŭ pyŏnhwa kwajŏng yŏn'gu: Yi Sanghyŏp ŭi *Haewangsŏng* ŭl chungsim ŭro" (A study of textual change process in adapted novels: Focusing on *Neptune* by Yi Sanghyŏp), *Minjok munhwa nonch'ong* 56 (2014): 316–317.

But Yi never gave Ruikō credit. Although he indeed indicated that the novels were "translations" (*pŏnyŏk*), he omitted any acknowledgment of Ruikō in his works. Rather, he introduced the two novels as "a novel (*A Virtuous Woman's Resentment*) written by a British writer that is famous in the West"[7] or "a very famous French novel."[8]

The erasure of Ruikō stemmed from Yi's general ambition to authenticate the Western origins of the novels through his translations, especially *Neptune*. Despite some of the radical changes he made to the original texts, Yi tried hard to convince his readers of the Western origin of his translations. The thrilling events, the catharsis, and the intense feeling of sympathy reflected in the translation of *Diavola*'s, he states, cannot be experienced in any other novels except Western ones.[9] When Yi's translation of *A Virtuous Woman's Resentment* was serialized in *The Daily*, along with illustrations of the story's Western scenes, he kindly offered extra text to explain things about the West with which his readers would not have been familiar. This functioned more or less like a footnote—though the illustrations and notes disappear in his subsequent serial *Neptune*. In addition, the illustrations that accompanied *A Virtuous Woman's Resentment* enhanced the Western flavor by showcasing foreign cityscapes, architecture, and objects along with characters in Western dress, producing an "illusion of direct contact with the foreign," as Heekyoung Cho points out.[10]

The successful construction of the "illusion," however, was not made through a direct translation of the text. In order to enhance the illusion, Yi Sanghyŏp created distance between the original and his translation, making his translation a hybrid. He used pictures of characters with "Western looks" but Korean names who travel from one Western city to another (Fig. 5-1). Yi Sanghyŏp did not create names that were phonetically similar to those in Western fiction. Instead, the names served ideographical purposes (such as naming the female protagonist "virtuous and wise") that first cohere with the title of the fiction, and second, that probably felt more

---

7. Yi Sanghyŏp, "Sinsosŏl yego" (Announcing a new novel), *Maeil sinbo*, 22 October 1914.

8. *Haewangsŏng, Maeil sinbo*, 3 February 1916.

9. Yi Sanghyŏp, "Sinsosŏl yego" (Announcing a new novel), *Maeil sinbo*, 22 October 1914.

10. Heekyoung Cho, "Imagined, Transcultural, and Colonial Spaces in Print: Newspaper Serialization of Translated Novels in Colonial Korea," *East Asian Publishing and Society* 34 (2013): 160.

Figure 5-1. An opening scene from *Chŏngbuwŏn, Maeil sinbo*, 29 October 1914 (Photo credit: Korea Press Foundation).

familiar to his readers. Presumably, Yi's distancing strategy was to narrow the epistemological distance between colonial Korea and the West. The strategy of distancing and narrowing the gap that translators like Yi went through was a complicated process, and no matter how he tried to complete the "radical" task of having his readers experience "the West as it is," Yi could not make a radical departure from previous translation practices. He had to accommodate readers whose familiarity with the text would be established through the use of native names and native sentiments just as was done by his predecessor, Cho Chunghwan.

Nonetheless, the illusion of their radicalness became a significant selling point for Yi Sanghyŏp's translations. Numerous responses from readers appear throughout the serialization.[11] Displayed right below each installment, readers reacted to the authenticity of the novel, expressing thoughts along the lines of "A Virtuous Woman's Resentment is the first case in the literary world in Korea where novels with a Western origin are read like a Western novel."[12] Yi's various statements about his philosophy of "translating Western novels as they are"[13] in fact differentiate him from previous translators for his conscious attempt to remain a translator, not an author. This attitude was perhaps derived from the acknowledgment of the emerging translations of Western novels that were gaining popularity among the educated populace. Established by Ch'oe Namsŏn in 1914, Youth (Ch'ŏngch'un) was one magazine that began to introduce foreign novels penned by literary giants that include Victor Hugo, Ivan Turgenev, Leo Tolstoy, Miguel de Cervantes, and others, though its readership consisted only of a small circle of the educated—especially educated young men. In a sense, The Daily was competing against Youth for the educated and for students by assuming the magazine's role of exposing the colonized to the "superior" forms of culture from the West. The Daily then was in a better position than a single literary magazine like Youth to promote the new literature and the West more widely. This is because its reports on international affairs were an important component for informing readers about the world "out there," as seen in its West-focused editorials around the time of the serialization of A Virtuous Woman's Resentment.

As Ham T'aeyŏng points out in his study of The Daily readership, the timing of The Daily's serialization of A Virtuous Woman's Resentment was

---

11. Readers' responses to social and cultural events began to appear in 1913, and their responses to fiction began to appear with the serialization of Chŏngbuwŏn. Most of these were addressed to the translator, praising his ability to translate the piece and expressing their impressions of the story, characters, events, and so on. See Heekyoung Cho, "Imagined, Transcultural, and Colonial Spaces in Print," for a detailed analysis of readers' responses to A Virtuous Woman's Resentment.

12. A note from a reader, "Chŏngbuwŏn ŭl pogo" (On A Virtuous Woman's Resentment), Maeil sinbo, 22 April 1915.

13. Yi Sanghyŏp, "Kŭnkŭn yŏnjae hal kŭkhi chami innŭn sinsosŏl" (On the upcoming of an extremely entertaining new novel), Maeil sinbo, 25 October 1914.

the newspaper's attempt to appeal to a new set of readers with "genuinely Western novels" as Yi Sanghyŏp advocated.[14] In fact, the kind of readers who identified themselves in *The Daily*'s "Reader's Column" in the mid-1910s were mostly students,[15] whose avid reading of fiction was a sign of their growing curiosity about Western culture. These "students" were likely high school students, since there were no colleges or universities in colonial Korea at that time. Available records show that the number of female students was extremely small compared to male students during the entire colonial period.[16] By the mid-1920s there were only about 2,800 female high school students,[17] and the illiteracy rate among women remained high at around 93 percent by 1920.[18] Even though the newspaper promoted the importance of equal education as seen in the previous chapter, these figures show that the main readership may well have been male students and adults.

A majority of the readers who sent responses to *The Daily* in fact appear to be males. They also seem moved by Yi Sanghyŏp's focus on men's intelligence and the spiritual resilience that young Korean men must possess. One male reader, for example, addresses his fellow male readers as "*sanai*," a term that is often associated with militaristic masculinity, and encourages them to be as courageous and faithful as the protagonist in *A Virtuous Woman's Resentment*.[19] A number of male readers expressed much sympathy for the protagonist's innocence (*kyŏlbaek*), fidelity (*chijo*), and elegant beauty (*kosang*). The repetitive praise in these responses of the female protagonist's feminine qualities is then contrasted with the male

14. Ham T'aeyŏng, "1910 nyŏndae *Maeil sinbo* sosŏl yŏn'gu" (A study of serial novels in 1910s *Maeil sinbo*)," PhD diss., Yonsei University, 2009, 176–179.

15. Ibid., 190–199.

16. By 1918, there were: 454 ordinary (elementary) schools established by the colonial government, whose pupils totaled 88,000, 15 percent of whom were female; 26 private ordinary schools with 555 females out of a total of 2,830 students; and 24,000 traditional private academies (*sŏdang*), which included 3,504 females out of 1,148,516 students. Patricia Tsurumi, "Colonial Education in Korea and Taiwan," in *Japanese Colonial Empire 1895–1945*, ed. Ramon H. Myers and Mark R. Peattie (Princeton, NJ: Princeton University Press, 1984), 299.

17. Based on the statistics published in the women's journal *Sinyŏsŏng*, January 1925. cited in Mun Okp'yo et al., *Sinyŏsŏng* (New women) (Seoul: 2003), 90.

18. Yoo, *The Politics of Gender in Colonial Korea*, 71.

19. Mun Chŏngho, "*Chŏngbuwŏn* ŭl pogo" (On *A Virtuous Woman's Resentment*), *Maeil sinbo*, 2 May 1915.

villains' manipulative actions; thus the paper continuously depicts the idea of womanhood that is devoid of economic and social independence. The literary magazine *Youth* did not give significant consideration to female readership either. Founded and operated by male writers and translators, *Youth* concentrated on reproducing the image of wise mothers and good wives while promoting male leadership as a way to civilize Korea.[20] In short, it is likely that the target readers of *The Daily*'s serialized crime fiction were young men who would in this way be repeatedly exposed to this gendered vision of civilization through their reading practice.

The Daily began to allocate considerable space to reporting on World War I starting in early August 1914. Reports of the war appeared frequently, along with relevant photographs, maps, illustrations of warfronts, and war technologies (Fig. 5-2). Yi Sanghyŏp in turn associated his novels with the war, advocating learning about the West through war and through his writing.[21] The content of his translations, however, was far from warfare itself; rather, they were stories about individuals who sought justice for themselves. Nonetheless, the reports on the war were significant enough to direct the readers' interest toward the West. Their exposure to Western stories of revenge, however personal, expanded their imagination of a world beyond the Korean peninsula.

In these novels, the absence of Korea served Yi Sanghyŏp better than simply encouraging his readers to immerse themselves in Western culture. Yi's persistent rhetoric about "knowing the West through novels" seems to address the colonial reality by borrowing Western examples, questioning Japan as the agent of modernity. While the notion of the West as the source of modernity is hinted at, the colonized desire for modernity places Japan at a lower cultural power level than the West. The Chinese settings in *Neptune* may be considered a retreat from this, but Yi had taken a more radical step toward the criticism of colonialism through *Neptune* without making any direct reference to colonial Korea. Both *The Daily*

---

20. Chŏn Ŭn'gyŏng, "1910 nyŏndae chisigin chaptchi wa 'yŏsŏng': *Hakchikwang* kwa *Ch'ŏngch'un* ŭl chungsim ŭro" (Women and magazines established by male intellectuals in the 1910s: Focusing on *Hakchikwang* and *Youth*), *Ŏmunhak* 93 (2006): 499–530.

21. Yi Sanghyŏp, "Kŭmil put'ŏ keje toenŭn *Chŏngbuwŏn* e taehayŏ" (On *A Virtuous Woman's Resentment* that is serialized from today), *Maeil sinbo*, 29 October 1914.

Figure 5-2. Introducing a Krupp cannon. "The Business of the Cannon Queen," *Maeil sinbo*, 29 November 1914 (Photo credit: Korea Press Foundation).

and Yi emphasized the French origin of the novel,[22] but the geographical and historical proximity of the setting—turn-of-the-nineteenth-century China—to colonial Korea was an intriguing strategy to mirror Korea's geopolitical reality. Yi's technique of spatializing—the expansion and contraction of Korea's distance from the Japanese empire—resulted in the realistic rendering of the paradox of the modernity in the colonial space.

Some argue that Yi Sanghyŏp's privileged position as one of the major contributors to the newspaper proves him a collaborator.[23] However, like Ruikō, Yi seems to have been conscious of social justice, and his con-

22. "Yŏnjae yego" (Announcement of a new serial novel), *Maeil sinbo*, 3 February 1916.

23. Chŏn Ŭn'gyŏng, "1910 nyŏndae Yi Sanghyŏp sosŏl kwa singminjibae tamnon: *Maeil sinbo* dokjawa ŭi sanggwanssŏng ŭl cungsimŭro" (Colonial discourses in Yi Sanghyŏp's

sciousness manifested clearly in his active engagement in newspaper journalism while colonial rule was relatively relaxed from the early 1920s. He was one of the critical voices in Korean journalism in the 1920s: he reported the massacre of Koreans during the Kanto earthquake in Japan, and he was imprisoned and fined for his newspapers' accusations about the unfairness and brutality of the Japanese colonial police.[24] The selected novels translated by Yi Sanghyŏp emphasize the cultural superiority of Japan at times, but the overall content of his works reflects critical views on Korea's situation in light of Europe and China. Yi's criticism of the Japanese empire was expressed in his alteration of Ruikō's works where he implicitly denies Japan as the agent of modernity in his description of law. Although there is no direct criticism or mockery of law and policing in the translations, it is evident that the heroine in *A Virtuous Woman's Resentment* and the hero in *Neptune* are thrown into a lawless world. They free themselves by circumventing the law, a powerful criticism of the Japanese colonialist discourses of justice and criminality.

The manifestation of colonial subjectivity in these works leads us to see the complexity of cultural production that suggests the masculine sense of rivalry over modernity. By turning the original context on its head, Yi Sanghyŏp's translation alluded to the frustrated masculinity of colonized men whose imagination of mobility and freedom was to be fulfilled by stories of perfect revenge, like *Neptune* and the rescue of a damsel in distress in *A Virtuous Woman's Resentment*—stories that defy the convention of law and policing as a marker of modernity.

THE STORIES OF SUFFERING HEROES AND HEROINES IN THE LAWLESS WORLD

Mary Elizabeth Braddon was a popular novelist and the female characters in her novels have strong personalities; for example, the diabolical woman Audley in one of her most well-known works, *Lady Audley's Secret* (1862).

novels in the 1910s: Focusing on the relationship between *Maeil sinbo* and its readership), *Hyŏndae sosŏl yŏn'gu* 25 (2005): 394.

24. Chŏng Chinsŏk, *Kŭkppi Chosŏn ch'ongdokbu ŭi ŏllon kŏmnyŏl kwa t'anap* (Top secrets of the governor general of Korea's censorship and suppression of press in Colonial Korea) (Seoul: Communication Books, 2008), 123–130.

Pure-hearted and resilient women are rewarded with happiness at the end for their endurance of misfortunes, such as the protagonist Jenny in *Diavola*. Jenny is a gifted singer and an orphan who runs away from her foster father's home on witnessing his murder of a sea captain. She then comes under the guardianship of a baron, Sir Oswald Eversleigh, who marries her but soon abandons the pregnant Jenny after a false accusation of infidelity by his nephew. The accusation was part of the nephew's scheme to become the baron's sole heir. When her husband is ultimately murdered by his nephew and Jenny is left with no adequate material resources, she supports herself and her daughter through her singing career. The nephew, with a medical doctor friend, commits a series of crimes even after the baron's death, and through the help of detectives that Jenny encounters coincidently, the villains' crimes are revealed. At the end, she reunites with her biological father, an Italian nobleman, and concentrates on advancing her singing career in Italy and England.

The Count of Monte Cristo was one of the most popular novels by Alexandre Dumas, and it was serialized in *Journal des débats* in 1844. Like his other novels, *The Count* is an adventure story in which the protagonist, Edmond Dantès, brings justice to those who wronged him. In *The Count*, Dantès is a Spanish sailor who is about to marry his fiancée, Mercédès, when he is falsely accused of treason and arrested. He is imprisoned in Château d'If for fourteen years, during which time his father dies of starvation and his fiancée marries his friend who in fact was the one who had set him up out of jealousy. Dantès escapes from the prison, and with financial resources and intellectual guidance provided by his fellow prisoner, a highly educated Italian named Abbé Faria, he carries out his revenge on those who destroyed his future and family.

Both Jenny and Dantès are uprooted from their homes by evil forces, the former by a kidnapper and the latter by his coworkers and a public prosecutor. However, they receive moral and material support from the alternative families they meet on the way, a husband and a mentor, respectively. In Jenny's case, her husband is more than a partner. He also nourishes Jenny's gift by providing the means for her to build her musical career. Jenny's continuous efforts to build her singing career will eventually make her financially independent, which is especially important after she is left penniless following her husband's murder. The independent figure of Jenny disappears in both the Japanese and Korean translations, in which her happiness is found within a family. Similar to the way the baron becomes a father figure for Jenny in *Diavola*, the Italian Abbé Faria is an important figure for Dantès, educating Dantès on various subjects and transferring his accumulated wisdom to his disciple. The world the protagonists venture into is devoid of familiarity and their alternative fathers are crucial for their survival and spiritual growth.

Although both protagonists are strong-willed and independent in the originals, Japanese and Korean translations reduced the female protagonist's agency. As examined in the previous chapter in the examination of Japanese domestic fiction, the late Meiji government was deeply concerned over descriptions of women who pursue individualistic interests over familial duty in fiction works. By the late 1890s, around the time when Ruikō was concentrating on his translations of crime fiction, the Meiji government stressed educating women to become wise mothers and good wives to the extent that it designed a curriculum for women's higher education to serve this ideological purpose. Ruikō's omission of the protagonist's independence may have reflected the social milieu, but another possible explanation for this omission is his emphasis on justice that manifests in the form of "rewarding" the victimized protagonist with domestic peace. In the Korean translation, the suffering protagonist serves a purpose that cannot be explained by the ideology of wise mothers and good wives alone. Making the suffering women safely return home reflects colonized male writers' anxiety over the control of the domestic sphere. The obsession with bringing a woman home, so evident in this particular translation, also speaks to this anxiety, although the translator of *Diavola*, Yi Sanghyŏp, differs from previous writers and translators for his criticism of the Japanese colonial state's exploitation of the colonized in the altered figure of the protagonist.

Ruikō, who has been primarily identified as a translator of French and English detective fiction in Japan and Korea, was a political activist before he undertook his career as a newspaper journalist and translator. He had two ambitions in translating crime fiction: to educate the general populace about democratic principles and to criticize the Meiji government's legal system.[25] Ruikō was deeply concerned about the fairness of the court

---

25. Sari Kawana, *Murder Most Modern: Detective Fiction and Japanese Culture* (Minneapolis: University of Minnesota Press, 2008), 8.

system in particular, which, in his view, did not meet the Western standard that he felt the Meiji government should emulate.[26] These aims resulted in alterations of original texts such as adding didactic prefaces, addressing the readers directly, emphasizing the role of law, and so on, while leaving the original geographical background and the overall plot intact.[27]

The legal system of Meiji Japan became the model for colonial Korea's legal system, which was established in 1912, and was worse than the "unfair" system Ruikō had criticized. The Ordinance of Criminal Action in Korea (*Chosŏn hyŏnsaryŏng*), for example, grants prosecutors the authority to investigate as well as prosecute, and to imprison a person under suspicion even when he or she is not caught in the act.[28] The unconditional authority given to prosecutors emblematizes the violence of an empire that justifies its abuse of the colonized in the name of scientific rationality.

In the Korean versions of these texts, law enforcement significantly contributed to the characters' displacements. When Jenny, or Chŏnghye in the Korean version, is arrested after she is falsely accused of the attempted murder of her husband, the trial process is described as unfair, with the prosecutor's treatment of the accused during the interrogation process described as "illicit."[29] The translator, Yi Sanghyŏp, adds that such a process is a thing of the past "unlike trials done [fairly] now,"[30] a line that can only be described as wry humor considering the colonial situation. In *Neptune*, the Chinese Dantès, Chunbong, is accused but never tried by a public prosecutor Yang (M. de Villefort in the French original), defying the law and the role of law enforcers. When Chunbong, now under his false identity as the Count of Neptune, hears the prosecutor Yang advocating the merit of law, he responds, "I am not subject to the law of just one country called China. My law is the law of the world. I can, for example,

---

26. Satoru Saito, *Detective Fiction and the Rise of the Japanese Novel, 1880–1930* (Cambridge, MA: Harvard University Asia Center, 2012), 73.

27. Mark Silver, *Purloined Letter: Cultural Borrowing and Japanese Crime Literature, 1868–1937* (Honolulu: University of Hawai'i Press, 2008), 62 and 66.

28. Clause 1 and 2 in Article 12, Ordinance of Criminal Action in Korea. Korea Ministry of Government Legislation. Accessed on 16 May 2016, http://www.law.go.kr/lsInfoP.do?lsiSeq=67431#AJAX

29. Yi Sanghyŏp, *Chŏngbuwŏn II*, ed. Pak Chinyŏng (Seoul: Hyŏnsil munhwa, 2007), 36.

30. Ibid.

punish the bad and reward the good if I want to regardless of their countries of origin, and this is the way to follow the law of God."[31]

For Yi Sanghyŏp, this statement about law functions as more than a criticism of a society ruled by the corrupt. It was also intended to reveal the colonial reality that severely limited the freedom of the colonized in the translator's re-creation of Dantès and the people around him. The backdrop of the original *The Count* is Spain and Dantès's fiancée is from the then-Spanish-ruled Catalonia; Dantès's mute servant Ali is Nubian; his father starves to death due to poverty. These characters, including Dantès himself, are socially vulnerable and have limited means to fight injustice. Dantès's close relationship with these figures challenges the exploitative nature of imperialism. He detests the society that fails to protect the powerless, stating, "I never seek to protect society which does not protect me, and concerns itself with my affairs only to injure me; in this way giving them a low place in my esteem, and preserving a neutrality toward them, it is society and my neighbor who are indebted to me."[32] In Yi's translation, Chunbong develops close relationships with marginalized individuals such as the abandoned son of the prosecutor Yang, the colonized, slaves, and a failed revolutionist, all of whom come from diverse national backgrounds. These individuals are unable to escape their unfortunate situations on their own and the law cannot save them; rather, it only injures them further.

Yi Sanghyŏp followed the overall plot of Ruikō's work faithfully,[33] but presented characters that implicitly reflect the colonial situation. One good example is the replacement of Abbé Faria with the Indian Buddhist priest called Tara, who was involved in the support for India's independence and is imprisoned for his association with "revolutionists" in China.[34] Although *Neptune* describes Tara as a failed revolutionist but an out-

---

31. Yi Sanghyŏp, *Haewangsŏng*, vol. II, ed. Pak Chinyŏng (Seoul: Hyŏnsil munhwa, 2007), 146.

32. Alexandre Dumas, *The Count of Monte Cristo*, translation revised by Peter Washington; Introduction by Umberto Eco (New York: Alfred A. Knopf, 2009), 441.

33. The background of Ruikō's translation adheres to Dumas's original, but he changed the names of characters into Japanese equivalents. Kuroiwa Ruikō, *Gankutsuō* (The king of the cave), in *Kuroiwa Ruikō zenshū* vols. 1 and 2 (Tokyo: Haru shobō, [1901–1902)] 2006).

34. The "revolutionists" implicitly indicate those who were in support of Sun Yat-sen (1866–1925). Yi Sanghyŏp, *Haewangsŏng*, vol. I, 134.

standing human being who possesses courage, intelligence, and patience, the priest is destined to be forgotten by the world and to die in the prison. It is Dumas's Dantès alone who can bring himself out of the pit of despair and take revenge on those who wronged him. Dantès's kingdom is "bounded only by the world"; he is "neither an Italian nor a Frenchman, nor a Hindu, nor an American, nor a Spaniard" but a "cosmopolitan."[35] He "adopt[s] all customs, speak[s] all languages ... therefore, that being of no country, asking no protection from any government, acknowledging no man as my brother, not one of the scruples that restrain the powerful, or the obstacles which paralyze the weak, paralyze or restrain me ... I wish to be Providence myself, for I feel that the finest, noblest, most sublime thing in the world, is to recompense and punish." [36]

In the Korean translation, Chunbong claims that he exists outside the convention of national boundaries. He is not "British or French, and not Korean or Japanese,"[37] but a man who is free to take whatever identity he wishes and be wherever he wishes to be. Chunbong can speak about Korea by identifying himself as a cosmopolitan (*segye ŭi saram*) who carries out the law of providence without being bound to legality and nationality. The true figure of the colonized is perpetually missing in Yi Sanghyŏp's translation, but it is through the state of absence that he speaks about justice on behalf of the colonized Koreans.

CRIMINALITY AND GENDER IN
A VIRTUOUS WOMAN'S RESENTMENT AND *NEPTUNE*

The validity of the civilizing process through the intervention of law enforcement was presented by Yi Injik and Yi Haejo earlier, but the criminality described in their works was related to domestic problems; they focused on crimes committed within the family. However, in *A Virtuous Woman's Resentment* and *Neptune*, the criminals and victims are not related to each other by blood. Protagonists in these works are uprooted from their close-knit port communities and are placed in urban settings that are alien to them, places in which the force of civilization becomes

---

35. Dumas, *The Count of Monte Cristo*, 535.
36. Ibid., 537.
37. Yi Sanghyŏp, *Haewangsŏng*, vol. II, 141.

ambiguous. Blind faith in civilization is absent in these works. Doubts about the civilizing force are expressed in these translations through the altered portrayal of female figures such as Chŏnghye in *A Virtuous Woman's Resentment* and the princess of Vietnam in *Neptune*, Kyŏngnang (Haydée in the French original), who is enslaved as a consequence of the colonization of Vietnam by the French.

The masculine force of civilization poses a danger of colonizing the vulnerable, who are feminized through their portrayal as female characters. In the works that I analyzed in the previous two chapters, female protagonists' exposure to foreign lands were described positively, representing their mobilization from domestic to foreign environments as a step toward civilization. However, the portrayal of the global cities, to which the protagonists are exposed, is ambivalent in these translations. The cosmopolitan lifestyle of people in high society and the highly industrialized urban landscape are alluring, but danger is lurking in the shadows of the glamorous cityscape. Cities are dangerous places, especially for women like Jenny in *Diavola* who is exposed to constant threats from criminals unknown to her. The Japanese and the Korean translations of *Diavola* emphasized the vulnerability of the protagonist in contrast to the plotting and pursuit among male criminals and heroes.

Cities such as London, Paris, Shanghai, and Beijing become the central background of *A Virtuous Woman's Resentment* and *Neptune*; they are places where both criminals and protagonists can easily fake and alter their identities. In the originals, both Jenny and Dantès change their names a number of times in various urban settings, and both the Japanese and Korean translations altered the names according to the translators' need to stress the victimization of women. As Ian McArthur and Mio Bryce note, the Japanese translation of *Diavola*, entitled *Abandoned Small Boat (Sute obune)*, changed the image of a strong-willed adult woman, Jenny, to underline the vulnerable young girl's recovery of her identity and reconciliation with her long-lost father through altering her names in Japanese.[38] If Ruikō altered the title and names in order to create sympathy for the protagonist, the Korean translator Yi Sanghyŏp emphasized Confucian female virtues in *A Virtuous Woman's Resentment*. Unlike the original and the Japanese translation, Yi consistently refers to

---

38. McArthur and Bryce, "Names and Perspectives in *Sute-Obune*," 141–151.

the protagonist as Chŏnghye, altering her last name only once when she runs away from her foster father. Her fidelity, frugality, and modesty are represented with a name that literally means "virtuous and wise," strongly reflecting the ideology of good wives and wise mothers.

Perhaps because of this danger, women in these two novels do not build social relationships outside their comfort zones. Their passivity in dealing with others is contrasted with the male characters' active collaboration with other men. The three main villains in *A Virtuous Woman's Resentment*, namely the baron's nephew, the nephew's doctor friend, and the kidnapper, maintain a relationship based on merit; they share the goal of stealing the baron's wealth. Chunbong in *Neptune* also develops numerous relationships with male characters, including enemies and their family members. In both works, the friendship among men is questionable, demonstrating how men's interest in personal wealth and status can nullify friendship and collaboration among them. The three villains in *A Virtuous Woman's Resentment* and Chunbong's enemies in *Neptune* fall because of their rivalry. The world where villains and heroes live is devoid of intimacy and compassion, a cold place where friendship holds no value; instead, masculine rivalry determines the direction of their fate.

Intimacy among characters is instead found in extremely challenging situations such as Chunbong's encounter with the Buddhist priest Tara in prison and Chŏnghye's encounter with her future husband on a dark street in London where she was singing to make a living. These encounters are outside the capitalist machine, which is also the machine of crime, and completely indifferent to social relations and human emotion. In this sense Chŏnghye's artistic ability and her noble manner stand as qualities that challenge the capitalist force, and that enable characters like her to maintain their integrity even in a time of extreme poverty.[39] Likewise, Chunbong's filial piety and loyalty to his father and former employer are powerful weapons with which to fight villains. The villains that the heroine and the hero face, however, cannot be defeated by moral superiority and virtues alone. Chŏnghye's talent must be nourished by her husband's material support, and both this support and the treasures Chunbong in-

---

39. Kwŏn Yongsŏn, "Pŏnyŏk kwa pŏnan sai hogŭn iyagi esŏ sosŏllo kanŭn kil: Yi Sanghyŏp ŭi *Chŏngbuwŏn* ŭl chungsim ŭro" (The gap between translation and adaptation or the way from storytelling to novel—Focusing on Yi Sanghyŏp's *A Virtuous Woman's Resentment*), *Han'guk kŭndae munhak yŏn'gu* 5, no. 1 (2004): 157.

herites from the Buddhist priest play decisive roles in making these characters independent and mobile. It takes a "superman" like Dantès in *The Count*, to borrow Umberto Eco's words,[40] to defeat the evil force of capitalism that produces villains. Now armed with intelligence, spiritual resilience, and an enormous fortune, the Chinese Dantès, Chunbong, can manifest his omnipotence and crush the machine of crime.

Intelligence like Chunbong's is not a result of education. If Yi Injik, Yi Haejo, and Cho Chunghwan criticized the uncivilized condition of Korea through their positive description of education, *A Virtuous Woman's Resentment* and *Neptune* reverse the civilization discourse: those who are educated, such as medical doctors, lawyers, and government officials, are the criminals. These professionals were introduced as agents of civilization in *The Daily*, but their corrupted morality, greed, and desire for material accumulation and social success are criticized in the two novels. This changed identity of criminals is rebellious in the colonial context, as it shows how the colonialist rhetoric of education can easily be overturned by these educated elites' criminal acts. In *A Virtuous Woman's Resentment* the most fearful character is a medical doctor, a friend of the main villain who uses his knowledge of medicine to murder Chŏnghye's husband (Fig. 5-3). The use of poison is more than the unethical conduct of the professional; it symbolizes the production of evils out of the "good system" that supposedly ensures social progress.

Two other notable villainous characters in *Neptune* are the public prosecutor Yang and the military general Yangun (Fernand in the original) who use their privileged positions to victimize the hero. These two men are opportunists whose drive for power and wealth drives them to sacrifice even their own kin. Their madness for power is contrasted with the Indian Buddhist priest who is crazy in the eyes of the prison guards but completely normal in the eyes of his fellow inmate Chunbong. This contrasting image of madness is ingenious for its depiction of the villains' abuse of knowledge for evil deeds and the priest's use of knowledge to bring justice to the marginalized. The distinction between normal and abnormal is reversed in the prison, where true knowledge is imprisoned by the corrupt. As Amelita Marinetti argues, Faria's role in Dumas's original is crucial for turning Dantès into a new man, and the knowledge, wisdom, and wealth transferred to Dantès from Faria will play a decisive

---

40. Umberto Eco, "Introduction," in Dumas, *The Count of Monte Cristo*, xiv.

Figure 5-3. Two villains in a medicine lab, *Chŏngbuwŏn, Maeil sinbo*, 26 November 1914 (Photo credit: Korea Press Foundation).

role in correcting injustice.[41] In *Neptune* the priest Tara's teaching of humanity through his attempts to bring justice to the colonized Indians is emphasized, and his knowledge and wisdom are materialized in a book he wrote entitled *A Theory of Revolution in India and China*. This is the most important treasure Chunbong inherits from the priest, a treasure written in a solitary confinement cell, containing the priest's aim to overturn the world full of madness.

AN ANTI-IMPERIALIST, THE COUNT OF NEPTUNE IN CHINA

The original text of *The Count*, as well as Ruikō's translation, begins with the appearance of Edmond Dantès, a fisherman who is tasked with delivering a

---

41. Amelita Marinetti, "Death, Resurrection, and Fall in Dumas's *Comte de Monte-Cristo*," *The French Review* 50, no. 2 (1976): 264.

letter from Napoleon to the Bonaparte faction in Paris without knowledge of the contents of the letter. This happens ten days before Napoleon escapes from the Island of Elba and the ensuing military campaigns of the Hundred Days in 1815. If Dumas's *The Count* reflected his generation's witnessing of the "fallen and resurrected in the person of Napoleon"[42] in the figure of Dantès, it may not be a coincidence that the historical background of the translation is the first Sino-Japanese War, one of the major historical moments that altered the geopolitical position of Korea. The war was an opportunity and a means for Japan to display its imperial power to the world while it enhanced Japan's penetration of imperial power into the Korean peninsula.

The translation is set in 1894 and begins when a Shanghai fisherman, Chunbong, delivers a letter from Hawai'i to Beijing written by the nationalist revolutionary Sun Yat-sen (1866–1925) who was then in political exile in Hawai'i. The letter is supposed to reach the Revolution Party of China (*Hyŏkmyŏngdang* in Korean). This is likely a fictitious name for the Revive China Society founded by Sun who was an inspiring figure for Korean nationalist intellectuals at the turn of the century for his leadership of political reforms in China.[43] Yi Sanghyŏp's radical appropriation of this historical background speaks to the significance of the changes made in China, which would transform from a feudal to a modern state. The Qing dynasty would be defeated by Japan in the first Sino-Japanese War (1894–1895), and the dynasty would be overthrown by revolutionaries in 1911, during what is now referred to as the Xinhai Revolution. However, the war was also fought in the Korean peninsula, giving Japan the power to intervene in Korean politics and economy. In the Korean translation, Chunbong is imprisoned during the fourteen years when Korea was under Japan's imperial power (from 1894 to 1908).

Yi also uses spatial references to revolution in his version. Shanghai and Beijing are the two most prominent cities in *Neptune*; Shanghai is the main setting in the first quarter of the text while the rest takes place in

---

42. Ibid., 266.

43. Sun's political vision is said to have inspired some high-profile Korean nationalists, such as Kim Kyusik, Sin Kyusik, and Kim P'ilsun, with some like Sin Kyusik even participating in the Xinhai Revolution. The revolution was thus a stimulus for Korean nationalists to organize and reshape their anticolonial activities, and Shanghai was a temporary haven for many Korean nationalists after Japan's annexation of Korea.

Beijing. While Beijing is portrayed as a place where tension between various political factions erupts continuously before the revolution, Shanghai is portrayed as a city with a strong foreign presence. In the original, Dantès's Catalonian fiancée, Mercédès, lives on the margins of French society. In *Neptune*, Chunbong's fiancée Sukchŏng lives close to Shanghai's French residential area. The significance of Shanghai, however, goes beyond the marginalization of the native Shanghainese due to the European hegemony in China. It is in Shanghai that Chunbong's fellow prisoner, the priest Tara, tries to strengthen India's relationship with China in his effort to bring independence to his country. Shanghai, together with Hong Kong, was in fact at the forefront of the organization and preparation of an Indian nationalist group, the Ghadar Party, in its resistance against Britain in the mid-1910s. Although the Ghadar Party members historically only consisted of Sikhs, Hindus, and Muslims, the Buddhist character in *Neptune* was meant to familiarize the Indian context for Koreans—and, more importantly, to parallel the Indian struggle to gain independence from the British with the Korean struggle to be free from Japanese colonial rule.[44]

The featuring of this Indian presence also seems inseparable from the political significance of Rabindranath Tagore's status at the time. Tagore was the first Asian to receive the Nobel Prize in Literature in 1913, and he was invited to Japan in 1916, since the Japanese saw him as a representative of "Asian spirituality." Tagore's internationally recognized status was connected with the Japanese media's promotion of pan-Asian unity at the time of his visit. He was an inspiring figure for the colonized through his poetry on hope and freedom. Thus the Indian presence in *Neptune* is ambivalent. On the one hand, the connection between the Chinese revolution and the Indian effort to gain independence can be viewed within the purview of Japan's effort to project the pan-Asian idea. On the other hand, *Neptune*'s frequent use of the term "revolution" (*hyŏkmyŏng*) evokes a potent imagination of independence in the minds of Korean readers.

Yangun (Fernand in the original), one of Chunbong's enemies, is another character that plays a role in revealing the colonial situation of Korea in terms of his presence in the Korean peninsula and Vietnam. In the

---

44. Many prominent Indian revolutionaries, such as Mathra Singh Chima (1883–1917), for example, participated in the Chinese Revolution, and they used Shanghai as an important base for organizing the party's activities. B.R. Deepak, "Revolutionary Activities of the Ghadar Party in China," *China Report* 35, no. 4 (1999): 440.

French original, Fernand, a French military officer, is dispatched to a small kingdom in Greece called Janina where he plots treason. He deceives the royal family of Janina and turns them into slaves in order to steal the family's wealth without being revealed to the French authorities. In *Neptune*, Yangun is sent to Vietnam as a Chinese soldier during the Sino-French conflict (1884–1885), but he betrays Vietnam by helping the French in order to steal the royal family's wealth. Later he is sent to Korea during the first Sino-Japanese War (1894–1895) and this time he helps the Japanese for his own personal gain while sacrificing his fellow Chinese soldiers. These two events, through which Yangun shows his selfishness, go beyond personal greed by causing loss to China and Chinese soldiers. They are a metaphor of the rise of Japan as a new global hegemony in East Asia by contrasting the positions of China and Japan: Japan's victory in the first Sino-Japanese War confirmed China as a fallen empire and Japan as a rising new empire.

However, Yi's attitude toward China in *Neptune* is ambivalent. While the power difference between China and Japan is delineated through the description of the war, Yi describes Chunbong, who fashions a Japanese identity for himself as "the marquis Tojin" (Lord Wilmore in the original) after his escape from prison, as "so proud of being Japanese to the point of arrogance … [the marquis] finds fault in every affair China does while showing blind support for Japan."[45] Further, unlike the French original text, where King Louis XVIII is portrayed negatively, incompetent and detached from the running of the country, Yi's portrayal of the head of state, the Empress Dowager Cixi in *Neptune*, is positive. The empress dowager, despite the country's internal disorder and external pressures around the time of the war, does not lose her cool-headedness. She remains calm, unlike Louis XVIII who runs about in confusion during the period of the Hundred Days. She also pays close attention to international relations of the time, including the urgent situation faced by her neighboring country, Korea. Korea is not mentioned by name, but considering the context of the war, it is obvious that the empress is refering to Korea. These portrayals of China and Japan cannot be separated from the unfortunate Indian priest Tara's involvement in the independence movement since these figures are products of imperialism.

---

45. Yi Sanghyŏp, *Haewangsŏng*, vol. II, 311.

Yi Sanghyŏp's anti-imperial stance becomes bolder in his insertion of the Vietnam situation, which he does by mentioning Liang Qichao's writing on the French colonization of Vietnam, *The History of the Fall of Vietnam* (*Wŏlnammangguksa*), published in 1905. A Korean translation of *The History of the Fall of Vietnam* was avidly read by Korean reformers at the turn of the century. Although the book was banned in Korea by the time of Yi's translation of *The Count*, Yi reminds his readers of how the unfortunate fate of Vietnam as described in Liang's book evoked sympathy among Chinese at the time of its publication. This section is unique to Yi's translation; his description of "sympathy" means more than the way it is contextualized on the surface. It is in fact a way of identifying with Koreans whose fate is similar to that of the Vietnamese, evoking emotional responses among Korean readers and allowing them to draw connections between the situation in Vietnam and the political predicament in Korea. Chunbong's protection of the Vietnamese princess who lost her family and kingdom is symbolic. The feminine position of Vietnam is identified with the position of Korea; powerless and enslaved, she has no ability to take revenge on her enemy except by relying on her hero, Chunbong, and his material wealth and mobility. As the portrayal of China and its empress dowager, the Indian priest, and the Vietnamese princess indicate, what appears to be a story of personal revenge against villains, as Pak Chinyŏng rightly notes, exposes the exploitive nature of imperialism.[46] It is Chunbong alone who can redress the injustice with his near-omniscient abilities.

THE FUTURE OF VENGEFUL MASCULINITY

Unlike Braddon's *Diavola*, the heroine in *A Virtuous Woman's Resentment* eventually returns home safely to her husband and unites with her father. Bringing suffering women home is not something new; there is a pervasive association of women with domesticity and reproduction in all the novels that I have analyzed to this point. What becomes increasingly palpable, however, is male anxiety over the control of domestic order and social mobility. As objects of blame for the uncivilized state of the nation, men

---

46. Pak Chinyŏng, *Pŏnyŏk kwa pŏnan ŭi sidae*, 412.

manifest their desire to gain controlling power. This masculine imagination powerfully reveals the dark side of modernity in crime fiction that questions the uneven relationship between the colony and the metropole.

The hero's act of perfect revenge in *Neptune* in particular challenges the exploitative nature of colonialism. The hero perfectly masters economic and social institutions and structures of the colonizer in order to expose the hypocritical nature of colonial logic. It must be noted that the mastering process and the act of revenge cannot be carried out with the hero's real name; he operates in the shadow of the supposedly rational world that, in fact, is dimmer than a shadow itself. Crime fiction such as *The Count of Monte Cristo* enable the translator to express the mastering process in the interplay of the real and the fictional, the visible and the invisible, the familiar and the unfamiliar, the possible and the impossible, all of which articulated the reality of the colonized under the colonial capitalist force.

Dantès in *The Count* is a mythical figure who can reverse abusive power relations. He is reborn in Yi Sanghyŏp's translation as an allegorical figure whose omnipotent ability speaks to the intense anxiety of the colonized standing before the colossal force of colonialism. Chunbong, in *Neptune,* is a hero who embodies such anxiety; he can never exist in reality but serves as a figure of hope. The ending of *Neptune* reflects Yi's hope for the future, however faint or uncertain that hope was. The subheading of the final chapter is "A Covert Future" (*Ŭnyŏnhan twit kiyak*) in Yi's translation, whereas Ruikō entitled it "The Finale" (*Daidanen* in Japanese). This ending is based on the French original, which shows a letter left by the hero for a young couple, Maximilien Morrel and Valentine De Villefort, whom he had come to love for their honesty and passion for life. Dantès's letter reads:

> There is neither happiness nor misery in the world; there is only the comparison of one state with another, nothing more. He who has felt the deepest grief is best able to experience supreme happiness. We must have felt what it is to die, Morrel, before we can appreciate the enjoyments of life.
>
> Live, then, and be happy, beloved children of my heart, and never forget, that until the day when God reveals the future to man, all human wisdom is contained in these two words, "Wait and hope."[47]

---

47. Dumas, *The Count of Monte Cristo*, 1178.

The letter is translated faithfully by Ruikō and Yi.[48] Yi, however, added a line that raises the question of his motivation in making the finale open-ended: "The count hinted his promise to return. Then where would he reappear again? As the count says, perhaps this translator"—referring to Yi Sanghyŏp himself—"may have to quietly wait and anticipate the future."[49] The fact that Chunbong "left for the East" (*tongbang*), which is not in the Japanese text, supports the conclusion that Chunbong is in fact an embodiment of hope for the colonized.

As the serialization of *Neptune* was ending, a new rising literary star, Yi Kwangsu, began to fascinate his readers with his first creative novel, *The Heartless* (1917), which was serialized in *The Daily*. Yi Injik and Yi Haejo had published creative novels prior to *The Heartless*, but the reappearance of a novel written by a native creative writer such as Yi Kwangsu signified a new chapter in the history of Korean literature, as shown through the embodiment of the complexity of human emotion, a stream of consciousness, and the problematization of capitalism in *The Heartless*, all of which meet the conditions of what is called modern novels. However, it is questionable whether *The Heartless* was conceived as something entirely new at the time. For one thing, the protagonist's conflict with the past and anxiety for the future, as well as the story of the troubled love triangle between a young man and two women in Yi Kwangsu's novel, were not alien to his readers who had experience with the novel genre in *The Daily*.

More important, however, modern novelists such as Yi Kwangsu, regardless of their direct exposure to Western and Japanese literature through education in Japan, would continually embody the ambiguity of nation and modernity through a hierarchy of gender relations, giving not only authoritarian but also spiritual voice to male protagonists who are morally and intellectually burdened with the development of national culture, as is strongly reflected in *The Heartless*. When the colonial state relaxed its colonial rule by allowing Koreans to establish political, social, and cultural organizations and to publish vernacular newspapers and magazines shortly after the March First Movement, young male intellectuals led the native culture industry with their intent to dedicate their

---

48. The letter is abbreviated in the Japanese and the Korean translations, which omitted the mention of the Christian notions of God and Satan. Also, the last two words of the count, "wait and hope," were altered to "wait with joy" in both translations.

49. Pak Chinyŏng, *Haewangsŏng*, vol. III, 395.

knowledge and talents to developing the nation. These educated young intellectuals, especially writers such as Yi Kwangsu, did not shy away from expressing their burden toward developing a national culture, a burden that they often authenticated by assuming their patriarchal position in the society. Patriarchal nationalism would thus persist for the rest of the colonial period: the attitude of male writers toward women, especially educated women, became increasingly dominating, consistently barring female writers from the literary scene. The emergence of Yi Kwangsu then indicates "the beginning" of modern literature in Korea and confirms the formation of the gendered institution called modern Korean literature.

Epilogue

The Fiction of Nation, Gender, and Modernity

> After finishing a lecture at his fourth-year English class at 2 o'clock in the afternoon, Hyŏngsik, an English teacher at Kyŏngsŏng School, walks toward the elder Kim's house in Andong while sweating heavily under the scorching June sun. He is invited as an English tutor for Kim's elder daughter Sŏnhyŏng and set to give her a one-hour lesson each day at 3 o'clock starting today so that she can be prepared for studying abroad [*yuhak*] in America next year.[1]

THE ABOVE LINES ARE FROM THE OPENING SCENE of *The Heartless*, the "first" modern Korean novel, written by Yi Kwangsu. The serialization of *The Heartless* began on January 1, 1917, in *The Daily*, while the serialization of *Neptune*, the Korean translation of *The Count of Monte Cristo*, was nearing its conclusion in the same newspaper. Instead of using foreign characters, the protagonist in this translation is Hyŏngsik, an educated, but poor young Korean man living in Korea. It is noteworthy that Hyŏngsik's knowledge of English is the "ticket" for him to enter the wealthy elder Kim's house, who has plans to have Hyŏngsik as his son-in-law and send him, along with his intended wife, Sŏnhyŏng, to America. Hyŏngsik and Sŏnhyŏng would ultimately travel to Chicago to further their education, intending to return to Korea and dedicate their lives to civilizing their society.

The imagination of social mobility with a heavy dose of "free love" (*jayu yŏnae*), one of the main themes in *The Heartless*, in fact was nothing new to readers. They were already familiar with these themes through novels such as *A Dream of Long Suffering*. However, *The Daily* attempted to target a different readership with *The Heartless*: young elites and students rather than general readership. *The Daily*'s strategy turned out to be

---

1. Yi Kwangsu, *Mujŏng, Maeil sinbo*, 1 January 1917.

a great success. Writing from the center of the Japanese empire, Tokyo, the appearance of the twenty-five-year-old young Korean author as a rising literary star was inspiring to Korean readers, and the book's message of self-advancement and dedication to "society" (*sahoe*), a term that more or less meant the Korean nation for Yi,[2] was well-received.

Yi's geographical position and his status as a college student demonstrated a new possibility of transnational mobility that the Japanese empire could offer. This new possibility manifests in the novel's use of language, such as the reference to English and Japanese and the idea of free love that was none other than an imagination of individuality. Yi's appearance was a turning point in the development of the novel genre not just because of the "traits" of modern novels such as subjectivity that have been discussed so much, but also because of the very space where it emerged: *The Daily*, where differing interests and literary influences collided and had been negotiated since its inception. *The Heartless* has been discussed innumerable times since the colonial period as the beginning of the modern novel, thus I would like to limit my discussion to two points: first, the intricate relationship between the newspaper and transnational literary contacts on the development of the Korean modern novel; and second, the gendered imagination of nation and modernity that is one of the most distinctive characteristics of the novel.

Characters in *Neptune* as serialized in *The Daily* supposedly speak different languages, though their dialogue is written in Korean. However, despite the fact that it is set in colonial Korea, transliterations of English appear frequently in *The Heartless*. What is more significant is the transliteration of Japanese, which hardly appeared in novels prior to *The Heartless*. At times transliterations of English and Japanese words and phrases appear in a single sentence, especially in dialogues between educated young men. Reflecting Yi Kwangsu's brief career as a teacher at a high school after his return from his first sojourn in Japan from 1910 to 1913, the protagonist also studied in Japan before becoming an English teacher. In short, in the novel Japanese is presented as a living language for educated men such as Hyŏngsik, while English is a language that will open another

2. Kim Hyŏnju, "Singminjiesŏ ŭi 'sahoe' wa 'sahoejŏk' konggongsŏng ŭi kwejok: 1910 nyŏndae *Maeil sinbo* esŏ Yi kwangsu ŭi sahoe tamnon ŭi ŭimi" (The trajectory of "society" and "social" publicness in the colony: The meaning of Yi Kwangsu's discourse on society in *Maeil sinbo* in the 1910s), *Han'guk munhwa yŏn'guso* 38 (2010): 221–261.

door of opportunity for him to further his career. The reference to English and Japanese functions as an epistemological ground to link the colony with the metropole, and it also confirms how *The Daily* played a crucial role for writers to negotiate foreign literary forces.

The Daily was more than a space to publish fiction works; it was a space for writers and translators to appropriate their linguistic familiarity and literary sensibility in order to communicate with their fellow Koreans. By the late 1910s, native writers "framed the novel in Japanese but had to write it in Korean," as Kim Tongin described the writing of his first novel, *The Sorrow of the Weak* (*Yakk'an ja ŭi sŭlp'ŭm*), in 1919. This involved the translation of the overall content of a novel as well as the translation from Japanese, the writers' literary language. In fact, while in Japan Yi Kwangsu and Kim Tongin both produced their first short stories in Japanese prior to their production of novels. Yi in particular transliterated all the Chinese characters in his original manuscript of *The Heartless* into Korean for the serialization of his novel in *The Daily*. We must recall that in their works, writers in the previous decade had to "translate" their written language from the Chinese script to Korean vernacular. Like Yi and Kim, these writers also faced the linguistic dilemma of changing their linguistic life as a way of establishing the nation since the Chinese script remains their everyday language as far as their writing was concerned. This translation process, of course, signifies more than the ways in which writers and translators dealt with the linguistic dilemma; it also demonstrates how they negotiated foreign literary forces in order to communicate with readers. Within little more than ten years, the so-called modern Korean novel was formed "between empires," to borrow Andre Schmid's expression, but also "across empires" in terms of Korean writers' and translators' negotiation of transnational literary forces.

The historical consciousness of national identity and modernity was a driving force behind the formation of the new novel genre. However, it is equally important to point out how gender became an ideological anchor for the manifestation of the imaginations of nation and modernity. For many native writers, the sense of anxiety from being caught between the anticipation for and the instability of the future is persistently reflected in novels, the increasingly suppressive process of colonization often led them to express their anxiety through assigning symbolic powers to male characters, arming them with modern knowledge and superior morality. On the other hand, male writers' handling of female characters, as signs of the past or the future, exposed their fear of the loss of control over material and spiritual resources to external forces. The themes of rape and suicide attempts are the two most distinctive literary conventions that represent this fear. Rape functions as a symbolic act that signifies the victimization of the Korean nation and society while a suicide attempt is often a catalyst for a spiritual renewal or the severance from the past for members of Korean society.

The representation of gender in novels thus should be seen as a contested field of ideologies, where differing political visions of society and culture collided and converged; and where gender hegemony was produced and circulated. Although the coupling of women and domesticity reflects cultural practices shaped by the neo-Confucian view of gender roles, a close examination of the emphasis on female domesticity during the period of my investigation reveals issues that cannot be explained by existing traditions alone. Rather, the construction of gender during this time was a product of political hegemony that differentiated men from women as a way of sustaining colonial, national, and patriarchal interests. Gender, in other words, was an epistemological ground on which native writers and translators negotiated with the colonial force in their descriptions of gender roles, hierarchy, and domesticity. In this book I have sought to comprehend the power relations underlying the construction of gender in the novel genre that was enthusiastically adopted and explored at the time.

While the attempt to keep women at home as wise mothers and good wives is persistent in the works that are examined in this book, there is an increasing sense of anxiety and ambiguity in speaking about nation and modernity in the early colonial period that manifests in the works' emphasis on patriarchal authority. Inasmuch as the desire for progress is strong in these works, writers' and translators' awareness of the uneven relationship between the colony and the metropole is revealed in their alterations of stories and characters from original texts. While Cho Chunghwan reveals the ambiguity of colonial capitalism through his male protagonists' oscillation between money and love—and by extension, between the capitalist force and the traditional world order—Yi Sanghyŏp took a bolder step toward criticizing the uneven relationship by challenging the judicial system and injustice of the Japanese empire. Translation became a strategic tool for these two translators in confronting their frustration with the colonial reality, as manifested in their male protagonists' strong desire to bring order to domesticity and redress injustice. As these works demonstrate, the historical conditions in Korea directed the development of the novel genre in which gender was the most important component in making sense of nation and modernity under colonial rule, an effect that would continuously appear in novels in the following decades.

Literature was redefined in both Japan and Korea around the turn of the century, when the influence of Western material—European romanticism in particular—led to a general recognition of literature as an autonomous form of art. At that time, the so-called Realist school, with the Japanese author of *The Gold Demon* (*Konjiki yasha*), Ozaki Kōyō, at its center,[3] lost its dominant status. Instead, the Naturalist school[4] became the mainstream in seeking "to know the 'Truth' of human life," as a response to "the demands of an intellectual age that would consider and critique the substance of life."[5] The Naturalist school's emphasis on "intellect," "feelings," and "inner reality" over "objective reality" resulted in the rejection of popular (*taishū*) literature's ability to critique that "substance." Thus, writers such as Ozaki Kōyō as well as readers—women in particular—became objects of criticism. Romance fiction was denigrated as a less refined form of literature that merely entertained the masses rather than helping them contemplate the meaning of life.

It is noteworthy that Naturalist writers were especially contemptuous of female writers; they perceived literature to be "men's career," and presented it as "pure" (*junsui*) as opposed to "popular." In other words, the new group of male writers authenticated the new mode of literary expression by avoiding popular literature, simultaneously buttressing their authority by placing women's works below theirs. Young Korean male writers were greatly inspired by Japanese literature at the time as they often

---

3. "Realist" writers sought ways to express their life experiences and criticize the collapse of morality that seriously constrained human relations, as shown in Kōyō's *Konjiki yasha*.

4. The Naturalist school in Japan was influenced by the French Naturalist school, which is characterized by its attempt to scrutinize social reality "scientifically." In Japan, however, characters reject the philistine world to examine the self rather than external reality. Yukiko Tanaka, *Women Writers of Meiji and Taishō Japan* (Jefferson, NC: McFarland and Company, Inc., 2000), 110–111.

5. Shirayanagi Shū ko, cited in Sadami Suzuki, *The Concept of "Literature" in Japan*, trans. Royall Tyler (Kyoto: Nichibunken, 2006), 207.

obtained higher education in Japan. One of the most influential figures leading modern Korean literature is Yi Kwangsu, whose literary sensibility was shaped in Japan. Shortly after a new generation of Korean writers returned to Korea, the literary scene changed: they would contribute to the divide between popular literature and artistic literature, "educating" readers on what modern novels were like in contrast to the popular novels they had been reading. *The Heartless* is on the front line of the division between "pure" and "popular" novels, as well as the novel's readership into "educated elites" and "ordinary people." In addition, these new writers' assertion of male authority in the literary world was layered with the complexity of producing literary works in the colonial situation, in which their expression of patriarchal nationalism became more prominent than it had been with the previous generation of writers and translators.

About one and a half months before he began to serialize *The Heartless*, Yi Kwangsu published an essay in the same newspaper, entitled "What Is Literature?" (*Munhak iran hao*) that in a nutshell discusses the relationship between literature and history. In it, he argues that literature determines the fate of a nation since it is the source of nourishment for people's thoughts and emotions, which in turn will lead the nation to accumulate and develop its "spiritual civilization." Yi tried to authenticate the spiritual value of literature by looking to Western civilization, viewing the European Renaissance in particular as the source of "today's science and civilization," for it "nurtured the freedom of thought."[6] His introduction to the history of the West since the Renaissance is written in a brisk manner with an oversimplified judgment about its "freedom," which, he argues, the Sinocentric world lacked.[7] There is no sense of respect or nostalgia about things from the past in this essay, in which Yi blatantly denies the cultural values of premodern Korean literature. In so doing, Yi negates Korean history altogether since, in his view, it had not developed independently from Chinese influences.

Yi's emphasis on "freedom of thought," as cultivated in the West directs us to see how the paradox of modernity and nation continuously underpinned works produced by native writers and translators through-

---

6. Yi Kwangsu, "What Is Literature?" (*Munhak iran hao*). Originally published in *Maeil sinbo*, 10–23 November 1916, trans. Jooyeon Rhee in *Azalea: Journal of Korean Literature and Culture* 4 (2011): 290.

7. Ibid., 298.

out the colonial period. For one thing, thinking freely about modernity and nation was not necessarily translated into freely *expressing* one's thoughts about them; and for another, the placing of national history outside of the Sinocentric world was possible only in rhetoric. Inasmuch as the denial of the past was evident in novels, the desire to maintain and restore certain parts of the past was also manifest in male writers' and translators' reconstructions of women in their works.

Yi Kwangsu's novel, *The Heartless*, thus is significant first because of its representation of the paradox of nation and modernity in colonial Korea in gendered terms, and second, because it confirms men's authority in leading the "cultural civilization" more firmly than any other works produced prior to it. In *The Heartless*, the male protagonist, similar to other male protagonists in romance fiction and crime fiction, has no family members. He alone suffers the burden for the historical progress of the nation, which manifests in his oscillation between individualistic desire and moral duty. The way Yi Kwangsu negotiates the paradox is by reconstructing the past; the male protagonist is detached from the past by being an orphan while female protagonists are renewed through education. In this novel, the split of the modern self in a colonial situation is vividly illustrated in the moral suffering of the male protagonist who must negotiate between the future and the past. The generation of writers from the late 1910s, such as Yi Kwangsu, was predominantly male, just like the previous generation of writers and translators I have examined, and their vision of Korea's future grew increasingly patriarchal.

The rhetoric of women's education consistently appears in works in the 1910s, just as it was promoted by the nationalist writers and translators shortly before Korea was colonized. However, the rhetoric was rationalized by placing women on the fringe of history in order to authenticate the male-led historical development. The novel in turn attributed patriarchal nationalism to this hegemonizing through reconfiguring ideal men and women in a modern nation that had yet to come. The hegemonizing process cannot be separated from the masculine force of colonialism that persistently and systematically propagated the image of a modernized future Korea, often juxtaposed with the backward past as represented in the feminine position of the present Korea. In this historical context, the novel genre served the purpose of manifesting ideological visions of national community in which gender played a crucial role, allowing native writers and translators to articulate the ambivalence of narrating about the nation in the absence of the very nation itself. In the midst of the clash between these two historical forces, nationalism and colonialism, however, women were doubly marginalized beyond the fictional space.

Korean students studying in Japan were exposed to the relatively liberal mood of Taisho democracy. Since, economically speaking, they were better positioned than most Koreans living in the peninsula, and they had greater access to various forms of cultural activities. Those who were interested in literature began to form literary circles in which to exchange their ideas and publish their works through their own journals. Socializing with fellow Korean students was also essential for those young students who were given many opportunities to mix with the opposite sex in literary functions. And yet, there was a general tendency for female students to rely on male students' financial and intellectual support for their literary activities. This power hierarchy would become even more salient once they returned to Korea.

The March First Movement in 1919 changed the cultural landscape of colonial Korea dramatically. The mass-scale movement alarmed the governor general of Korea who shifted the emphasis of colonial policy from military to cultural affairs, relaxing a series of restrictions and regulations concerning the media.[8] As a consequence, Korean-language newspapers and magazines began to appear from 1920 on. These print media became a channel for nationalist groups to disseminate a set of programs—educational, national consciousness-raising, capitalist, and social revolutionary[9]—in order to achieve Korea's independence. As Michael Robinson observes, the overall agenda of independence was carried out with a consensus

---

8. The governor general of Korea tolerated "moderate publications," though any publication that threatened the public order, such as those promoting socialist ideas, became an object of strict censorship. Michael E. Robinson, "Colonial Publication Policy and the Korean Nationalist Movement," in *The Japanese Colonial Empire 1910–1945*, ed. Ramon H. Myers and Mark R. Peattie (Princeton, NJ: Princeton University Press, 1987), 342.

9. There were generally two factions in the nationalist movement. The moderate nationalist group concentrated on education, national consciousness-raising, and capitalist development as a way of obtaining independence on a gradual basis while the radical group called for immediate action by stressing social revolutionary thought. Michael E. Robinson, *Cultural Nationalism in Colonial Korea, 1920–1925* (Seattle: University of Washington Press, 1988), 5.

that various programs must be utilized "in the service of remodeling Korean society,"[10] which more or less meant Western-style "moderniza-tion." Young Korean male elites played a crucial role in this movement in the cultural sector. However, their attitude toward gender was conserva-tive, advocating for women to become wise mothers and good wives for national progress. A small coterie of educated young women, in turn, started challenging the "wise mothers and good wives" ideology for its unrealistic expectations that failed to accommodate actual socioeconomic conditions.[11]

Male Korean intellectuals viewed Western European and American societies as ideal models for national development and they emphasized women's education as an important condition for bringing about women's liberation.[12] Overall, there was a broad consensus among Korean elites that the cause for the underdeveloped state of Korean society and discrim-ination against women was the intellectual gap between the West and Korea. The emphasis on Western knowledge as a way to narrow the gap, however, saw a paradoxical gender asymmetry: women's voices were often pushed to the periphery of the cultural sphere by educated men who justi-fied their paternalistic attitude toward women by exhibiting their intel-lectual authority. Yi Kwangsu is a good example. As a leader of the cultural nationalist movement, he was adamant about educating women to become good mothers.[13] Yi added that women must cultivate their artistic sense, exercise to improve their physical condition, pay attention to hygiene, and most of all provide "spiritual support" for their husbands. In short, male intellectuals in the 1920s confirmed that women's motherhood and sub-missiveness were conditions for national growth. This attitude toward women's liberation is reflected in their novels, in which learned women's demands for gender equality are ridiculed and criticized as individualistic and selfish acts that are differentiated from male intellectuals' heavy bur-den of national progress.

Present studies of Korean history and culture have attempted to show that readings of the colonial experience of Koreans must go beyond the

---

10. Ibid., 58.
11. Yoo, *The Politics of Gender in Colonial Korea*, 81.
12. "Chosŏn yŏja haebang kwan," *Kaebyŏk*, vol. 4 (April 1920), 33.
13. Yi Kwangsu, *Sinyŏsŏng*, January 1925, 19–20.

binary of coercion and resistance. These scholars find that colonialism, and the subsequent process of modernization, provided the conditions for Koreans to negotiate with, reconstruct, and modify their cultural identities, creating multiple alternatives through their acquisition and exploration of new technologies such as radio and cinema.[14] I find this approach useful for the reading of representations from multiple perspectives, and yet I would like to emphasize that these conditions must be carefully examined since they did not necessarily provide equal opportunity for men and women in their experiencing of the alternatives.

As many scholars have pointed out, the colonial history of Korea has been written from a nation-focused framework since the liberation (1945), with a tendency to look at its colonial history as a history of the anticolonial struggle of *minjok*—a hegemonic notion of nationhood that is dismissive of people's experience of capitalist modernity and nationhood itself, which was heterogeneous.[15] Furthermore, the anticolonial critique of colonial history cannot be completed without examining Japan's influence on Korean historiography.[16] Even before Korea was annexed, nationalists' writings on Korean history show that they were already sharing ideas about capitalist modernity similar to those of the Japanese, confirming the deep dilemma of contemporary Korean historians who try to separate nationalist thought from colonial thought.[17]

The troubling boundary between "originality" and "imitation" became more salient in Korea in the debate about the "authenticity of native culture" against the widespread American-inspired commodity culture in the 1920s, during which many nationalists tried to redefine "Korean spirit" to aggrandize nationalism. While the dual capacity of a society's ability to adapt to capitalist modernity and its strong desire to maintain "cultural authenticity" is not an unfamiliar mode of nationalism in other societies,[18] what is noteworthy in this case is the realm of representation

---

14. Equating colonialism as the beginning of the modernizing process in Korea, scholars tried to show the multiplicity of modern experiences of Koreans in Shin and Robinson, eds., *Colonial Modernity in Korea.*

15. Shin and Robinson, *Colonial Modernity in Korea.*

16. This point has been made in Andre Schmid's research on Korean nationalism between 1895 and 1919. Schmid, *Korea between Empires,* 265.

17. Ibid., 267.

18. Harry Harootunian, for example, saw the coexistence of the commodity culture promoted by Japanese media and the appeal to native culture by cultural nationalists as a

within which images of women were used to propagate not only nationalist but also colonial thought in Korea.

The study of the relationship between gender and literature requires
closer attention in Korea and elsewhere, since it was used as a way to challenge the masculine norms of nation and modernity that continuously
marginalized women in both colonial and postcolonial Korea. The anticolonial cultural milieu in the Cold War and post–Cold War eras led to
the binary reading of literary works produced in the colonial period, although this binary has begun to be challenged in recent years. Reading
novels produced in colonial Korea demands more of us than the simple
deconstruction of anticolonial ideology. We must attend to the ways in
which the representation of gender in these works produced the resilience
of gender hegemony. We may also gain better insight into the complexity
of the formation of modern Korean literature by focusing on gender—not
just in order to deconstruct the patriarchal institution called modern Korean literature but also in order to move beyond the nation-focused reading of history, which bars us from making a more balanced critique of
imperialism and its historical legacies.

---

sign of social contradiction in Japan's capitalist modernization. See Harootunian's *Overcome by Modernity: History, Culture, and Community in Interwar Japan* (Princeton, NJ:
Princeton University Press, 2000), and *History's Disquiet: Modernity, Cultural Practice,
and the Question of Everyday Life* (New York: Columbia University Press, 2000).

BIBLIOGRAPHY

Newspapers and Magazines
Maeil sinbo
Chosŏn ilbo
Taehan maeil sinbo
Tongnip sinmum
Nyŏjajinam
Nyŏjatokbon
Sinyŏsŏng

Altman, Albert A. "Korea's First Newspaper: The Japanese *Chōsen shinpō*." *The Journal of Asian Studies* 43, no. 4 (Aug. 1984): 685–696.

Ambaras, David. R. "Social Knowledge, Cultural Capital, and the New Middle Class in Japan 1895–1912." *The Journal of Japanese Studies* 24, no. 1 (1998): 1–33.

An Kuksŏn. *Sŏlchungmae. Han'guk kaehawgi munhak ch'ongsŏ: sin sosŏl/ ponan(yŏk) sosŏl* 3, 3–81 (1–79). Seoul: Asea munhwasa, 1978.

———. *Kŭmsu hoeŭirok.* In *Han'guk kaehawgi munhak ch'ongsŏ: sin sosŏl/ pŏnan(yŏk) sosŏl* 2, 449–497 (1–49). Seoul: Asea munhwasa, 1978.

Anderson, Benedict. *Imagined Communities: Reflections on the Origin and Spread of Nationalism.* Rev. New York: Verso, 2006.

Archer, John. *The Nature of Grief.* London and New York: Routledge, 1999.

Bakhtin, M.M. "Discourse in the Novel." In *The Dialogic Imagination*, edited by M. Holquist, 259–422. Austin: University of Texas Press, (1934) 1981.

———. *The Dialogic Imagination: Four Essays.* Austin: University of Texas Press, 1992.

Bassnett, Susan, and Harish Trived, eds. *Post-Colonial Translation: Theory and Practice.* New York: Routledge, 1999.

Braddon, Mary Elizabeth. *Run to Earth.* Adelaide, South Australia: eBooks@

Adelaide. Available at https://ebooks.adelaide.edu.au/b/braddon/mary_eliz abeth/run_to_earth/index.html. Accessed December 15, 2018.

Buck-Morris, Susan. *Hegel, Haiti, and Universal History.* Pittsburgh, PA: University of Pittsburgh Press, 2009.

Burton, Antoinette "The Unfinished Business of Colonial Modernities." In *Gender, Sexuality, and Colonial Modernities,* edited by Antoinette Burton, 1–16. New York: Routledge, 1999.

Caprio, Mark. *Japanese Assimilation Policies in Colonial Korea 1910–1945.* Seattle: University of Washington Press, 2009.

———. "Marketing Assimilation: The Press and the Formation of the Japanese-Korea Colonial Relationship." *The Journal of Korean Studies* 16, no. 1 (2011): 1–25.

Chang Chiyŏn. *Aeguk puinjŏn.* In *Han'guk kaehawgi munhak ch'ongsŏ: Yŏksa/chŏn'gi sosŏl* (A comprehensive series of literature produced during the Enlightenment period: historical and biographical novels), 337–379 (1–39). Seoul: Han'guk munhŏn yŏn'guso, 1979.

———. *Raran puinjŏn.* In *Han'guk kaehawgi munhak ch'ongsŏ: Yŏksa/chŏn'gi sosŏl* (A comprehensive series of literature produced during the Enlightenment period: historical and biographical novels), 385–425 (1–41). Seoul: Han'guk munhŏn yŏn'guso, 1979.

Chatterjee, Partha. *The Nation and Its Fragments: Colonial and Postcolonial Histories.* Princeton, NJ: Princeton University Press, 1993.

Cho Chunghwan. "Pŏnyŏk hoego: *Changhanmong* kwa *Ssangongnu* (Recalling the translation of *The Gold Demon* and *My Crime*)." *Samch'ŏlli* 6, no. 9 (1934): 234–236.

———. *Changhanmong* (A dream of long suffering). Edited by Pak Chinyŏng. Seoul: Hyŏnsil munhwasa, 2007. Published between 13 May and 1 October 1913.

———. *Purhyŏgwi* (The cuckoo). Edited by Pak Chinyŏng. Seoul: Hyŏnsil munhwasa, 2007. First published in 1912 by Keisha shoten in Tokyo, Japan.

———. *Ssangongnu* (Tears of twin jade). Edited by Pak Chinyŏng. Seoul: Hyŏnsil munhwa, 2007. Published between 17 July 17 1912 and 4 February 1913. *Maeil sinbo.*

Cho, Heekyoung. "Imagined, Transcultural, and Colonial Spaces in Print: Newspaper Serialization of Translated Novels in Colonial Korea." *East Asian Publishing and Society* 34 (2013): 153–183.

———. *Translations' Forgotten History: Russian Literature, Japanese Mediation, and the Formation of Modern Korean Literature.* Cambridge, MA: Harvard University Press, 2016.

Cho, Sook Ja. "Within and between Cultures: The Liang-Zhu Narrative in Korean Local Culture." *Harvard Journal of Asiatic Studies* 74, no. 2 (2014): 207–248.

Cho Susam. *Ch'ujae kii* (Ch'ujae's collection of strange stories), cited in Yi Sŭngwŏn, *Sarajin chigŏp ŭi yŏksa* (A history of jobs that disappeared). Seoul: Irum, 2011.

Ch'oe Ch'angsu. "Sinsosŏl: yŏsŏng ŭi kŭndaehwa wa chagi chŏngch'esŏng" (Modernized women and their identity). *Ŏmun nonjip* 28 (2000): 253–281.

Ch'oe Myŏngp'yo. "Somun ŭro kusŏng toen Kim Myŏngsun ŭi sam kwa munhak" (The life and works of Kim Myŏngsun, which has been constructed by rumors). *Hyŏndae munhakiron yŏn'gu* 30 (April 2007): 224–228.

Ch'oe Pyŏngch'an. "Nyŏja kyoyuk p'iryo" (The necessity of women's education). *Nyŏjajinam* 1 (1908): 16–19.

Ch'oe T'aewŏn. "Pŏnan iranŭn haeng'wi wa kŭ juch'e" (An act of adaptation and the adapting subjectivity). *Chōsen bunka kenkyūkai seminar*, Waseda University, 24 November 2007.

Choi, Hyaeweol. *Gender and Mission Encounters in Korea: New Women, Old Ways*. Oakland: University of California Press, 2009.

Chŏn Kyŏngok et al. *Han'guk yŏsŏng chŏngch'i sahoesa* (The political and social history of Korean women). Seoul: Sukmyŏng Women's University Press, 2006.

Chŏn Ŭn'gyŏng. "1910 nyŏndae chisigin chaptchi wa 'yŏsŏng': *Hakchikwang* kwa *Ch'ŏngch'un* ŭl chungsim ŭro" (Women and magazines established by male intellectuals in the 1910s: Focusing on *Hakchikwang* and *Youth*). *Ŏmunhak* 93 (2006): 499–530.

———. "1910 nyŏndae Yi Sanghyŏp sosŏl kwa singminjibae tamnon: *Maeil sinbo* dokjawa ŭi sanggwanssŏng ŭl cungsimŭro" (Colonial discourses in Yi Sanghyo's novels in the 1910s: Focusing on the relationship between *Maeil sinbo* and its readership). *Hyŏndae sosŏl yŏn'gu* 25 (2005): 381–405.

———. "*Mansebo* ŭi tokja t'ugoran kwa kŭndae taejung munhak ŭi hyŏngsŏng" (Readers' responses in *Mansebo* and the formation of modern popular literature). *Ŏmunhak* 111 (2011): 359–388.

Chŏng Chinsŏk. *Han'guk ŏllonsa yŏn'gu* (A study of Korean journalism). Seoul: Iltchogak, 1988.

———. "Ilche ha kŏmnyŏl kigu wa kŏmnyŏl kwan ŭi pyŏndong" (The censorship bureau and censors in colonial Korea). In *Singminji kŏmnyŏl*, 15–63. Seoul: Somyŏng, 2011.

———. *Kŭkppi Chosŏn ch'ongdokbu ui ŏllon kŏmnyŏl kwa t'anap* (Top secrets of the governor general of Korea's censorship and suppression of press in colonial Korea). Seoul: Communication Books, 2008.

————. *Ŏllon kwa han'guk hyŏndaesa* (Journalism and modern Korean history). Seoul: Communication Books, 2001.

Chŏng Haebaek. "Namnyŏ tongdŭng ron" (On equality between men and women). *Nyŏjajinam* 1 (1908): 19–23.

Chŏng Hwan'guk. "1900 nyŏndae ŭi yŏsŏng" (Women in the 1900s). *Han'guk kojŏn yŏsŏng munhak yŏn'gu* 8 (2004): 249–277.

Chŏng Sŏnhi. "18 segi Chosŏn munindŭl ŭi chungguk sosŏl toksŏ silt'ae wa toksŏ tamnon" (Reading patterns and literary discourses among Chosŏn literati in the eighteenth century). In *17/8 segi Chosŏn ŭi oeguk sŏjŏk suyong kwa toksŏ munhwa* (The reception of foreign texts and the reading culture in seventeenth and eighteenth-century Chosŏn), edited by Hong Sŏnp'yo et al., 51–92. Seoul: Hyean, 2006.

Chŏng Sŏnt'ae. *Han'guk kŭndae munhak ŭi suryŏm kwa palsan* (Essays on modern Korean literature and thought). Seoul: Somyŏng, 2008.

Courant, Maurice. *Han'guk sŏji* (Biliographic Coréenne). Translated by Lee Heejae. Seoul: Iljogak, (1894) 1994.

Deepak, B. R. "Revolutionary Activities of the Ghadar Party in China." *China Report* 35, no. 4 (1999): 439–456.

Deuchler, Martina. *The Confucian Transformation of Korea: A Study of Society and Ideology.* Cambridge, MA: Harvard University Press, 1992.

Duara, Prasenjit. *Rescuing History from the Nation.* Chicago: University of Chicago Press, 1997.

Dumas, Alexandre. *The Count of Monte Cristo.* Translation revised by Peter Washington, Introduction by Umberto Eco. New York: Alfred A. Knopf, 2009.

Duus, Peter. *The Abacus and the Sword: The Japanese Penetration of Korea, 1895–1910.* Berkeley: University of California Press, 1995.

Eagleton, Terry. *Literary Theory.* Minneapolis: The University of Minnesota Press, 1996.

Felski, Rita. *The Gender of Modernity.* Cambridge, MA: Harvard University Press, 1995.

Fraser, Nancy. "Rethinking the Public Sphere: A Contribution to the Critique of Actually Existing Democracy." *Social Text* 25/26 (1990): 56–80.

Gluck, Carol. *Japan's Modern Myth: Ideology in the Late Meiji Period.* Princeton, NJ: Princeton University Press, 1987.

Gu, Ming Dong. *Chinese Theories of Fiction: A Non-Western Narrative System.* Albany: State University of New York Press, 2006.

Ha Kyŏngsim. "Chosŏn yŏsŏng yŏnung sosŏl ŭi ch'urhyŏn paekyong e kwanhan siron" (An essay on the emergence of heroines in Chosŏn fiction). *Chungguk munhak nonjip* 54 (2011): 303–328.

Ham T'aeyŏng. "1910 nyŏndae Maeil sinbo sosŏl yŏn'gu" (A study of serial novels in 1910s *Maeil sinbo*), PhD diss., Yonsei University, 2009.

————. "Yi Injik ŭi hyŏnsil ŭishik kwa mosun" (The contradiction in Yi Injik's understanding of the reality). In *Kŭndae kyemonggi munhak ŭi chaeinsik*, edited by Munhak kwa sasang yŏn'guhoe, 7–30. Seoul: Somyŏng ch'ulp'an, 2007.

Han Wŏnyŏng. *Han'guk kaehwagi sinmun yŏnjae sosŏl yŏn'gu* (A study of serialized newspaper fiction works in the enlightenment period). Seoul: Ilchiisa, 1990.

Harootunian, Harry. *History's Disquiet: Modernity, Cultural Practice, and the Question of Everyday Life*. New York: Columbia University Press, 2000.

————. *Overcome by Modernity: History, Culture, and Community in Interwar Japan*. Princeton, NJ: Princeton University Press, 2000.

Hong Insuk. "Kŭndae kyemonggi kŭlssŭgi ŭi yangsang kwa yŏsŏng chuch'e hyŏngsŏng kwajŏng" (The writing patterns in the enlightenment period and the formation of female subjectivity). *Han'guk kojŏn yŏn'gu hakhoe* 14 (2006): 103–130.

Hong Sŏnyŏng. "T'ongsok e kwanhan isŏl" (Another theory of popular narratives). *Ilbon munhwa yŏn'gu* 29 (2009): 233–248.

Hong Yanghi. "Singminji sigi 'hyŏnmo yangch'ŏron' kwa 'modŏnit'i' ŭi munje" (The ideology of wise mothers and good wives in colonial Korea and the problem of modernity). *Sahak yŏn'gu* 99 (2010): 299–338.

————. "'Hyŏnmo yangch'ŏ' ŭi sangjing, Sin Saimdang: Singminji sigi Sin Saimdang ŭi chaehyŏn kwa chendŏ chŏngch'ihak" (The symbol of wise mothers and good wives, Sin Saimdang: The representation of and the politics of gender of Lady Sin). *Sahak yŏn'gu* 122 (2016): 155–190.

Howland, Douglas R. *Translating the West: Language and Political Reason in Nineteenth-Century Japan*. Honolulu: University of Hawai'i Press, 2002.

Hyun, Theresa. *Writing Women in Korea*. Honolulu: University of Hawai'i Press, 2004.

Ida Yūko. *Karera no monogatari* (Men's stories). Nagoya, Japan: Nagoya daigaku shuppankai, 1998.

Im Hwa. "Kaesŏl sinmunhaksa" (Establishing a history of new literature). *Chosŏn ilbo*, 2 September 1939–31 October 1939.

Im Sŏngnae. *Chosŏn hugi ŭi taejung sosŏl* (Popular fiction in late Chosŏn). Seoul: Pogosa, 2008.

Inoue, Miyako. *Vicarious Language: Gender and Linguistic Modernity in Japan*. Berkeley: University of California Press, 2006.

Irigaray, Luce. *Speculum of the Other Woman*. Ithaca, NY: Cornell University Press, (1975) 1985.

Ito, Ken. *An Age of Melodrama: Family, Gender, and Social Hierarchy in the Turn-of-the-Century Japanese Novel.* Stanford, CA: Stanford University Press, 2008.

Iwasaki Sōdo and Mikami Kifu. *Sekai jūni joketsu* (Twelve world heroines). Tokyo: Kōbundō shoten, 1902.

Joseph, Betty. *Reading the East India Company, 1720–1840: Colonial Currencies of Gender.* Chicago: University of Chicago Press, 2004.

Judge, Joan. "A Translocal Technology of the Self: Biographies of World Heroines and the Chinese Woman Question." *Journal of Women's History* 21, no. 4 (November 2009): 59–83.

Kal, Hong. *Aesthetic Constructions of Korean Nationalism: Spectacle, Politics, and History.* New York: Routledge, 2011.

Kawana, Sari. *Murder Most Modern: Detective Fiction and Japanese Culture.* Minneapolis: University of Minnesota Press, 2008.

Keene, Donald. *Dawn to the West: Japanese Literature in the Modern Era.* New York: Holt, Rinehart and Winston, 1984.

Kim Chuhyŏn. "Wŏlnammangguksa wa *it'aeri kŏn'guk samgŏljŏn* ŭi ch'ŏt pŏnyŏkja (The first translator of *The History of the Fallen Vietnam* and *The Three Heroes Who Found Italy*)." Haksul palp'yo charyojip (conference proceedings) in *Han'guk hyŏndae munhakhoe* (2009): 167–178.

Kim Hyŏnju. "Singminji esŏ 'sahoe' wa 'sahoe jŏk' kongongssŏng ŭi kwejŏk" (The stance of "society" and "social publicity" in colonial Korea). *Han'guk munhwa yŏn'gu* 38 (2016): 221–261.

Kim, Michael. "Literary Production, Circulating Libraries, and Private Publishing." *Journal of Korean Studies* 9, no. 1 (2004): 1–31.

Kim Tongin. "*Sosŏl e taehan Chosŏn saram ŭi sasang ŭl*" (Toward the embodiment of Koreans' thoughts in novels). Reprinted in *Kim Tongin chŏnjip* 16, 138–141. Seoul: Chosŏn ilbosa, (1919) 1988.

Kim Yŏngmin. "1910 nyŏndae sinmun ŭi yŏkhal kwa kŭndae sosŏl ŭi chŏngch'ak kwajŏng" (The role of newspapers in the 1910s and the formation of modern fiction). *Hyŏndae munhak ŭi yŏn'gu* 25 (2005): 261–300.

———. "1910 nyŏndae sinmun ŭi yŏkhal kwa kŭndae sosŏl ŭi chŏngch'ak kwajŏng" (The role of newspapers in the 1910s and development of the novel). In *A Study on the Relationship Between Modern Korean Narratives and Media*, edited by Kim Yŏngmin, 135–168. Seoul: Somyŏng ch'ulp'an, 2005.

———. *Han'guk kŭndae sosŏlsa* (A history of modern Korean fiction). Seoul: Sol, 1997.

———. *Han'guk ŭi kŭndae sinmun kwa kŭndae sosŏl I* (A study of modern Korean newspapers and modern novels, volume I). Seoul: Somyŏng, 2006.

Kim Yunsik and Kim Hyŏn. *Han'guk munhaksa* (The history of modern Korean literature). Seoul: Minŭmsa, 1973.

Ko Chaesŏk. "Yi Injik ŭi chugŭm, kŭ poiji annŭn yusan" (The death of Yi Injik and his invisible legacy). *Han'guk ŏmunhak yŏn'gu* 42 (2004): 221–252.

Kondō Haruo. *Chōgonka/Biwakō no Kenkyū* (A study of *chogōnka* and *biwakō*). Tokyo: Meiji shōin, 1981.

Kwon, Aimee Nayoung. *Intimate Empire: Collaboration and Colonial Modernity in Korea and Japan*. Durham, NC: Duke University Press, 2015.

Kwŏn Podŭre. *Han'guk kŭndae sosŏl ŭi kiwŏn* (The origin of modern Korean literature). Seoul: Somyŏng, 2000.

————. "Sinsosŏl e nat'anan kidokkyo ŭi ŭimi: *Kŭmsu heoŭirok* kwa *Kyŏngsejong* ŭl chungsim ŭro" (The meaning of Christianity in the New Novel: Focusing on *Kŭmsu hoeŭirok* and *Kyŏngsejong*). *Han'guk hyŏndae munhak ŭi yŏn'gu* 8 (1998): 7–30.

————. *Yŏnae ŭi sidae* (The age of love). Seoul: Hyŏnsil munhwa yŏn'gu, 2004.

Kwŏn Yŏngmin. *Han'guk hyŏndae munhaksa* I (A history of modern Korean literature I). Seoul: Minŭmsa, 2002.

Kwŏn Yongsŏn. "Pŏnyŏk kwa pŏnan sai hogŭn iyagi esŏ sosŏllo kanŭn kil: Yi Sanghyŏp ŭi *Chŏngbuwŏn* ŭl chungsim ŭro" (The gap between translation and adaptation or the way from storytelling to novel: Focusing on Yi Sanghyŏp's *A Virtuous Woman's Resentment*). *Han'guk kŭndae munhak yŏn'gu* 5, no. 1 (2004): 137–165.

Landes, Joan. *Women and the Public Sphere in the Age of the French Revolution*. Ithaca, NY: Cornell University Press, 1988.

Lauretis, Teresa de. *Technologies of Gender: Essays on Film, Theory and Fiction*. Bloomington: Indiana University Press, 1987.

Law, Graham. "Out of Her Hands: On the Charlotte M. Brame Manuscripts in the O'Neill Collection (MSS 0141)." *Waseda Global Forum*, no. 8 (2011): 109–128.

Ledyard, Gari. "Kollumba Kang Wansuk, an Early Catholic Activist and Martyr." In *Christianity in Korea*, edited by Robert Buswell Jr. and Timothy Lee, 38–71. Honolulu: University of Hawai'i Press, 2007.

Lee, Haiyan. *Revolution of the Heart: A Genealogy of Love in China, 1900–1930*. Stanford, CA: Stanford University Press, 2007.

Lee, Jae Hoon. *The Exploration of the Inner Wounds-Han*. Atlanta, GA: The American Academy of Religion, 1994.

Lee, Janet Yoon-sun. "Dilemma of the Lovesick Hero: Masculine Images and Politics of the Body in Seventeenth-Century Korean Love Tales." *Journal of Korean Studies* 21, no. 1 (2016): 45–69.

Lee, Ji-Eun. "Literary, Sosŏl, and Women in Book Culture in Late Chosŏn Korea." *East Asian Publishing and Society* 4 (2014): 36–64.

————. "Women in Book Culture." In *Women Pre-scripted: Forging Modern Roles through Korean Print.* Honolulu: University of Hawai'i Press, 2016.

Liang Qichao. "On the Relationship between Fiction and the Government of People" (Lun xiaoshuo yu qunzhi zhi guanxi). In *Modern Chinese Literary Thought: Writings on Literature 1893–1945,* edited by Kirk Denton, 74–81. Stanford, CA: Stanford University Press, 1996.

Liu, Siyuan. "The Impact of *Shimpa* on Early Chinese *Huaju.*" *Asian Theatre Journal* 23, no. 2 (Fall 2006): 342–355.

Loomba, Ania. *Colonialism/Postcolonialism.* London: Routledge, 2001.

Luhmann, Niklas. *Love as Passion: The Codification of Intimacy.* Translated by Jeremy Gaines and Doris L. Jones. Stanford, CA: Stanford University Press, 1998.

Luo, Xuanmin. "Ideology and Literary Translation: Liang Qichao." *Perspectives* 13, no. 3 (2005): 178–187.

Marinetti, Amelita. "Death, Resurrection, and Fall in Dumas' *Comte de Monte-Cristo.*" *The French Review* 50, no. 2 (1976): 260–269.

McArthur, Ian, and Mio Bryce. "Names and Perspectives in Sute-Obune: A Meiji-Era Adaptive Translation of the Mary Braddon's Mystery Novel, *Diavola.*" *The International Journal of Humanities* 4, no. 3 (2007): 141–151.

McClintock, Anne. *Imperial Leather: Race, Gender and Sexuality in the Colonial Contest.* New York: Routledge, 1995.

Min, Kwandong, and Sŭnghyŏn Yu. "Chosŏn ŭi chungguk sosŏl suyong kwa chŏnp'a ŭi chuch'edŭl" (The acceptance of Chinese fiction and its agents in Chosŏn). *Chungguk sosŏl nonch'ong* (A treatise on Chinese fiction) 33 (2011): 175–205.

Moretti, Franco. *Atlas of the European Novel 1800–1900.* London and New York: Verso, 1998.

————. "History of the Novel, Theory of the Novel." *Novel: A Forum on Fiction* 43, no. 1 (2010): 1–10.

Mun Okp'yo et al. *Sinyŏsŏng* (New Women). Seoul: Ch'ŏngnyŏnsa, 2003.

Nakagawa, Akio. "*Changhanmong* ŭi pŏn'an hyŏngt'ae e taehan chaegŏmt'o" (A reevaluation of the translation of *Konjiki yasha*). *Kugŏ kyoyukhak yŏn'gu* 12 (2001): 454–489.

Niranjana, Tejaswini. *Siting Translation: History, Post-Structuralism, and the Colonial Context.* Berkeley: University of California Press, 1992.

No Yŏnggu. "'Yŏngung mandŭlgi' yŏksa sok ŭi Yi Sunsin insik" (The reception of Yi Sunsin in the history of 'making heroes'). *Yŏksa pip'yŏng* (2004): 338–358.

No Yŏnsuk. "20 segi ch'o tong asia chŏngch'i sŏsa e nat'anan 'aeguk' ŭi yangsang" (Expressions of "patriotism" reflected in political writings in the beginning of twentieth century East Asia). *Han'guk hyŏndae munhak yŏn'gu* 28 (2009): 7–34.

Noguchi Takehiko. *Kindai nihon no renai shōsetsu* (Modern Japanese romance novels). Osaka: Osaka shoseki, 1987.

Ortolani, Benito. *The Japanese Theatre: From Shamanistic Ritual to Contemporary Pluralism.* Princeton, NJ: Princeton University Press, 1995. Revised edition.

Ōtani Morishige. *Chosŏn hugi sosŏl tokja yŏn'gu* (A study of fiction readership in late Chosŏn). Seoul: Korea University Press, 1985.

Ozaki Kōyō. *Konjiki yasha* (The gold demon). Tokyo: Kadowaka Shoten, 1971.

Pak Chinyŏng. *Pŏnyŏk kwa pŏnan ŭi sidae* (The age of translation and adaptation). Seoul: Somyŏng ch'ulp'an, 2011.

———. "'Yi Suil kwa Sim Sunae iyagi' ŭi taejungmunyejŏk sŏngkkyŏk kwa kyebo: *Changhanmong* yŏn'gu" (Characteristics of "Yi Suil and Sim Sunae" and its popularization: A study of *Changhanmong*). *Hyŏndae munhak ŭi mŏn'gu* 23 (May 2004): 231–264.

Pak Ch'ŏlsang. *Sŏjae e salda: Chosŏn chisigin 24in ŭi sŏjae iyagi* (Stories of private libraries of 24 intellectuals in Chosŏn). Seoul: Munhak tongnae, 2014.

Pak Sŏnyŏng. "Yi Injik ŭi sahoe ch'ŏrhak kwa ch'inil ŭi hamŭi" (Yi Injik's social philosophy and the implication of his collaboration). In *Sahoe wa yŏksa* 89 (2011): 193–231.

Pak T'aegyu. "Yi Injik ŭi yŏn'gŭk kaeryang ŭiji wa *Ŭnsegye* e mich'in ilbon yŏn'guk ŭi yŏnghyang e kwanhan yŏn'gu" (A study of the influence of Japanese theater on Yi Injik's *Ŭnsegye* and his involvement in the reforming of Korean theater). *Han'guk ilbon hakhoe* 47 (2001): 287–303.

Pak Ŭnsik. *Sŏsa kŏn'gukchi. Yŏksa/chŏn'gi sosŏl*, vol. 6 of *Han'guk kaehwagi munhak ch'ongsŏ*, compiled by Han'gukhak munhŏn yŏn'guso, 197–257 (1–35). Seoul: Asea munhwasa, 1978. Originally published in Seoul: Kwanghak sŏp'o, 1908.

Pierson, John D. *Tokutomi Sohō 1863–1957.* Princeton, NJ: Princeton University Press, 1980.

Poole, Janet. *When the Future Disappears: The Modernist Imagination in Late Colonial Korea.* New York: Columbia University Press, 2014.

Poulton, Cody. "Drama and Fiction in the Meiji Era: The Case of Izumi Kyōka." *Asian Theatre Journal* 12, no. 2 (Autumn 1995): 280–306.

Pratt, Mary Louise. *Imperial Eyes: Travel Writing and Transculturation*, 2nd edition. New York and London: Routledge, (1992) 2008.

Ragsdale, Kathryn. "Marriage, the Newspaper Business, and the Nation-State Ideology in the Late Meiji Serialized Katei Shōsetsu." *The Journal of Japanese Studies* 24, no. 2 (1998): 229–255.

Rhee, Jooyeon. "Between Words and Images: Gender and Cultural Productions in Colonial Korea." PhD diss., York University, Canada, 2011.

————. "'No Country for the New Woman': Rethinking Gender and Cultural Nationalism in Colonial Korea through Kim Myŏngsun." *Acta Koreana* 17, no. 1 (June 2014): 399–427.

Robinson, Michael E. "Colonial Publication Policy and the Korean Nationalist Movement." In *The Japanese Colonial Empire 1910–1945*, edited by Ramon H. Myers and Mark R. Peattie, 312–343. Princeton, NJ: Princeton University Press, 1987.

————. *Cultural Nationalism in Colonial Korea, 1920–1925*. Seattle: University of Washington Press, 1988.

————. *Korea's Twentieth-Century Odyssey*. Honolulu: University of Hawai'i Press, 2007.

Rodriguez Garcia, Jose Maria "Introduction: Literary into Cultural Translation." *Diacritics* 34, no. 3/4 (Autumn/Winter 2004): 2–30.

Ruikō Kuroiwa. *Gankutsuō* (The King of the cave). In *Kuroiwa Ruikō zenshū*, vols. 1 and 2. Tokyo: Haru shobō, (1901–1902) 2006.

Ryu Chunghee. "Kaehawgi Chosŏn minhoe hwalttong kwa ŭihoet'ongyong kyuch'ik" (Activities of civil societies in the kaehwagi period and Accommodation of General Rules for the Assembly). *Tongbang hakchi* 167 (2014): 1–32.

Saeki Junko. *Renai no kigen* (The origin of love). Tokyo: Nihon keizai shimbunsha, 2000.

Saito, Satoru. *Detective Fiction and the Rise of the Japanese Novel, 1880–1930*. Cambridge, MA: Harvard University Asia Center, 2012.

Sakaki, Atsuko. "Kajin no Kigū: The Meiji Political Novel and the Boundaries of Literature." *Monumenta Nipponica* 55, no. 1 (2000): 83–108.

Sand, Jordan. *House and Home in Modern Japan: Architecture, Domestic Space, and Bourgeois Culture, 1880–1930*. Cambridge, MA: Harvard University Asia Center, 2005.

Scheff, Thomas J. "Shame and the Social Bond: A Sociological Theory." *Sociological Theory* 18, no. 1 (2000): 84–99.

Schmid, Andre. *Korea between Empires 1895–1919*. New York: Columbia University Press, 2002.

Scott, Joan W. "Introduction to Revisiting 'Gender: A Useful Category of Historical Analysis.'" *The American Historical Review* 113, no. 5 (2008): 1344–1345.

Shin, Gi-Wook, and Michael Robinson, eds. *Colonial Modernity in Korea*. Cambridge, MA: Harvard University Press, 1999.

Shin Jiyoung. *Pu/jae ŭi sidae: kŭndae kyemonggi mit singminji sigi Chosŏn ŭi yŏnsŏl/chwadamhoe* (The age of absence/presence: Public speeches and roundtable discussions in the enlightenment period and in colonial Korea). Seoul: Somyŏng ch'ulp'an, 2012.

Silver, Brenda R. "Periphrasis, Power, and Rape in *A Passage to India*." In *Rape and Representation*, edited by Lynn A. Higgins and Brenda R. Silver, 115–140. New York: Columbia University Press, 1991.

Silver, Mark. *Purloined Letter: Cultural Borrowing and Japanese Crime Literature, 1868–1937*. Honolulu: University of Hawai'i Press, 2008.

Sin Ch'aeho. "Sosŏlga ŭi ch'use" (A trend among fiction writers). *Taehan maeil sinbo*, 2 December 1909.

———. *Ŭlchi Mundŏkjŏn*. Reprinted in *Sin Ch'aeho chŏnjip: pyŏlchip*, in *Tanjae Sin Ch'aeho chŏnjip: pyŏljip*, 4th edition. Seoul: Tanjae Sin Ch'aeho kinyŏm saŏphoe, 1977.

———. *Yi Sunsinjŏn*. Reprinted in *Sin Ch'aeho chŏnjip: pyŏljip*, in *Tanjae Sin Ch'aeho chŏnjip: pyŏlchip*, 4th edition. Seoul: Tanjae Sin Ch'aeho kinyŏm saŏphoe, 1977.

———. "Yŏngung kwa segye (Heroes and the world)." *Taehan maeil sinbo*, 16 September 1908, reprinted in *Tanjae Sin Ch'aeho chŏnjip: pyŏlchip*, 4th edition. Seoul: Tanjae Sin Ch'aeho kinyŏm saŏphoe, 1977.

Sin Yŏngju. *Chosŏn sidae songsa sosŏl yŏn'gu* (A study of songsa sosŏl in Chosŏn). Seoul: Sin'gu munhwasa, 2002.

Sŏ Chŏngja. *Han'guk kŭndae yŏsŏng sosŏl yŏn'gu* (A study of modern Korean novels written by women writers). Seoul: Kukgak charyowŏn, 1999.

Son Sŏngjun. "Rolang puin chŏn'gi ŭi tongasia suyong yangsang kwa kŭ sŏngkkyŏk" (Adaptations of the biography of Madame Roland in East Asia and their characteristics). *Pigyo munhak* 53 (2011): 116–123.

———. "Yŏngung sŏsa tong asia suyong kwa chungyŏk ŭi wŏnbonssŏng: sŏgu t'eksŭt'ŭ ŭi han'gukjŏk chae mangnakhwa rŭl chungsim ŭro" (Second-hand translations of Western biographical fictions and their originality: Focusing on localization of Western biographical fictions). PhD diss., Sungkyunkwan University, 2012.

Song Minho. "Yŏlchae Yi Haejo ŭi saengae wa sasangjŏk paegyŏng" (The life and the philosophical background of Yi Haejo). *Kugŏ kungmunhak* 156 (2010): 241–271.

Stockton, Sharon. *The Economics of Fantasies: Rape in Twentieth-Century Literature*. Columbus: Ohio State University Press, 2006.

Stoler, Ann. *Along the Archival Grain: Epistemic Anxieties and Colonial Common Sense*. Princeton, NJ: Princeton University Press, 2010.

Suh, Serk-Bae. *Treacherous Translation: Culture, Nationalism, and Colonialism in Korea and Japan from the 1910s to the 1960s.* Berkeley: University of California Press, 2013.

Suzuki, Sadami. *The Concept of "Literature" in Japan.* Translated by Royall Tyler. Kyoto: Nichibunken, 2006.

Suzuki, Tomi. *Narrating the Self: Fictions of Japanese Modernity.* Stanford, CA: Stanford University Press, 1996.

Tanaka, Yukiko. *Women Writers of Meiji and Taishō Japan.* Jefferson, NC: McFarland and Company, Inc., 2000.

Taylor, Charles. *Modern Social Imaginaries.* Durham, NC: Duke University Press, 2004.

Thornber, Karen L. *Empire of Texts in Motion: Chinese, Korean, and Taiwanese Transculturations of Japanese Literature.* Cambridge, MA: The Harvard-Yenching Institute, 2009.

Tikhonov, Vladimir. "Masculinizing the Nation: Gender Ideologies in Traditional Korea and in the 1890s–1900s Korean Enlightenment Discourse." *The Journal of Asian Studies* 66, no. 4 (2007): 1029–1037.

Tikohnov, Vladimir, and Yi Hye Gyung. "The Confucian Background of Modern 'Heroes' in the Writings of Sin Ch'aeho: In Comparison with Those of Liang Qichao." *Acta Koreana* 17, no. 1 (2014): 339–374.

Tokutomi, Roka. *Hototogisu.* Tokyo: Sinchōsha, 1930.

Torrance, Richard. *The Fiction of Tokuda Shūsei and the Emergence of Japan's New Middle Class.* Seattle: University of Washington Press, 1994.

Tsurumi, Patricia. "Colonial Education in Korea and Taiwan." In *The Japanese Colonial Empire 1895–1945,* edited by Ramon H. Myers and Mark R. Peattie, 275–311. Princeton, NJ: Princeton University Press, 1984.

Tymoczko, Maria. "Ideology and the Position of the Translator: In What Sense is a Translator 'In Between'?" In *Apropos of Ideology: Translation Studies on Ideologies in Translation Studies,* edited by Maria Calzada Peraz, 181–201. Manchester, UK: St. Jerome Publishing, 2003.

———. *Translation in a Postcolonial Context: Early Irish Literature in English Translation.* Manchester, UK: St. Jerome Publishing, 1999.

Venuti, Lawrence. "Translation, Community, Utopia." In *The Translation Studies Reader* (2nd ed.), edited by Lawrence Venuti, 468–488. New York: Routledge, 2000.

Williams, Raymond. *Marxism and Literature.* London: Oxford University Press, 1977.

Yang Sŭngin. *Hanmun sosŏl ŭi t'ongsoksŏng* (The popular appeal in fiction written in Chinese script). Seoul: Pogosa, 2008.

Yang, Yoon Sun. *From Domestic Women to Sensitive Young Men: Translating the*

Individual in Early Colonial Korea. Cambridge, MA: Harvard University Asia Center, 2017.

————. "Nation in the Backyard: Yi Injik and the Rise of Korean New Fiction, 1906–1913." PhD diss., University of Chicago, 2009.

Yi Haech'ang. *Han'guk sinmunsa yŏn'gu* (A study of the history of Korean newspapers). Seoul: Sŏngmungak, 1971.

Yi Haejo. *Chayujong.* In *Sin sosŏl, pŏnan(yŏk) sosŏl,* vol. 4 of *Han'guk kaehwagi munhak ch'ongsŏ* compiled by Han'gukhak munhŏn yŏn'guso, 5–44 (1–40). Seoul: Asea munhwasa, 1978. Originally published in Seoul Kwanghak sŏp'o, 1908.

————. *Ch'unoech'un. Maeil sinbo,* 1 January 1912–14 March 1912.

————. *Hwa ŭi hyŏl. Maeil sinbo,* 6 April 1911.

————. *Sanch'ŏnch'omok, Han'guk sin sosŏl chŏnjip.* Seoul: Ŭlyu munhwasa, (1908) 2011.

————. *Pinsangsŏl.* In *Sin sosŏl, pŏnan(yŏk) sosŏl,* vol. 4 of *Han'guk kaehwagi munhak ch'ongsŏ,* compiled by Han'gukhak munhŏn yŏn'guso, 3–44. Seoul: Asea munhwasa, 1978. Originally published in Seoul: Kwanghak sŏp'o, 1908.

————. *Ssangokchŏk.* In *Sin sosŏl, pŏnan(yŏk) sosŏl,* vol. 4 of *Han'guk kaehwagi munhak ch'ongsŏ,* compiled by Han'gukhak munhŏn yŏn'guso, 415–532. Seoul: Asea munhwasa, 1978. Originally published in Seoul: Kwanghak sŏp'o, 1908.

Yi Injik. *Hyŏl ŭi nu.* In *Sin sosŏl, pŏnan(yŏk) sosŏl,* vol. 1 of *Han'guk kaehwagi munhak ch'ongsŏ,* compiled by Han'gukhak munhŏn yŏn'guso, 1–96 (1–94). Seoul: Asea munhwasa, 1978. Originally published in Seoul: Kwanghak sŏp'o, 1908.

————. *Kwi ŭi sŏng.* in *Sin sosŏl, pŏnan(yŏk) sosŏl,* vol. 2 of *Han'guk kaehwagi munhak ch'ongsŏ,* compiled by Han'gukhak munhŏn yŏn'guso, 109–385 (1–146; 1–125). Seoul: Asea munhwasa, 1978. Originally published in Seoul: Kwanghak sŏp'o, 1908.

————. *Moranbong. Maeil sinbo,* 5 February 1913–3 June 1913.

Yi Kwangsu. *Mujŏng. Maeil Sinbo,* 1 January–14 June 1917.

————. "What Is Literature?" (*Munhak iran hao*). Originally published in *Maeil sinbo,* 10–23 November 1916. Translated by Jooyeon Rhee in *Azalea: Journal of Korean Literature and Culture* 4 (2011): 293–314.

Yi Kyŏngha. "Taehan cheguk yŏin dŭl ŭi sinmun ilkki wa tokja t'ugo" (A study of female readership of newspapers and 'women's opinion section'). *Yŏ/sŏng iron* 12 (2005): 78–296.

Yi Manyŏl. "Kaehwagi ŏllon kwa chungguk: Yang Kyech'o rŭl chungsim ŭro" (The Chinese influence on Korean journalism during the enlightenment period: Focusing on Liang Qichao). In *Han'guk kŭndae ŏllon ŭi chaejomyŏng* (Rethinking Korean modern journalism), 78–118. Seoul: Communication Books, 2001.

Yi Mihyang. *Kŭndae aejŏng sosŏl ŭi yŏn'gu* (A study of modern romance novels). Seoul: P'urŭn sasang, 2001.

Yi Minhi. *Chosŏn ŭi pest'ŭssellŏ* (Bestsellers in Chosŏn). Seoul: Pronesis, 2010.

Yi Sanghyŏp. *Chŏngbuwŏn* (A virtuous woman's resentment), vols. I and II. Edited by Pak Chinyŏng. Seoul: Hyŏnsil munhwa, 2007. Published between 29 October 1914 and 19 May 1915.

————. *Haewangsŏng* (*Neptune*), vols. I, II, and III. Edited by Pak Chinyŏng. Seoul: Hyŏnsil munhwa, 2007. Published between 10 February 1916 and 31 March 1917.

Yi Soyŏn. "Ilche kangtchŏmgi yŏsŏng chapchi yŏn'gu" (A study of women's journals in colonial Korea). *Ehwa sahak yŏn'gu* 29 (2002): 217–235.

Yi Sŭnga and No Sangnae, "Pŏnan sosŏl ŭi t'eksŭt'ŭ pyŏnhwa kwajŏng yŏn'gu: Yi Sanghyŏp ŭi Haewangsŏng ŭl chungsim ŭro" (A study of textual change process in adapted novels: Focusing on Neptune by Yi Sanghyŏp). *Minjok munhwa nonch'ong* 56 (2014): 297–328.

Yi Yumi. "Kŭndae ch'ogi sinmun sosŏl ŭi yŏsŏng inmul chaehyŏn yangsang yŏn'gu" (A study of the image of women in fiction in modern Korean newspaper). *Han'guk kŭndae munhak yŏn'gu* 16 (2007): 75–98.

Ying, Hu. *Tales of Translation: Composing the New Woman in China, 1899–1918.* Stanford, CA: Stanford University Press, 2000.

Yoo, Theodore Jun. *The Politics of Gender in Colonial Korea: Education, Labor, and Health, 1910–1945.* Oakland: University of California Press, 2008.

Yoo, Jamie Jungmin. "Networks of Disquiet: Censorship and the Production of Literature in Eighteenth-Century Korea." *Acta Koreana* 20, no. 1 (2017): 249–280.

Youn Young-Shil. "Tong asia chŏngch'i sosŏl ŭi han yangsang" (A case of political novel in East Asia). *Sanghŏ hakpo* 31 (Feb. 2011): 13–49.

Yu Kilchun. *Sŏyu kyŏnmun* (The impression of the West). Translated by Hŏ Kyŏngjin. Seoul: Sŏhaemunjip, (1895) 2004.

Yun Haedong. "Singminji kŭndae wa konggongsŏng" (Colonial modernity and publicness). *SAI* 8 (2010): 163–195.

————. *Singminji ŭi hoesaek chidae* (The gray zone in colonial Korea). Seoul: Yŏksa pip'yŏngsa, 2003.

Index